SIGHTHOUNDS

Their Form, Their Function and Their Future

SIGHTHOUNDS

Their Form, Their Function and Their Future

David Hancock

THE CROWOOD PRESS

Previous Books by the Author

Dogs As Companions – 1981
Old Working Dogs – 1984 (reprinted 1998 and 2011)
The Heritage of the Dog – 1990
The Bullmastiff-A Breeder's Guide Vol 1 – 1996
The Bullmastiff-A Breeder's Guide Vol 2 – 1997
Old Farm Dogs – 1999
The Mastiffs – The Big Game Hunters – 2000–06 (six editions)
The Bullmastiff-A Breeder's Guide – 2006 (one volume hardback edition)
The World of the Lurcher – 2010
Sporting Terriers – Their Form, Their Function and their Future – 2011

———————————————————

First published in 2012 by The Crowood Press Ltd,
Ramsbury, Marlborough, Wiltshire, SN8 2HR

www.crowood.com

British Library Cataloguing-in-Publication Data
A catalogue record for this book is available from the British Library.

ISBN 978 1 84797 392 4

Page 1: The Irish Wolfhound Dog, Ch. Marquis of Donegal.
Page 2: The greyhound family: back left, Persian; centre, English Greyhound; back right,
Deerhound; front left, Italian; and front right, Siberian Wolfhound.
Page 3: Greyhound with pups by Joseph Gott 1825.
Page 5: 'The Friend of Man' by Pisanello c.1430

Typeset and designed by D & N Publishing, Baydon, Wiltshire

Printed and bound in India by Replika Press Ltd

CONTENTS

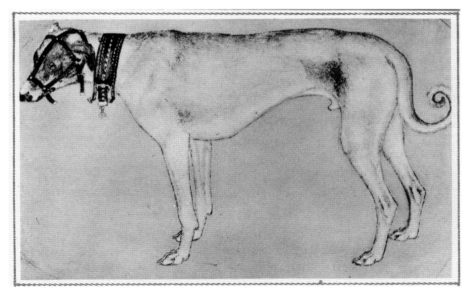

DEDICATION

This book is dedicated to all those pioneer breeders, to whom I pay tribute in the text, who brought these magnificent sighthound breeds to our kennels and homes today, boldly introducing new breeds from overseas and bravely persevering with the minor breeds that never seem to capture the dog-owning public's affection. In an increasingly urban society, the sighthound breeds are under unprecedented threat, their sporting role severely curtailed by contemporary moral judgements and their design so often victim of show ring fashion. These distinguished pioneer breeders deserve not just our gratitude but our admiration too for leaving behind them such superb canine athletes. This alone should inspire us to breed the coursing breeds to their high standards and with their depth of selfless vision.

> Let the brisk greyhound of the Celtic name
> Bound o'er the glebe and show his painted frame.
> Swift as the wing that sails adown the wind,
> Swift as the wish that darts along the mind,
> The Celtic greyhound sweeps the level lea,
> Eyes as he strains and stops the flying prey,
> But should the game elude his watchful eyes
> No nose sagacious tells him where it lies.
> John Whitaker (1735–1808)

Coursing Greyhounds. Trainer Edward Dent (left);
owner Colonel North (right).

PREFACE

This book is a celebration of the speedsters of the dog world, an expression of admiration for their astonishing athleticism, remarkable hunting skills and sheer stylishness, right across the world. It is not a manual, advising on training, nutrition, care and maintenance, breeding and hunting techniques. It is, if anything, the story of the 'canine cursorials' – dogs with limbs adapted for running, that find their prey in open country and hunt it using great pace, often over considerable distances. It is no surprise therefore to find their most effective use in deserts, on steppes and prairies or level rocky terrain, from Syria and Iraq to Afghanistan and Russia. They were valued by hunters from ancient Egypt and classical Greece, then in turn, by tsars, sheikhs and western noblemen. Arrian, the

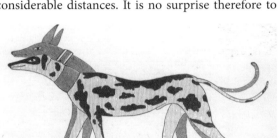

Egyptian Hounds Circa 3000BC.

Deerhunt detail from Devonshire Tapestries.

Hunting with sighthound in Ancient Greece.

15th century hunt detail from Devonshire Tapestries.

is a timeless description of the sighthound function and nature.

The Devonshire Hunting Tapestries of the early fifteenth century, in the collection of the Victoria and Albert Museum, vividly display the sheer pageantry of the hunting scenes of those times, featuring hounds and hawks – with the hounds mainly being of the greyhound type, illustrating the high value in the hunting field of these hounds at that time. Such scenes typified the hunting scene right across Europe and western Asia in the fifteenth century – the style of the pageantry may have differed but the significant employment of sighthounds and their immense value to man at that time is evident. The tapestries indicate the wide range of quarry pursued by such hounds. They illustrate too the close companionship of man and dog in the hunt.

Greek historian, wrote in AD124: 'I myself have bred a hound whose eyes are the greyest of grey. A swift, hard-working, courageous, sound-footed dog, and she proves a match at any time for four hares. She is, moreover, most gentle and kindly-affectioned...' That

It is not surprising that, unlike some types of dog at the mercy of human whim, the sighthounds have retained their timeless type. An immediate similarity can be detected between, say, Dürer's sketch of a small sighthound of around 1500 and Augustus John's

Whippet by Augustus John, c. 1948.

Greyhound by Dürer, c. 1500.

Detail from Paolo Uccello's Hunt in the Forest, 1465.

portrayal of a whippet in 1948. The hounds depicted in Paolo Uccello's *Hunt in the Forest* of the mid-1400s and in Piero della Francesca's *Portrait of Sigismondo Malatesta* of 1451 could have featured in Franz Luycx's portrayal of the Kaiserin Eleonora Gonzaga of 1651. The anatomy of the sighthound has been shaped by function and decided by function. Changes in hunting itself may have lessened the sighthound role but speed, if not the same level of agility, is still in demand on the track.

In his *Of English Dogs*, published in 1576, Dr Caius mentions two types of hunting dogs: 'One which rouseth the beast, and continueth the chase. Another which springeth the bird, and bewrayeth the flight by pursuit.' This book is about the former. He further subdivided such hunting dogs into five functional categories: 'The first in perfect smelling, the second in quick spying, the third in swiftness and quickness, the fourth in smelling and nimbleness and the fifth

in subtlety and deceitfulness'. This book is about the second and third categories, the type relying on sight and speed. The athleticism of the sighthound breeds embraces sprinting, hurdling and middle-distance running; they are canine athletes that also clear obstacles and turn at great speed, sometimes facing formidably fanged or dangerously antlered quarry. They thoroughly merit our admiration and totally deserve our patronage in these difficult days for hunting dogs. I hope this book promotes both deserved admiration and selfless patronage.

Detail from Sigismondo Malatesta, 1451.

Kaiserin Eleonora Gonzaga by Franz Luycx, c. 1651.

ACKNOWLEDGEMENTS

The author is grateful to the staff at Sotheby's Picture Library, Christie's Images Ltd., Bonhams, Arthur Ackermann Ltd., David Messum Galleries, Richard Green & Co., The Bridgeman Art Library, The Nature Picture Library, The National Art Library, The Wallace Collection, R Cox & Co., Lane Fine Art, The Kennel Club, The American Kennel Club, The National Trust, The Royal Collection – Photographic Services, and private collectors, (especially the late Mevr AH (Ploon) de Raad of Zijderveld, Holland, who gave free use of her extensive photographic archive of sporting paintings), for their gracious and generous permissions to reproduce some of the illustrations used in this book.

AUTHOR'S NOTE

A number of the illustrations in this book lack pictorial quality but are included because they either uniquely contribute historically to or best exemplify the meaning of the text. Old depictions do not always lend themselves to reproduction in today's higher quality print and publishing format. Those that are included have significance beyond their graphic limitations and I ask for the reader's understanding over this.

Where quotes are used, they are used verbatim, despite any vagaries in spelling, irregular use of capital letters or departures from contemporary grammar. For me, it is important that their exact form, as presented by the author originally, is displayed, as this can help to capture the mood of those times.

Lady with Companion Greyhound by F.R. de Leub (American, late 19th century).

THE COURSING DOGS

Ancient History

Much is made by breed historians of the hounds of Egypt, Greece and Rome but there is ample evidence

An Egyptian bronze figure of Anubis, Late period.

of hound-like dogs long before these times. In the Mesolithic period, 9,000 years ago, one or two species of larger animal provided the main source of meat in the human diet. In Europe these were red deer and wild boar, in North America the bison and in western Asia the gazelle and wild goat. One survey (Jarman, 1972) carried out in 165 sites of late Palaeolithic and Mesolithic age throughout Europe revealed the meat sources of the hunter-gatherers: 95 per cent of the sites indicated the presence of red deer, 60 per cent showed roe deer, 10 per cent revealed elk and chamois and a few had bison and reindeer. Twenty per cent of the sites indicated the presence of dog.

Early evidence

One of the earliest records of dog remains comes from the Palaeolithic cave of Palegawra in what is

Hunters in Ancient Greece.

Hyena hunt in Egypt, 1550–1080BC.

now Iraq, which is some 12,000 years old. Canid remains found at Vlasac in Romania date from c.5400–4600BC and the other remains there indicate no other domesticated animals. There were huge hefty hunting dogs throughout western Asia from well before 2000BC and a variety of hunting dogs in ancient Egypt, their white antelope dog resembling our modern harriers in conformation. The Celts, the Greeks and the Romans greatly prized their hunting dogs and left descriptions of them. Hounds were extremely valuable as pot-fillers and were therefore extensively traded. Well before 2000BC, the Sage Kings of the Yellow River valley in China, the Dravidians of the Indus valley in India and the Sumerians in the valleys of the Tigris and the Euphrates were, especially by European standards of that time, sophisticated hunters. Discoveries from near Ergani in Turkey, dated from 9500BC, and from east Idaho in the United States, dating from 9500 to 9000BC, prove the existence of tracking dogs in cave settlements. Ivory carvings from Thebes, dating from 4400 to 4000BC, depict fast running hounds. The Phoenicians had hounds hunting both by speed and by stamina using scent. In Babylon powerful short-faced hounds were used to hunt wild asses and lions. The Assyrian kings, assisted by their keepers of hounds, hunted lions, wild bull and elephant. From 2500BC onwards hunting with hounds was a favourite entertainment for noblemen in the Nile delta.

Development of Breeds

One Egyptian scribe of the 19th dynasty described a pack of hounds, 200 of one type, 400 of another, stating that: 'The red-tailed dog goes at night into the stalls of the hills. He is better than the long-faced dog, and he makes no delay in hunting …' In the Rig-Veda, an ancient Sanskrit record of Hindu mythology, we can find hound-like dogs described as 'broad of nostril and insatiable …' In time the specialist hounds developed physically to suit their function, the 'long-faced' dogs needing a slashing capability in their jaws backed by excellent long-sighted vision, to become, in time, our sighthounds. The 'broad-nostrilled', wider-skulled, looser-lipped dogs needed plenty of room for scenting capacity in both nose and lips where scent was tasted, to become, in time, our scenthounds.

As hounds became linked with human preferences in method of hunting and choice of quarry, so the breeds developed.

Greyhound-like Dogs

It is possible to find in Greek and Latin literature some sixty-five breed types by name although some are merely synonyms. The Greeks had hound breeders who insisted on the importance of pure bloodlines. Not all their hounds were Greek in origin, for the Greeks were a maritime people, with knowledge of the whole of the Mediterranean and the Black Sea. Pollux and Oppian referred to a breed coming from the Spanish peninsula as the Iberian; in Italy there was the Ausonian – discovered by Greeks settling in Naples – the Salentine, the Tuscan (a hunting dog which indicated concealed game, not a ground scent-seeking hound) and the Umbrian, able to run down game but not kill it. Arrian, in the second century AD, described two Celtic breeds, the Segusiae (named after a tribe from a province which included what is now Lyons) with excellent noses, good cry but a tendency to dwell on the scent and the Vertragi (literally 'lots of foot'), rough-haired greyhound-like dogs.

Medieval Hunting

As described in the preface, the sighthound type was widely used in the medieval hunt. Terms used

Medieval par force hunting.

Grehoundes in medieval deer hunt.

then were often loosely applied, with perhaps the best explanation being in the Appendix to Walter Baillie-Grohman's 1904 edition of *The Master of Game,* the Duke of York's translation of Gaston de Foix's *Livre de Chasse* of 1387. Hunting mastiffs were alauntes; brachets or bercelets were hunting dogs that accompanied those who shot their game, rather like the Bavarian Mountain Hounds of today, with their valued tracking skills (but could also mean small bitch hounds); lymers were leashed scenthounds, used rather as 'tufters' are used in the staghound packs; raches were the smaller, mainly white packhounds rather like the once-famous Curre pack here (but could also mean bitch hounds); bandogges were the ferocious 'seizers', slipped at the kill, to save

the more valued running hounds; greyhounds were the grehoundes or levriers, not the modern breed of Greyhound, with the fierce and shaggy Irish and Scottish deerhound called the '*levrier d'attache*' or 'held-dog' and the smaller, smooth-coated hound, the '*petit levrier pour lievre*' or small hare-hound. A brace, or more usually three, was handled by a fewterer. Heyrers were the tricolour Harriers of today; gazehounds were used in packs 'at force'.

Central European Terms

In his exhaustive *Lexicon of the Medieval German Hunt* (1965), David Dalby lists the various terms

Hunter restraining bandogges.

Bandogges released. Harry Bates, 1888.

for hunting dogs used then. The word *wint* was used to denote both the purpose-bred Greyhound and the heavier *veltre* or *zwic-darm,* which was a blend of Mastiff and Greyhound, resembling the bull lurchers of today. The *habech-wint* or *beiz-wint* was the Greyhound used with the hawk. The Greyhound was also called *wint-spil,* and *hasen-wint* when used to course hares. It is clear from the long list of sources referred to by Dalby that coursing in medieval Germany and the surrounding small states was carried on at a vast scale and it's surprising that a German sighthound did not emerge and survive, but the Germans do not have a good record at conserving their old hound breeds. There is reference in the German hunt to the *wind-bracke,* which could be translated as the hound that hunts by speed and scent, perhaps their gazehound.

Different Function of Gazehound

In his *Of English Dogs,* published in 1576, Dr Caius mentions the gazehound and the Greyhound *quite separately*, clearly not considering the latter to be a type of the former. Nowadays, wrongly, we blur the gazehound and the sighthound, regarding the two words as synonyms. Caius writes 'Our countrymen call this dogge a Gasehounde because the beames

of his sight are so stedfastly settled and unmoveably fastened.' Caius uses the word Greyhound for 'another kinde of Dogge' – as a general term for hounds that hunt using speed, not for a distinct breed, mentioning their 'incredible swiftness' and their 'principal service in starting and hunting the hare'. He goes on to describe them with phrases such as 'For it is a spare and bare kind of dog (of flesh, but not of bone): some are of a greater sort and some lesser; some are smooth skinned, and some are curled. The bigger therefore are appointed to hunt the bigger beasts, and the smaller serve to hunt the smaller accordingly'. That is a fair summary of the sighthound group and certainly no word picture of just today's recognized breed of Greyhound.

Rough and smooth 'Windhunde', c. 1780.

Levriers. Henri d'Ainecy, c. 1840.

Seventeenth-Century Differentiation

In *The Gentleman's Recreations* of 1674, Nicholas Cox mentions the eleven breeds of hound of that time. He describes the gazehound as being 'used for catching the fox and hare, hunting chiefly by sight in open country, employed by people riding … popular in the north of England', but adding later a reference to the gazehound as 'our little beagle with swift foot and ready voice'. He then describes the Greyhound, quite separately, as being still of grahound type, not so big as the wolf-dog in Ireland, being used for coursing. He clearly considered the Greyhound and the gazehound as being wholly different hounds.

Wider use of word Greyhound

The *Sportsman's Cabinet* of 1803 continues the use of the word Greyhound as a substitute for sighthound rather than as a breed title but errs in stating, 'it being evidently demonstrable, that gazehound was the original appellation in applicable allusion to that particular kind of dog running by sight and not by scent'. The editor of this valuable tome had clearly not read Caius' words of nearly three centuries previously before his rather tortuous words over-confidently stated his case. In his valuable book *The Dog in Health and Disease* (1867), the celebrated 'Stonehenge' records: 'THE GAZEHOUND – This breed is now lost, and it is very difficult to ascertain in what respects it differed from the greyhound.' I don't believe the great man got that right. It is not justifiable to refer to this type as a *breed*; the word Greyhound has long been utilized to cover any hound with the sighthound function. In his authoritative *Hounds in Old Days* (1913), Sir Walter Gilbey, who knew his hounds, wrote of the gazehound, extending the words of Dr Caius:

> This was not the greyhound – which is concisely summed up as a 'spare and bare kind of dog' – and the statement that the 'gazehound' hunted by sight, depending little or not all on its nose, forbids the assumption that Caius refers to the Northern Hound or Northern Beagle; which, as Gervaise Markham shows, had a very good nose.

The gazehound may well have been an ancestor of types like the Fell Hound, which tracks its quarry using scent and then pursues it at pace or par force.

Old Meaning of 'Gaze'

Par force hunting fell out of favour in Britain, especially in the south, the slower 'hunting cunning', using scenthounds, replacing it. But boarhounds and staghounds across mainland Europe were employed in this style of hard-pursuit quarry-hunting for much longer. In otter hunting to 'gaze' meant to view the otter. Shakespeare wrote of 'the poor frighted deer, that stands at gaze'. The word 'gaze' clearly had a more precise meaning than merely 'see' or 'sight'; it has a Scandinavian origin and meant to fix one's eye on an object. Par force hounds located their prey by using scent and, once they caught sight of it, fixed their eye on it and went, often with reckless speed, wearying the beast to death, as Caius recorded. Sighthounds don't

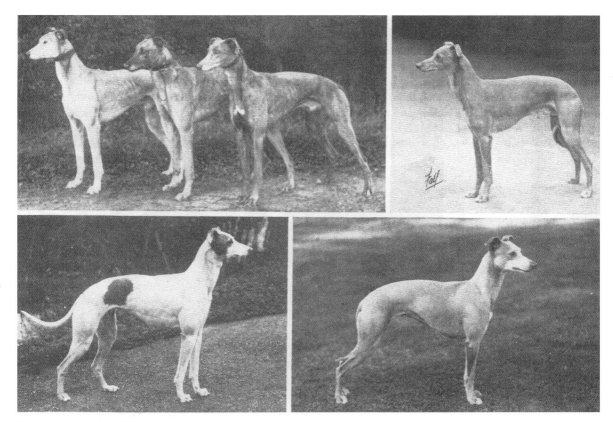

The Greyhound and the Whippet.
Top left: Mr E. Baxter's Greyhounds Elder brother, Ever Bright & Entry Badge. Bottom Left: Mr E. Baxter's Greyhound Edna Best (Bitch).
Top right: Mr J Emlyn-Owen's whippet Watford Breeze (Dog). Bottom right: Mrs E. Scarlett's Whippet Neptune's Sunshine (Bitch).

(1) and (2): Gazelle Hounds, the property of Hon. Florence Amhurst. (3): Greyhound, Champion Fire Water, exported to the USA. The Gazelle Hound is an ancient breed, true to type of a thousand years ago. Greyhounds in King John's reign were accepted in lieu of money. The Greyhound was not the Gazehound. (from Ash's Dogs of 1926).

hunt in packs 'at force'; they hunt at speed, sometimes as a brace, but using athleticism, agility, inherited skill, recalled experience, immense stamina over hundreds of yards, maintaining astonishing pace and applying great determination. It is belittling to blur them with the gazehounds, which have quite different skills and need a different anatomy to succeed in the hunting field. Researching a gazehound in historical references, having assumed the word refers to a sighthound, is not wise. Taking historic references to 'Greyhounds' to refer only to the breed of that name can be just as misleading.

The Eternal Sighthound Physique

The sprinters of the canine world have become known, in modern times, as sighthounds, although they hunt by speed, using sight mainly, but scent too. The need for their extreme pace has bestowed upon them a distinctive anatomy, right across the breeds, and with it a physical stylishness and a natural elegance that makes them the aristocrats of the dog world. They rely on long legs, deep chests, lightness of build, strong feet and keen eyesight. Their detection of movement, often at great distances, is astonishing. In silhouette, size and coat texture apart, the various sighthound breeds resemble each other, function deciding form. A big Whippet can be mistaken for a small Greyhound; a smooth Saluki can be confused with a Sloughi; both the Spanish Galgo and the Hungarian Magyar Agar can be taken for Greyhounds and the bat-eared breeds of the Mediterranean littoral are easily misidentified. They look similar because their function is similar; no sighthound can function with anything other than a sighthound physique. Hounds that hunt using their stamina, and rely mainly on scent to pursue their quarry, are governed by very different design criteria.

Sighthound is a Modern Word

In *The Kennel Encyclopaedia* (1908), J. Sidney Turner writes under the heading of the Eastern Greyhound: 'Before discussing the various breeds of Greyhounds, it may be of interest to note the various names by which they are called. The term Tazi Kutha, or running dog, is a Persian word, now indiscriminately applied by natives of India and Persia to all breeds of Greyhounds be they English or Eastern.' If he were writing today, he would use the word sighthound instead of the word Greyhound. In the whole four-volume encyclopaedia he does not list the word sighthound at all. Similarly, in his valuable but strangely underrated two-volume *The Dog Book* (1906) the extremely knowledgeable Scottish writer James Watson records on the Greyhound:

There is no doubt that the name was made to cover a great many dogs that were not what we call greyhounds. It is not so long ago that deerhounds and wolfhounds were called Scottish and Irish greyhounds. The Russian wolfhound was mentioned as the Russian greyhound and his close relative of Persia had also the same breed name and if we go further back we cannot find traces of dogs that must have

Magyar Agar – Hungarian Greyhound.

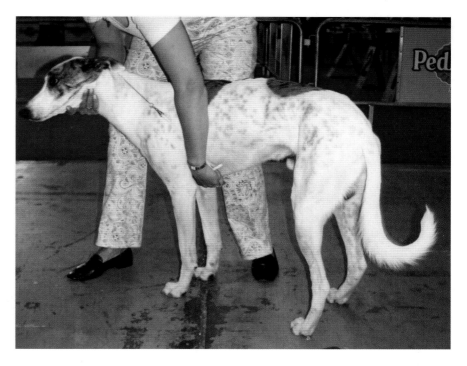

existed in England and could only have been included in the general group of greyhounds.

He did not use the generic term sighthound in his 800-page masterpiece.

Need to Subdivide Hound Breeds

Another expert of those times, Robert Leighton, in his comprehensive *The New Book of the Dog* (1912), a 650-page tome, covers the 'sprinter' breeds extensively but without using the word sighthound. He has ten pages on Oriental Greyhounds too. Nearly a century later, we have Juliette Cunliffe in her *Sighthounds – Their History, Management and Care* (2006) opening with: 'The group classified as Sight Hounds can just as easily be called Gaze Hounds or, indeed, from the natural history point of view, the Greyhound group.' I do not think Dr Caius would support that opening sentence and he lived in times when gazehounds and Greyhounds coexisted! In his authoritative *A History of Domesticated Animals* (1963), Frederick Zeuner writes extensively on the early history of the dog but writes of the greyhound type not the sighthound type. Of course

he did not need to collect breeds into groups for show purposes and perhaps kennel clubs in the pedigree dog world found a need to divide the speedsters from the scenthounds and chose the group name sighthounds; that is useful but should never be taken to mean that the speedsters only hunt using their eyes, because they do not. Less sophisticated sportsmen in East Anglia called their lurchers 'look-dogs', knowing they mainly relied on their eyes when hunting.

Common Purpose

The various breeds of sighthound can sound, from their breed names, designed for a specific task – as the titles Wolfhound and Deerhound exemplify; very exotic – as the name tags Saluki, Azawakh and Cirneco dell'Etna illustrate; or simply down to earth – as breed names such as Whippet, Rabbit Dog and Caravan Hound indicate. But whether sounding specialist, exotic or mundane, they all have the same purpose, catching their quarry using speed, sight, agility and sheer athleticism. Their owners ranged from the highest in the land, with their elaborate hunting pageantry, to the lowly peasant or nomad hunter, relying on a skilful hound to feed his family. They were admired for their grace, physical beauty

The high head of the Sighthound.

and stylish charm, but valued for their hunting prowess. No hungry man gives food to a useless dog.

Conservation Need

Sighthounds are found all over the world and in some unexpected places. In Admiral Anson's report on his historic circumnavigation of the globe in 1740–44, there is mention of Goat Island off the coast of Chile, where 'the place is covered with dogs of an enormous size resembling the greyhounds'. Wherever any sighthound breed comes from and whatever its coat length, we should respect their heritage, perpetuate them as honourably as Bedouins do and 'control' their breeding just as strictly as the latter do. Is any sighthound *not* physically constructed for hunting really a sighthound at all? This book argues for real sighthounds to be conserved both in their anatomical and their spiritual content; they are a precious feature of our canine coverage. We really must find alternative sports for them, simulating the chase and testing their ancient long-treasured talents. This is discussed in the conclusion.

Coursing Dogs – These were generally smooth, short-haired animals with slender bodies set on long legs, pointed heads, either small pointed or larger floppy ears and a long thin tail. It is one of the most frequently represented of all the breeds and clearly held a position of some esteem both as a valuable hunting hound and as a companion of the gods. The earliest representation is of a Saluki-like hound on a leash appearing on pottery from the Halaf period (5300–4300BC). A seal impression in sun-dried clay from the Chalcolithic period c.5000BC at Tell Arpachiya in Mosul reveals 'some kind of coursing dog, perhaps a greyhound.'

Brewer, Clark & Phillips, *Dogs in Antiquity, Anubis to Cerberus* (2001)

CHAPTER 1

THE SIGHTHOUND CULTURE

Moving at Speed

In estimating the Greyhound's claim to be the handsomest of the canine race we must remember for what his various excellencies, resulting in a whole which is so strikingly elegant, are designed. Speed is the first and greatest quality a dog of this breed

Chiens de chasse et chèvre, 1880.

can possess; to make a perfect dog there are other attributes he must not be deficient in; but wanting in pace, he can never hope to excel.

Hugh Dalziel, *The Greyhound* (1887)

All sighthounds are 'high drive' dogs, being stimulated to chase by moving objects. I've seen young coursing dogs, out for the first time on the flat fens of East Anglia, take off after a car speeding along a distant by-road, maybe a quarter-of-a-mile away. They have been stimulated purely by the moving object with no thought as to what it might be. The drive in sighthounds, particularly the coursing Saluki-type lurchers, has been so enhanced that it overrides just about every other trait.

Lurcher expert Penny Taylor, writing in *The Countryman's Weekly* (September 2011)

Using Their Speed

The hounds that hunt using their speed would have been better named the cursorial canines or better still, 'coursers', but have become known as sighthounds.

Inherited prowess. Colonel Charlett's Greyhounds, W.H. Davis, 1850.

Saluki at Speed.
D. Copperthwaite.

The German word for sighthound is '*windhund*' and their expression '*von Wind haben*' means to get wind of; in some ways that is better, for whether by sight or scent, all sporting dogs become aware of their quarry by getting wind of it. Hunting by speed depends on the pace of the dog and its willingness to speed after a fast-moving quarry. Sighthounds without hard muscle and an alert eye are a sad sight; to me they have simply lost the right to be regarded as sighthounds. To develop a type of dog to excel at a particular function, with a physique specially designed to do so,

Borzois racing in Germany.

and then let it waste away is a betrayal. To deny it the chance to run fast is a form of indirect cruelty; that is what it is for! It is therefore cheering to hear not just of Greyhound Racing but of Whippet and Lurcher racing, and of Afghan Hound racing being conducted too. Dogs bred to race need to exercise their sheer muscular power.

Astonishing Power

The Whippet, for its size, may well be the swiftest of all animals. Some years back, in a lecture at the Royal Institution on 'The Dimensions of Animals and Their Muscular Dynamics', Professor A.V. Hill made a number of salient points. He remarked that a small animal conducts each of its movements quicker than a large one, with muscles having a higher intrinsic speed and being able proportionately to develop more power. The maximum speeds of the racehorse, Greyhound and Whippet are apparently in the ratio 124:110:110 but their weight relationship is in the ratio 6,000:300:100. The larger animal can, however, maintain its pace for longer periods. Professor Hill suggested that up a steep hill, the speed of a racehorse, Greyhound and Whippet could be in reverse order to that on the flat. It is generally held that a Whippet's best performance is over a furlong on the flat, when it

Big lure-chasing Whippet.

can capitalize on its ability to provide the maximum oxygen supply per unit weight of muscle. This is a very efficient running dog.

Performing the Function

It is not just sheer speed – agility comes into the equation as well. Agility matters hugely in, say, a wolf hunt too, for the wolf is a daunting adversary: brave, strong and athletic. Bigger quarry, such as deer, are naturally agile too. Stamina has to accompany speed and agility. In the Middle East I have watched two Salukis race out of sight over ground which would have broken some dogs' legs and over a distance which would have taken the pace out of many hounds. I was not surprised when a lurcher breeder once told me that the greatest benefit from the blood of the Saluki came in the feet. The Afghan Hound also needs remarkable feet to cope with the terrain in its native country. We may not want our Afghans and

Salukis to sprint over rocks or our Borzois to hunt wolves, but they came to us as breeds developed for a function and with an anatomy which allowed them to perform that function. We ignore that original function and we imperil the breed.

Hazel's Pal – racing whippet. D. Clarke.

Whippet at speed.

Magyar Agar.

Show Ring Changes

We have to be extraordinarily careful that in the pursuit of show success, whether in lurcher rings or at KC-licensed events, we do not end up destroying the key elements in these handsome, *functional* speedsters. A sighthound needs lung and heart room in abundance; it must have great forward extension, facilitated by sound shoulders. Short straight upper arms are creeping into so many sporting breeds these days and it is introducing quite untypical and most undesirable movement. The importance of sound shoulders can never be stressed enough in any hound breed. A hound built for speed, whether a

Spanish Galgo.

Afghan Hound as originally imported.

Modern Afghan Hound.

Spanish Galgo, a Hungarian Agar, a Tasy or a Taigon from mid-Asia, a Moroccan Sloughi or an Azawakh from Mali, *must* have the anatomical attributes that provide sprinting power. Some foreign sighthound breeds look different now from the original imports; the Afghan Hound certainly has more coat and the Borzoi can feature a markedly convex back as opposed to the more or less level topline of the early imports.

Energy and Heat Storage

Hunters and sportsmen the world over know that the ability to catch game using speed demands a very distinctive build. The sighthounds bound; they must have the height/weight ratio, the leg length and the liver size to sprint. Sighthounds race entirely on liver glycogen, sugar activated from the liver. Sprinting demands long legs and a sizeable liver. The bigger the liver the more sugar can be stored. A sighthound over 65lb in weight would theoretically have more

of a problem through heat storage, although its streamlined build allows the presentation of a greater surface area. We are good at getting rid of excess heat and not very good at storing it. Dogs are the reverse, removing excess heat from their surfaces rather as a radiator gives off heat.

Measuring Performance

When sighthounds were traded, such technicalities were not known but the radiator-like build, size without weight and long legs meant something to their traders. The most successful sprinters had the build to succeed and were traded and perpetuated. In breeding for appearance only we need to bear in mind those anatomical essentials that made sighthounds what they are: internationally renowned sprinters. An 85lb Borzoi will experience difficulties when running flat out; a Greyhound of any weight with a small liver will have an even bigger handicap. Traders in

Hurdling Track Greyhound.

Muscular commitment.

Poetry in Motion – contrasting aspects of the gallo, Cranog Bet and (below) Hack Up Chieftain.

such hounds could not measure livers but they could measure performance. Some of these overseas breeds are being perpetuated here only in the show ring. The worry is that, in time, show ring criteria will shape them, not function. If you look at the Afghan Hounds first imported here and then compare them with today's breed, you can immediately spot the heavier coat, with upright shoulders and short upper arms.

Wrong Breeding Criteria

It is so pleasing to know that Afghan Hound (and Saluki) racing is conducted in Britain; what a release for the hounds! Less pleasing is the knowledge that the best Afghan Hound racer, Fox Ellis, which won the national individual championship a record five successive times, was never used at stud. A litter sister became a champion but for Fox Ellis not to be used at stud tells you more about breeders seeking show-winner blood ahead of proven construction than I ever could. The sighthound breeds only survived to enter the show arenas because of their ability to race. And to race in their native terrain they needed

sighthound characteristics, not show points aimed at impressing an ignorant judge. It is insulting to import a magnificent foreign breed and then alter it for local preferences – which is also almost certain to introduce highly undesirable anatomical flaws.

Show Critiques

In 2009, two show judges' critiques on Afghan Hounds depressed me. One read: 'The more I observe modern day judges, the more I come to the conclusion that many seem to have little conception or complete lack of understanding of "true type". The second read: 'So on to the most major problems which are prevalent no matter where one looks… You either have to accept it or stand alone in an empty ring.' A 2011 judge in the same breed commented in the show critique:

> Although the entry was large for these days, 91 dogs entered and few absentees, the quality could not compare to previous occasions when I had the opportunity to judge Afghan Hounds in England. From what I saw, it appears that few of the many imports used at stud over the years have really been of any great help, and there appears to be little left of the beautiful, dignified, yet quietly fierce type I remember from the early days…

What sad reading! The grooming fetishists have prevailed in this breed and this insults the painstaking work done by primitive hunters in unforgiving terrain over many centuries in their native country. Our noble infantrymen sweating away in Afghanistan in recent years would much prefer not to have to wear body armour, bulky equipment round their waists

In Full Flight. Two Aces – the 1964 Grand National Winner, at the White City.

Racing Afghan Hound.

and carry packs on their backs. Afghan Hounds do not need a similar hindrance on their bodies!

Forbidden Use

When lamenting the misguided, contemptible class warfare behind the malicious Hunting with Dogs Act, which now denies many a working-class sportsman his chance to fill his family's cooking pot, it is easy to overlook the previous prohibitions of coursing large and small game with sighthounds on mainland Europe: in France in 1844, in Germany in 1848 and in Holland in 1924. Before this legislation, northern Europe had a distinguished heritage of hunting with sighthounds: *levriers* in France, *Windhunden,*

Flemish hunter. Jan Wildens, 1624.

14-year-old Archduke Albrecht with his zwickdarm or 'strong Greyhound'. After A Sanchez Coello.

Windspielen or *Windhetzen* (literally, speed-hounds, with even a separate name for those that went for the underbelly: *Zwickdarmers*) in Germany and the rough and smooth-coated Friese Windhond of the Netherlands. It is relevant to keep in mind too that in 10000BC, in a world population of 10 million, everyone was a hunter. By AD1500, in a world population of 350 million, only 1 per cent were hunters. By 1972, in a population of 3 billion, only 0.001 per cent were hunters. Even 2,000 years ago, in many parts of the world, the success of hunting dogs was the difference between eating and starving. Hunting by speed, relying on the eyes and long legs of our sighthounds, has left us a rich heritage of canine cursorial prowess.

Although hunting as Xenophon practiced it was still carried on, particularly by the Cretans and the Carians, and although the Romans hunted in much the same manner as the Greeks (as well as in great hunts of the Persian sort), a new sport was introduced into the ancient world by the Celts some time before the second century after Christ. Although it may have been called hunting, it was in fact almost exactly the same sport as what we call 'coursing', and its purpose was not to catch the hare but to watch the hounds

'Windhetzen' by Ridinger, late Middle Ages.

The agile Greyhound.

Sizing up the sighthounds. Greyhound, Whippet and Italian Greyhound by Strebel, 1905.

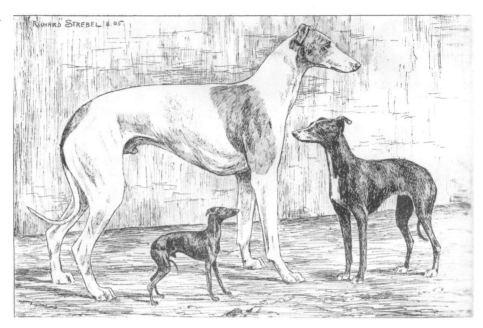

race her...The hounds used were the Vertragi, a breed of greyhounds...

> Denison Bingham Hull, *Hounds and Hunting in Ancient Greece* (1964)

Before buying a dog, always see him gallop, as freedom of movement counts for a great deal. Dogs that sprawl all over the track seldom get anywhere near the winners. Correct, symmetrical movement tending to speed and true running, can come only from dogs which are nearest to the accepted standard of perfection. It is very difficult to advise which is the most suitable size and weight. Good performances are put up by large and small dogs alike. If any special lists of sizes and weights had been kept, it is probable that dogs of between sixty and sixty-five pounds weight would be found the most suitable for both mechanical hare racing and the plumpton [that is, coursing], but no hard and fast rule can be laid down. B.A. McMichan, RVS, *The Greyhound* (1937). He was

Coursing on Epsom Racecourse.

the Official Veterinary Surgeon to The Greyhound Breeders and Trainers Association of Australia at that time.

The Nature of the Canine Speedsters

Greyhounds [here the word is used to denote sighthounds] are by far the commonest hunting dog to appear in late medieval illustrations … illustrations show them in all manner of domestic situations, in living- and bedrooms, at the board when their owners are at meals, sitting by the fireside and even at mass. Of all dogs, they appear to have been the most constant of companions of their masters during journeys, in war and at home.

Richard Almond, *Medieval Hunting* (2003)

Sighthounds share common personality characteristics. They exude dignity and a sense of self-importance, but can also act like court jesters. Occasionally, they may 'fire up' and stand firm according to their own perceptions and thresholds. The Borzoi in the clown suit, for instance, can quickly become a frightening force to reckon with: a large, powerful hound with lightning-fast reflexes, and the inherent abilities that enabled him to pull down and pin a wolf in years past. The wolves may have gone, but the Borzoi's imprinted genetic code is not forgotten. Instinct is a powerful force.

Denise Como, *Sighthounds Afield* (2004)

We hear a lot about what different breeds will bring into the lurcher – Saluki for stamina, Greyhound for speed, collie for toughness, Deerhound for coat, Whippet for take-off speed – but each breed brings in mental as well as physical attributes and these are given less importance or even forgotten when people are thinking of getting a lurcher … these character attributes will make all the difference to how it will respond to training and how it will behave when it goes through developmental fear periods and rebellious stages. Once mature, the lurcher will work – can only work – according to its genetic legacy.

Lurcher expert Jackie Drakeford, in *The Countryman's Weekly* (September 2011)

Compassionate Wolfhound.

Sighthounds at play.

The fact is, that for perfect working a considerable degree of mental activity and quickness is required, which shall enable the dog to do enough to distress the hare, without distressing himself. A good greyhound is never a fool, whatever may be said by some old-fashioned coursers. Depend upon it, that a greyhound soon learns to know all the motions of the hare, and is prepared to defeat them; and this tact he learns often before he has ever seen a hare, by chasing his companions in their play. Cunning is often acquired in this way…

J.H. Walsh, *The Pursuit of Wild Animals for Sport*
(1856)

Reserved Nature

The greyhound is said to be deficient in attachment to his master and in general intelligence. There is some truth in the imputation; but, in fact, the greyhound has, far less than even the hound, the opportunity of forming individual attachments, and no other exercise of the mind is required of him than to follow the game which starts up before him, and to catch it if he can. If, however, he is closely watched he will be found to have all the intellect that his situation requires.

Those words are from William Youatt's *The Dog* (1854) and reflect the timeless view of many on the running dogs: those who know them well rate them, those knowing them only from afar misjudging them. And they can be aloof, withdrawn – away from the hunting grounds, undemonstrative and reserved. They will never have the vivacity of a Jack Russell or make the demands for affection of a spaniel. In many cases you have to earn their affection, rather than expect it.

Using their Brains

In his book *The Dog – Structure and Movement* (1970), R.H. Smythe, sportsman, vet and exhibitor, writes:

> When galloping on a circular race track the fore limb nearest to the centre of the course takes the greater part of the weight and so becomes the leading leg. If by any reason the dog is thrown temporarily off its stride and changes legs, there will be a loss of speed and the winner is more often the dog that uses its brain to retain its balance and maintain the same type of gait throughout the race.

When you see a sighthound tearing round a track at flat-out speed, it is difficult to think of the racing dog using its brain, either to learn from experience or to adjust quickly to a split-second problem. But such a hound can so easily be underestimated; the great winners are often the brainiest dogs too. The hunting dog instincts work on the track as well.

Born to Hunt

Many of these breeds are glamorous, like the Afghan Hound; physically beautiful, like the Saluki; aristocratic, like the Borzoi; and seemingly gentle-natured, like the Deerhound. But they were designed and then bred to hunt and kill, whatever their gentleness away from the hunting field. They are favoured by some because of their sheer handsomeness and I have no criticism of that. But I am concerned that such attractive breeds can end up being valued only for their looks, and their spiritual needs overlooked. Their instinct to chase and catch other animals too needs to be acknowledged. There are dangers in overlooking the basic fact that sighthounds were selectively bred and specifically intended to kill small mammals. Instincts, however deeply buried, are still there. They need to be exercised but in a controlled way.

Some years ago, I lived near a well-meaning lady who rehomed two racing Greyhounds. They were delightful dogs and I support her kindness and compassion. She looked puzzled when I warned her that they needed retraining if exercised off the lead, because the only world they knew was chasing small furry moving objects. Her two new pets appeared so gentle, so unaggressive and so shy that she relaxed, a bit too much. A tradesman left a sidegate open one

Active Deerhounds.
G.D. Giles, 1911.

day and her retiring retired Greyhounds got out – and killed two cats and savaged a Dachshund within half an hour. The poor lady was devastated; but whatever their disposition, these two dogs were only doing what their inbred instincts told them they should be doing. If you own a sighthound do not be surprised if it acts like one!

Some years before that, I used to walk to work in London through St James's Park and often passed a lady walking her beautifully groomed Borzoi. The hound was very well trained, never pulled on the lead and seemed to ignore the many wildfowl that crossed its path. Then one day a grey squirrel dared to dash across the ground moving from one huge tree

Inactive Deerhounds by Landseer.

to another. The Borzoi shot forward so strongly and unexpectedly that the lady was unable to hold him and the grey squirrel had a nasty surprise but met a quick end. The lady was distraught, saying that the dog had never even seen a grey squirrel before. Her chosen breed was however a hunter, one bred for centuries to catch and kill. For all their elegance and reticence all sighthounds were designed to hunt and kill.

More recently, a Whippet owner wrote in one of the dog papers that she had had a distressing incident in the New Forest with her dog. She had taken her dog into an official car park and let her dog out of

Afghan Hound in repose.

the car for its usual walk, as she had many times before. On this occasion the dog suddenly dashed into nearby undergrowth and disappeared. The lady went after her dog only to see it seize a small deer by the hamstring after the briefest of chases. She was able to call the dog off but had to call a ranger to deal with the crippled creature, which was later destroyed. The lady was aghast at what her Whippet had done, understandably so in those circumstances. This dog had never hunted before but it had gone straight for the deer's hock. Canine instincts are often well buried but are still potentially active; owner empathy is essential, for we breed dogs for specific purposes and should never be surprised when their elemental nature emerges.

Natural Behaviour

Of course, any dog can chase cats, pursue deer or ambush a grey squirrel, but a sighthound stands a better chance of succeeding than most. Being built for extreme speed, having exceptional eyesight, acute hearing and a good nose for air scent are all very well but if the hunting instinct is not there too you do not have a hound at all. In his book *The Mind of the Dog*, R.H. Smythe, vet, exhibitor and sportsman, writes:

Relaxed Greyhound.

Much of the work carried out by dogs, whether it be chasing the live or dummy hare, hunting and tracking and so on, is really natural behaviour adapted to certain ends… One can only marvel at the instinct which compels a pack of greyhounds to chase a mechanical hare several times a week with no hope of ever catching it.

When dog's natural behaviour is harnessed by man, it is reinforced by dog's equally natural desire to please its human owner; training a member of the speedster breeds, however, is not a recommended task for a new dog owner. Dog breeds are often selected by their future owners because of their appearance, which potentially leads to mismatches. Owners must always be aware of the reason their potential purchase came into being – what they were *for*.

Training Challenge

Stanley Coren points out in *The Intelligence of Dogs* (1994):

Sighthounds, for example, will chase things that move. This means that attempting to work or train your greyhound, whippet, saluki, or Afghan hound in a busy area, such as a park where children and other dogs will be running around, will simply make the task more difficult. If you must train outdoors, use a relatively empty field or yard … you can take advantage of these breeds' responsiveness to visual stimuli by using large and exaggerated hand signals during training rather than simply depending upon voice commands.

In his forthright *Secrets of Dog Training* (1992), Brian Plummer, who knew a thing or two about the use of hunting dogs wrote: 'Sight hounds usually respond to commands with infuriating slowness despite the fact that when they so choose they can galvanise into action with an astonishing and often quite terrifying speed... All Middle Eastern greyhound types are singularly resistant to formal conventional training' – putting this down to a 'rather remote disposition'. All hound breeds need a certain independence of mind as well as immense determination in order to perform their allotted task at all. This demands both a measure of control by the owner but also a recognition that the dog's natural instincts need to be exercised.

Writing in *The Countryman's Weekly* in September 2011, lurcher expert Penny Taylor gave the view that:

> The 'shape' or 'wiring' in a dog's brain is something inherited through hundreds of years' breeding for a particular function and we must never forget the original purpose of our dogs if we are to succeed in training them. Some people say that the Saluki-type is untrainable but nothing could be further from the truth. You can't apply 'conventional' training methods to a dog which was never bred for trainability in the first place and you need to think outside the conventional training box to engage these dogs on your terms.

There is an awful lot of sense in this approach to sighthound training. Equally perceptively, a fellow lurcher expert, Jackie Drakeford, wrote in the same issue of the magazine:

> We may have a Deerhound stage where the pup may be a shy feeder, a clumsy great lout and not a great thinker; through a Saluki stage where the Deerhoundy cooperation is lost and a sensitive, stubborn, independent solver of problems emerges; to a Bedlington stage where fire and no reverse gear take over from the Saluki careful consideration of everything before acting; and a collie stage of hypersensitivity, cringing and refusing to leave your side...

It is so important with sighthounds to know your breed or the contributing ingredients in your hybrid.

Gentle giant.

Civilised Wolfhound.

Eagerness to Run

In their account of the first London greyhound track meeting, *The Times* of 21 June 1927 reported:

> The card consisted of eight races. The finishes, perhaps, were not quite so close as usual, but cleverness and experience told nearly every time, and the keenness and gameness of the dogs were indicated, first, by their howling and pawing at the doors of the starting box and, then, by their refusal to give in so long as a breath of wind remained to them. Trainers already tell stories of the older dogs' hatred of being beaten by another dog – a hatred that far transcends the desire for the mechanical hare's blood.

It is unwise to underestimate the powerful instincts of the sighthounds, especially their eagerness to run after a moving quarry, and most unwise to underrate the sheer competitiveness of the speedsters. However aloof their demeanour, however gracious their movement and however reserved in nature, these dogs are 'hot-wired' to run and to win! Julian Grenfell, in his poem *To a Black Greyhound*, has neatly captured the contrast between the hound in the field and the one on the hearth.

See him lie when the day is dead,
Black curves curled on the boarded floor.
Sleepy eyes, my sleepy-head –
Eyes that were aflame before.
Gentle now, they burn no more,
Gentle now and softly warm,
With the fire that made them bright
Hidden – as when after storm
Softly falls the night.

For me, the most perfect Greyhound, both in conformation and running style, was the stunning black racing Greyhound star Westmead Poncho of thirty years ago, the beau ideal of a sighthound, combining great beauty of form with an immense desire to run.

Greyhound faces convey every thought and feeling. Their eyes seem to reflect the wisdom of the ages. Bright intelligence shines from those eyes and captures your soul. They are soft, yet piercing, and reflect great intuitiveness and understanding. But they can convey other messages as well. At different times they express sympathy, sensitivity, amusement, keenness, anticipation, mischievousness, and sometimes, just

Racing Greyhound:
Westmead Poncho.
Greyhound magazine.

Good-natured but not fawning.

can be malformed to an extent which it is for ever impossible to counteract. The greyhound is one of the most peaceable of dogs, and is as happy as the day is long when wandering about on a farm.

> James Matheson, *The Greyhound – Breeding, Coursing, Racing, Etc* (1930). This advice can of course be applied to most sighthound breeds, not just the Greyhound.

Greyhounds were in fact so various in size that they were used for hunting all manner of game, and were so constantly with their masters that they were as much companions as working dogs.

> A. Compton Reeves, writing of the fifteenth-century sighthound in *Pleasures and Pastimes in Medieval England* (1997)

plain stubbornness. 'Just watch me!' is a challenge many owners have met in their Greyhound's eyes.

> Sue LeMieux, *The Book of the Greyhound* (1999)

The mild, affable, and serene aspect of the greyhound in its domestic state constitutes no drawback to its innate sagacity, or grateful attention to its protector; of which the unfortunate King Charles the First was so truly observant, that the remark he made during his troubles is upon record, and strictly, just as applicable to the instinctive fidelity of the animal, as well as its satirical effect upon the herd of sycophants who surrounded him. In the course of a familiar conversation, respecting the canine species in general, a doubt was started what particular kind of dog was entitled to pre-eminence, when it was universally admitted to rest between the spaniel and the greyhound; to which the monarch gave a polished finish in favour of the latter, by saying it possessed all the good nature and solicitous affability of the spaniel without the fawning.

> *The Sportsman's Cabinet* (1803)

Of all dogs, the greyhound is the one which requires the greatest amount of freedom. His great activity makes it essential that he has space upon which to gallop and roam at will. His conformation and nature demands it from earliest infancy, and it is a fact that young greyhounds, if shut away, never do any good. Even in the first two months of life they

Sighthounds for Sport

The Need to Pursue

The sighthound breeds came to us from the sporting field, from being used as coursing hounds; they will only stay with us as real sighthounds if we retain a sporting use for them, whether it's on the track or on the lure. We owe a great deal to those coursers who bequeathed such remarkable hounds to us; we will only honour their memory by *using* them. The very expression 'companion dog' hints at the dog being there for our benefit, but to regard a sighthound purely as a pet is to insult its distinguished heritage; we really must use them. I think it is fair to claim that coursing, all over the world, shaped the sighthound breeds of today into formidable canine athletes. To

Greyhound coursing, 1900.

Greyhound racing. Harringay, 1982.

maintain the sighthound's long history in providing excellence is going to prove a challenge. Lure racing is valuable exercise; track racing tests sheer speed and bend handling skills but coursing was the supreme test. All sighthounds need to run, but the pursuit of prey at speed in the hunting field is their instinct.

Coursing Prowess

'The aim of the true sportsman with hounds is not to take the hare, but to engage her in a racing contest or duel, and he is pleased if she happens to escape.' wrote Arrian in AD150. Those words succinctly capture the ethos of coursing across the centuries: it never has been about two hounds striving to catch a hare but a brace of sighthounds striving to outrun each other. The quarry is respected, allowed a fair start or law, and unlike shooting or fox-hunting, permitted to escape at any stage during the chase. In his *An Encyclopaedia of Rural Sports* (1870), Delabere Blaine wrote:

> The practice of modern coursing may be dated from the time of Elizabeth. Under her auspices it became a fashionable pursuit; nor has time diminished the hold it took on the regards of the sporting public. To further, methodise, and give stability to its practice, a code of laws was framed by the Duke of Norfolk, himself a lover of the leash, that became the stock on which the rules observed at coursing meetings were ingrafted.

Coursing Stars

Another Norfolk landowner, Lord Orford, started a line of coursing Greyhounds of remarkable prowess.

Orford's Czarina won forty-seven matches without ever being beaten; when Orford died, she went, with her co-star son Claret, to the Yorkshire kennel of Colonel Thornton. Claret was put to a high-quality bitch owned by another Yorkshire coursing man, Major Topham, to produce three of the best Greyhounds ever seen: Snowball, Major and Sylvia. All three won every match for which they were entered. Snowball was considered to be the finest Greyhound ever bred; he won in every type of country, was famed for his stamina and for his sheer power when running uphill. This blend of Yorkshire and Norfolk blood started perhaps the best ever line of coursing Greyhounds from England and provided the breeding basis for the breed from

THE GREYHOUND.

"Ah! gallant Snowball! what remains,
Up Fordon's banks, o'er Flixton's plains,
Of all thy strength — thy sinewy force,
Which rather flew than ran the course?
Ah! what remains? Save that thy breed
May to their father's fame succeed;
And when the prize appears in view,
May prove that they are Snowballs too."

Author unknown.

Benjamin Marshall – Colonel Thornton's Greyhound.

Major – winning Greyhound, 1803.

Czarina and Maria. Sawrey Gilpin, 1801.

Famous coursing Greyhound Claret.

then on. Snowball sired nearly fifty litters, with the bitches coming from all over Britain. Forty years after Snowball's whelping, the 'Blue Riband of the Leash', the Waterloo Cup, was held at Altcar and from then on this cup was the pinnacle of coursing fame. It was run on ground where the hare was protected and almost revered.

Winning Facets
Coursing Greyhounds like Czarina, Claret, Major and Snowball, then, later, Fullerton and Master McGrath, became the sporting icons of their time. Rawdon Lee, the prolific Victorian canine chronicler, used depictions of Fullerton and Master McGrath to illustrate the Greyhound as a breed in his several-volumed *Modern Dogs* series of the late 1890s and early 1900s. But in the text, surprisingly for him, he describes Snowball as a white dog, perhaps confused by the name itself. He could not have seen Chalon's celebrated painting of Snowball, showing very clearly the shining black coat. Colour 'prejudice' in Greyhound coats is discussed in Chapter 2. Coursing

needs have not always coincided with others. In *The Working Longdog* (1999), Frank Sheardown writes:

There has been a tendency with English-bred Greyhounds for the coursing ones to be bred with too much emphasis on strength, as they may run four times in the day in a 16 dog stake and not enough on speed. The track ones on the other hand tend to be

Snowball. H.B. Chalon, 1807.

bred for early pace but with not enough consideration given to the physical attributes necessary to withstand the punishing demands of a coursing meeting...

Track Racing

Out of coursing came the urban equivalent, track racing. As long ago as 1876 mechanical lure racing was conducted, at first as a spectacle at a sporting show, when two Greyhounds pursued an artificial hare raced along a groove in the track over a 400yd grass track. The first race was won by Charming Nell, owned by Edward Dent, breeder of the famous coursing Greyhound Fullerton. But it was after interest in America spread back to Britain, in the mid-1920s, that this new sport really took off. In 1926 the average crowd at a track meeting was 11,000. By 1932, the attendances had reached 20 million. With big money now accruing from the sport, the tricksters soon moved in, with doping scandals rife. The National Greyhound Racing Club has worked hard to drive out match-fixing and dog-faking. Bend racing does still have its critics due to the stress placed on the limbs of the racing dog.

Racing the Sighthound Breeds

Around 1960, four sighthound breeds were raced, one after the other, over a 425m course, with the following times for the different breeds: Greyhound: 27.68 seconds; Whippet: 30.97; Borzoi: 35.07; Afghan Hound: 36.11. The times reflect the build as well as the purpose of each type. In a recent report on an Afghan Hound race meeting at Ellesmere Port, these words were used in the introduction: 'Those of you who have never taken your dogs racing – you really do not know what you are missing – find your nearest meeting and go along and see what happens. They – and you! – deserve the fun.' This meeting was attended by twenty-two Afghan Hounds and twenty-seven others: four Lurchers, four Pharaoh Hounds and three Salukis, as well as Whippets, Border Collies, Siberian

Held in the slips – coursing Greyhounds.

Fullerton – winner of the Waterloo Cup in 1890–1–2.

Australian track race, 1936.

Huskies, even Jack Russells and five Border Terriers. In the 260s, the best Afghan time was 22 seconds; in the 440m run timings varied between 45 and 55 seconds; with some sub-seven-second times in the 100 metres. What fun and yes, the dogs do deserve it!

Organized Sport

In the wake of the Hunting with Dogs Act, the various coursing clubs for Greyhounds, Salukis and Whippets and the staging of the British single-handed longdog/lurcher coursing championships have been suspended. We are left with admirable organizations like the Working Whippet Club, the Whippet Club Racing Association, the New Lancashire Whippet Racing Club, Afghan Racing (open to all breeds) and a number of lure-racing groups, alongside the highly organized, very professional track racing world for Greyhounds, to exercise the sighthounds here. Lure coursing aims to stimulate the hounds' natural instincts to chase quarry. The 'lure', a bag or bunch of plastic bags tied to a line powered by an electric motor, using a system of pulleys to drag the lure along a set course, seems to excite the hounds' innate desire to chase even such an artificial quarry. Something is better than nothing in this crucial need to preserve the sighthound urge. The instinctive desire to pursue, the athleticism needed in the chase and the basic need to exercise speed all require an outlet. Running really quickly by dogs must never become archival.

Sprinting Prowess

A Greyhound can cover 5/16 of a mile in 30 seconds. In each decade the feats are repeated: in 1932, Ataxy did 525yd in 29.56 seconds, and, in 1936, 725yd in 41.69 seconds. In 1971, Dolores Rocket did the 525yd course in 28.52 seconds. In 1944, Ballyhennessy Seal set what was then a new world record for 500yd in 27.64 seconds. The legendary Mick the Miller did the 600yd in 34.01 seconds in 1930. He was spoken of as combining 'tranquillity with trackcraft'. In other words he never wasted energy nervously and used the circuit cleverly. When he died he was found to have a heart weighing 1½oz above the normal for a Greyhound of his size. In 2010 the TV Trophy was won by defending champion Midway Skipper, who completed the 844m course in a new track record, for Kinsley, of 52.91 seconds. Of course hounds with a comparable build can also achieve great speed: a 32lb Whippet was once recorded as covering 150yd in 8.6 seconds. At the Whippet Club Racing Association Bend Championships held at Moreton-in-Marsh five

Lure racing with Whippets, 2011.

Coursing: Greyhounds in Slips. Coloured lithograph by T. Fairland, after W.J. Shayer, 1841.

years ago, 130 dogs ran on a horseshoe-shaped 240yd track in nine different weight groups, with a fastest time of 14.9 seconds.

Until coursing becomes legal once again, this is a great way to keep the speedsters tried and tested. In 1895 there were more than 150 coursing clubs in Britain; we could do with the same number of racing/lure chasing clubs today – sighthounds need to run! Each year more than 15,000 supporters attend the National Coursing Meet in Powerstown Park, Clonmel, County Tipperary, bringing an estimated £15 million into the local economy. The sprinting prowess of canines can clearly be an economic benefit as well as a sporting contest.

A Greyhound in tip-top condition should be all fire, animation, and sprightliness; his gaiety, expressed in the sparkle of his eyes and the bounding elasticity of his limbs, should be so refreshing to the beholder as to produce the idea that the excellences of the animal could be carried no further.

Thomas Thacker, *The Courser's Companion* (1834)

If the private courser is a pot-hunter, these dogs (i.e. Greyhounds) are often the best killers; but as I am assuming that he pursues coursing as an amusement, for the purpose of competing with his neighbours in a friendly way, and not solely to kill hares, I do not for a moment look at his wishes from that point of view. The man who habitually takes a brace of cunning greyhounds out solely to kill hares is no sportsman…

J.H. Walsh, *Manual of British Rural Sports – The Pursuit of Wild Animals for Sport* (1856)

Coursing Greyhounds, 1990.

CHAPTER 2

BREEDS OF THE BRITISH ISLES

The Racing Gre-hund

Cultivated Breed

In his wide-ranging *Encyclopaedia of Rural Sports* (1870), Delabere Blaine writes:

> The cultivated English Greyhound exhibits a model of elegance, and a combination of symmetric proportions, probably unrivalled by any other animal but the race-horse. The perfection of the mechanism for speedy progression is apparent throughout his structure. Whether we regard his organs separately or conjunctively, they are admirably adapted for vast powers of locomotion: nor can we view him without being struck with surprise at the great alterations which can be effected in the animal frame by culture…

In those rather quaint words, he is pointing out that man, not nature, created the Greyhound and for a specific purpose. The appearance of the Greyhound has been shaped by man for speed, linked to a

Detail from Colonel Charlett's Greyhounds. W.H. Davis, 1850.

Two Greyhounds in a landscape. Henry Calvert, 1840.

Mr Reid's Greyhounds. William Barraud, 1831.

hunting or sporting role, and so long as this role was valued, this design prevailed. Modern man, willing to discard the role of so many companion rather than working dogs, has the relative luxury of breeding for a subjective goal – appearance – rather than an objective one – performance. Unless we respect the Greyhound's role, we ignore the long, distinguished history of this type in the service of man.

Breed Name

There is every need to respect the noble heritage of the Greyhound, as this breed is so much more than a 'grey-hound'. The inclusion of the letter 'Y' in the Greyhound's breed name gives an immediate hint that this breed earned its title by being a hound coloured distinctly grey. As with far too many breed titles, with those of the Tibetan breeds of dog standing out as classic examples, that of the Greyhound is misleading. The word grey, meaning colour, was not used by medieval writers when listing the coat colours of this hound. The importance of this misnomer lies in the fact that gre-hund meant a 'noble, great, choice or prize-hound'. Th ree notable authorities, Jesse, Dalziel and Baillie-Grohman, all agree on this and their word is good enough for me. A Welsh proverb stated that a gentleman might be known, and judged, 'by his hawk, his horse and his greyhound'. By a law of Canute, a greyhound was not to be kept by any person inferior to a gentleman. The greyhound was clearly the companion of noblemen and deserves the more distinctive title of Grehund, or noble hound.

In her *Bridleways through History* (1936), Lady Apsley wrote of the famous Celtic hounds:

> They were universally praised as brilliant in the chase of wolves and deer and magnificent in appearance. They were the grae hounds, or hounds of grew or gre – ie 'high degree' – which became in Old English

gradus, 'graded hounds of the best breed', wrongly translated sometimes as 'greyhounds'… it is likely they were smooth-coated, of the modern greyhound build and much stronger and larger, very courageous, clever and hunted by scent as well as by sight…

She quoted an ancient Irish law regarding hounds that valued a trained Irish grae-hound belonging to the king at a pound, with an untrained one worth 120 pence. In his masterly *Researches into the History of the British Dog* (1866), George Jesse wrote: 'Originally it was most likely grehund, and meant the noble, great, choice, or prize hound', pointing out it was written as greihounde by Chaucer and Edward, Duke of York (in his *Master of Game*), and grehounde by William Brocas in Henry VI's reign and by Dame Julyana Berners too. He added that the word 'gre' in time became obsolete. It is unlikely that the word grey in Greyhound referred to coat colour.

Early Role
Delabere Blaine, writing in 1870, stated that the early type of Greyhound was brought into Britain by the Celts:

> Distribution, however, gradually effected changes in his form and covering. In Scotland and Ireland his bony form and rough coat marked him; in England also he was seen as a large, bony, gaunt animal, less rough certainly, but with a coat of coarse texture. He was, at those times, employed in coursing the largest animals, as boars, bears, wolves, etc., as long as the country afforded them. When these disappeared, and when there was less required from his strength,

but more from his quickness of motion, as already hinted at, he was bred somewhat finer, and was then much employed in fox coursing, in those days a very favourite diversion.

More was required from his strength in Scotland and Ireland, and his form there did not develop away from the original one as it did in England. Inevitably the anatomy of sporting dogs responds to changes of role.

Loose Use
Confusingly, in the Middle Ages, the word Greyhound was used loosely, before the introduction of the word sighthound, to refer to such diverse types as the Irish Wolfhound, the Scottish Deerhound and the dainty diminutive Italian Greyhound. Such dogs were the close companions of men involved in war and travel to far-off countries. It is therefore most unwise to link the contemporary breed of Greyhound with portrayals of such men. Greyhound researchers usually make much of an early reference to the breed in England by Dame Berners in her *Boke of St Albans*. But her memorable description 'Heded like a snake, and necked like a drake. Fottyed lyke a catte. Tayled like a Rat', is a clear plagiarism of Gace de la Buigne,

Greyhounds coursing a fox. Thomas Gainsborough, 1784.

Sloughi.

Rajapalayam dog.

Spanish Galgo.

written some time previously and not in England. The Ancient Greeks prized their sighthounds, Arrian writing: '…the fast running Celtic hounds are called vertragi in the Celtic language … these have their name from their speed … the best bred of them are a fine sight.' The Italian for a Greyhound is *veltro* and the Old French *veltre*, from the Celtic word *guilter*. The Spanish for a Greyhound is *galgo*, derived from *gallicu*, a word meaning Gaullish hound.

Universal Look

Today the Galgo is the breed of Spanish Greyhound, just as the Chart Polski is the Polish one and the Magyar Agar the Hungarian version. At a distance all could be confused with a smooth Saluki, a Sloughi or an Azawakh, such is the universal silhouette of a smooth-haired sighthound (although the Galgo can feature the rough coat too). No doubt the Shilluk

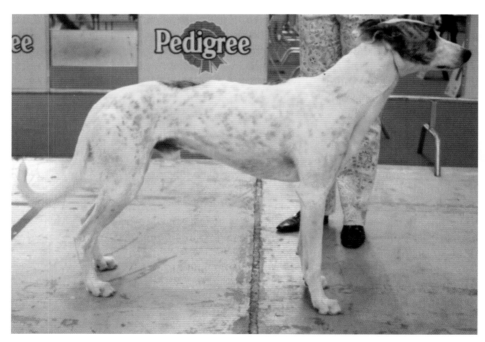

Magyar Agar.

*Colonel North's
Simonian and Fullerton.*

Greyhound from the plains of the White Nile in southern Sudan displays the same characteristic phenotype too. In India, there are the Vaghari and Pashmi hounds, the Rajapalayam and Rampur dogs, the Poligar and the Chippiparai dogs, all with clear smooth-haired sighthound anatomies along what we would term greyhound lines. To run fast a dog needs long legs, a long body, great muscular development but not too much weight. A sighthound is the perfect illustration of the old dictum 'function fashions form'. The form of early show Greyhounds was very much fashioned by the function of coursing.

In *The Kennel Gazette* of April 1891, the report covering the Greyhound entry at the Kennel Club's 35th annual show contained these words:

> These were far larger classes than usual at Kennel Club shows, and were particularly interesting from the fact of Col. North's entries of Huic Holloa and Gay City for competition, and Fullerton, Young Fullerton and Simonian not for competition. Five dogs of a similar high running form have never before been seen at a dog show. Fullerton is a very much better looking dog than ever Master McGrath was, showing more quality and much better made in front. He was exhibited in most perfect condition, full of muscle, and his feet and legs were a treat to see; in this respect Young Fullerton is also very good, although

of course he has not the power of his older brother. Simonian is a beautifully topped dog with immense quality, but his feet will never stand the work of either his brothers.

At this show the top coursing dogs were on show from the leading coursing kennel of the time. The sentiment behind the report was the crucial link between function and form.

Show Greyhounds

The show Greyhound fanciers might argue that they never expected their hounds to compete at the Waterloo Cup. But that argument is destroyed by the wording of their breed standard. This is a breed clearly designed to run fast, very fast. The section under 'Gait/Movement' asks for a 'straight, low-reaching, free stride enabling the ground to be covered at great speed. Hindlegs coming well under body giving great propulsion.' The need for a good slope to the pelvis to allow great forward extension in the hindlegs is not mentioned. Strangely, too, the characteristics of the breed are listed as: 'Possessing remarkable stamina and endurance': no mention of speed, the principal value of the breed to man down the ages. But as far as word pictures for breeds of dog go, this one is well written. A show Greyhound is expected to be: strongly not finely built, upstanding – that is, have

Treetops Golden Falcon – Crufts Best in Show, 1956.

Local Interprize, one of the fastest sprinters in the history of the sport.

presence, generously proportioned – a curvaceous rather than an angular dog, a dog of substance with great suppleness of limb, a clearly defined torso and muscular without being loaded. The hindquarters should hint at great propelling power and the foot should not be too cat-like but more hare-footed than

Quarter Day, winner of the 1938 Oaks and one of the greatest bitches of all time.

many judges deem necessary. The dog should be a graceful mover and a genuinely handsome dog.

A judge's critique from a 2011 Greyhound Club conformation show, after stating that many of the entry were carrying too much weight, which affected movement and the elegance the breed should have, went on to comment: 'I feel for the racing owners as they strongly support the breed at all levels; although all Greyhounds come from the same foundation stock, the racing dogs simply do not conform to the show standard [that is, the written breed standard] and are usually placed down the line...' In other words, dogs that are useful are less valued!

In 1928 the Greyhound Primly Sceptre won Best in Show at Crufts, the first to win the new award. Racing Greyhounds have been regularly shown and entered for Crufts, perpetuating a long tradition. In 1929, the entry was 252 from 187 Greyhounds, of which only seventeen were show bred, the coursing entry prevailing. Ernest Gocher's brindle 70lb dog Endless Gossip is the most famous racing Greyhound to appear at Crufts; he won the 1952 Greyhound Derby and performed well at the 1953 Waterloo Cup. An outstanding show Greyhound, Treetops Golden Falcon, won Best in Show at Crufts in 1956, only the second member of the breed to win this supreme award. It is good to learn that Ireland's annual Dublin show is to schedule special racing Greyhound classes, with each of the twenty-two tracks asked to send one dog to compete. At Crufts in 2009, in the racing/coursing entry, there was a striking black bitch Luvina Lexine Lacers Louise, which perfectly exemplified the correct conformation for the breed.

Faithful Hope – 1966 Derby winner in 28.52 seconds, the fastest time for the event.

Monday's News – one of the greatest since Mick the Miller.

Yellow Printer – the fastest Irish Greyhound Derby winner when he won in 1968.

Quare Times, one of the fastest in the sport's history.

Mick the Miller after winning the 1930 Greyhound Derby for Mrs Kempton.

Colour Discrimination

Black Greyhounds have been noticeably successful in the coursing fields; in 1830, an analysis of one year's coursing results showed that blacks or black/whites won 617 prizes against 318 by reds, fawns, and fawn/whites. Blues and blue/whites came next with 134 wins. On the track, many of the best dogs have been black: Local Interprize, Quarter Day and Dolores Rocket in particular. Black, long associated with short sprinting skills, has always matched white over the longer distances, with white often linked with stamina. White has been the predominating

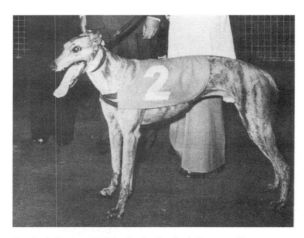

Butcher's Trac – a 30.8-kg dog by Butcher's Tee out of Outcast Trac, established the 845-metre track record of 52.44 seconds at Wembley in April 1976.

colour of many long-distance champions on the track, but only one, Canaradzo, won the Waterloo Cup, in 1861. One of Canaradzo's fellow runners in that win was Cardinal York, a red and white dog, described as 'coarse and common looking, built like a Bulldog, with a hard coat and a very hairy stern'. When the famous kennel of Lord Rivers was sold in 1825, out of fifty-two dogs, twenty-three were all black, fourteen were all blue, four were blue and white, six were red and there was one all white; brindle was not represented. Yet subsequently, on the track, some really great brindles made their name: Mick the Miller, Monday's News, Faithful Hope – as did a blue, one of the fastest of all time, Quare Times, and a fawn, the great Yellow Printer.

Speed and Agility

Poets have paid homage to the sheer antiquity of the Greyhound:

> The Greyhound, the great Hound, the graceful
> of limb,
> Rough fellow, tall fellow, swift fellow and slim;
> Set them round o'er the earth, let them sail o'er
> the sea,
> They will light on none other more ancient than he.

but surprisingly have usually paid less attention to the reason for that long history: the dog's astounding speed. Dogs can achieve astonishing speeds when serving man. On the racetrack, the records are fairly constant: over 500yd from 1927 to 1962 winners' times ranged from that of Oregan Prince at 27.17 seconds in 1961, to Entry Badge's 29.01 in 1927. Over 525yd between 1930 and 1974, Easy Investment ran at 28.17 seconds against Mick the Miller's previous best of 29.96. Over 700yd in the same period the fastest was O'Hara's Rebel in 39.54 seconds, against the earlier Mick the Miller's best at 41.31. In 1976, Butcher's Trac set up a track record of 52.44 seconds on the 845m Wembley track. Over the middle distance sprints there is nothing to match a Greyhound, even amongst the other sighthound breeds. But speed alone does not make a successful sporting Greyhound: the dog's agility, especially on the turn or 'wrench', and athleticism over or around obstacles decides hunting success, not sheer speed.

Famed Localities

Many parts of England achieved fame for their locally bred Greyhounds; renowned at various times were the High Wolds of Yorkshire, the farms of Cornwall (especially for the early show dogs, especially from the famous exporter of Greyhounds to America, Harry Peake), the flat fenland of Cambridgeshire, the Sittingbourne area of Kent, from where the earlier King Edward I took greyhounds to hunt in Gascony, and the East Riding of Yorkshire, where it was claimed the stock were the descendants of the wolfhounds once used there to hunt down the remaining wolves of England. The Lancashire dogs, like those of the Fawcetts, were often trained on the Fells to increase stamina; the Norfolk dogs were renowned for their long-distance sprinting powers. The Wiltshire dogs had their own imprint and reputation – well into the twentieth century, with the highly successful 'Melksham' kennels of Henry Sawtell, which were near the town of that name. Melksham Tom was the fastest dog of his day and

the sire of more coursing winners than any other dog of his time. This dog was sired by Staff Officer, who produced four out of five Waterloo Cup winners between 1921 and 1925. Melksham Tom's sheer pace was legendary but he was not always a great winner – on his debut at Avon Valley he led by seven lengths but was still beaten. His two sons, Melksham Endurance and Melksham Denny ran successfully in Ireland, where their father retired to stud in 1925. All three were very handsome dogs, very symmetrical and sleekly muscled but not huge.

Size Matters

In the Duke of York's *The Master of Game* (1406), the size of the Greyhound is considered important: 'The good greyhound should be of middle size, neither too big nor too little, and then he is good for all beasts. If he were too big he is nought for small beasts, and if he were too little he were nought for the great beasts.' These words may have referred to French sighthounds or levriers and not the Greyhound breed of today,

Melksham: Tom, Endurance and Denny. A. Wardle, 1929.

but it does indicate the need to link the size of the quarry with the size of the pursuing running dog. If you look at nineteenth-century portraits of wealthy landowners pictured with their Greyhounds, such as John Dalby's *Portrait of Sir Richard Sutton* (1845) and Grant's *Portrait of a Gentleman* about the same time, you can see the smaller Greyhound favoured then. On the track and in the coursing field there never was a need for a 100lb dog; the coursing dogs were the first show winners. Track Greyhounds range from 65 to 80lb for males and 55 to 70lb for females.

This is a breed that can get too big for its actual function. In the 120 years to the early 1970s, coursing Greyhounds increased in size by roughly 10lb or 16 per cent. From 1970 to 1990, they grew by a further 20lb, or 28 per cent. A dog called React Fagan won the 1989 Waterloo Cup weighing 95lb, but he crashed out of the very first round of the Altcar 1000, a £1,000 sweepstake for eight dogs. In *The Greyhound and Greyhound Racing* (1975), Roy Genders writes: 'But the larger weights serve no purpose, for some of the smallest dogs were the best and are so today. They are able to turn better when coursing and are more easily able to negotiate the bends round the tracks.'

Hard Going

Greyhounds at great pace possess injury-susceptible feet and legs; firm going makes it not only difficult to work their quarry as needed but can inflict quite serious injuries. This problem has been multiplied by coursing dogs achieving such substantial size increases since the early 1980s. Then, dogs over 70lb were considered too large by some, most averaging 66lb. By 1990, most would weigh over 80lb, with two successive Waterloo Cup winners being over 90lb. This trend shows the Irish influence in coursing Greyhound breeding. In most Irish 'park' coursing, only the run to the first turn decided the course and so sheer short-sprint power became the fashion of the

Sir Richard Sutton and Greyhound. John Dalby, 1845.

Portrait of a Gentleman. Sir Francis Grant, c. 1850.

day. In dry weather the course was watered, like a race course, and the surface then broken up, to lessen the impact on the running dogs' feet and the subsequent leg strain. As long ago as 1887, Hugh Dalziel was writing in *The Greyhound* that: 'to breed Greyhounds for coursing in enclosures of half-a-mile in length is to take the most certain means of destroying one of the most valuable qualities of the breed'.

Track Injuries

The racing Greyhound community is not short of handsome dogs, despite the overriding priority given to performance. I do have concerns about two aspects of this industry: the number of dogs abandoned to the rescue system (about 35,000 are bred; only 14,000 get adopted) and the penalties to so many dogs of bend racing. Hard surfaces and heavier dogs combine to increase the danger of serious injuries to Greyhounds when racing round bends at tracks. Statistics show that over the years, by the time the Greyhound Derby fi nal is run each year, at least forty of the entries will have sustained injury (Sweeney, 1980). I suspect that the heavier dogs suffer the highest injury rate. Greyhounds have very vulnerable feet and legs, especially over sun-baked or frozen going. Expecting them to cope with unyielding ground *and* considerable weight is not wise.

An organization called Greyhound Watch monitors track injuries and some of its findings cause concern. In 2010, the number of runners not finishing their race or coming in having slowed down was 4,513. Of these, 1,812 broke down or pulled up lame. Hock fractures were found to be common on oval tracks, with 2,315 out of 5,565 runners falling, with a breakdown over the course of: turn one:1,309; turn two: 283; turn three: 272; turn four: 81; other: 370. Long-bone fractures occurred in some falls. In Britain, up to six dogs are pitted against each other on a track basically made up of two straights leading into tight bends. The sheer force generated through the dogs' limbs on negotiating the turns, the likelihood of losing footing and inevitable bumping, are key elements in the distressing amount of injury suffered by these runners each year. Nearly 2,000 of the runners listed in the injuries total never raced again, giving the rescue organizations huge challenges. This is a problem needing to be faced on welfare grounds alone.

Health Issues

On the credit side, the Greyhound seems resistant to the worrying increase in cranial cruciate ligament rupture in dogs. A study of 821 cases of this disorder found that while seventy-seven were Rottweilers, not one was a racing Greyhound. The straighter stifle joint of the Rottweiler may play a part in this tendency but it is encouraging to note the greater robustness of the Greyhound's hindlimbs. The Greyhound is less liable to hip dysplasia than any other breed.

On the debit side is the worrying sensitivity of the Greyhound to anaesthetics, due to its lack of body fat. It is scarcely surprising for a breed capable of such speed to suffer more injuries in the chase; injuries creating a need for the administration of anaesthetics before treatment do, however, cause concern in the breed. Bloat has been reported as a problem in this breed; cardiospasm, an affliction of the oesophagus, is listed as a common problem in American dogs; Greyhounds have higher blood pressures, their cardiac output is higher, their blood volume is higher and their packed cell volume is higher than other breeds. But their red blood cell count is lower. The breed can be characterized as having a naturally occurring, significantly higher mean arterial pressure and cardiac output than other breeds (*see* Clark and Stainer, *Medical & Genetic Aspects of Purebred Dogs*, 1994).

Welfare Measures

With Greyhound welfare in mind, it is good to see new legislation in Ireland on this in the Welfare of Greyhounds Bill 2011. This bill affects all Greyhounds in the racing and coursing industry, not only those on premises registered as a Greyhound breeding establishment under the bill. Ireland's Greyhound industry sustains around 11,000 full-time and part-time jobs, mainly in rural areas, and accounts for an estimated £100 million in funding for local economies. Designed to regulate the operation of breeding premises, the bill applies to any person who breeds, trains, rears, transports, races or courses a Greyhound. Activists have argued for some years that far too many racing Greyhounds are being bred and far, far too many of these are later discarded to an uncertain fate. The Greyhound bill in Ireland limits to six the number of litters a bitch may have, restricts the breeding age to a minimum of 15 months and bars puppies born outside those limits from being registered for racing or coursing. It was good to learn that in America, nearly 3,000 fewer litters were recorded by their racing body in 1995 than in 1991, although three states have actually banned Greyhound racing, with three others due to follow suit.

Show–Track Crosses

It is significant that in lure-racing in Canada over the 1970s and 80s the most successful hounds were the 'half-and-halfs', that is, show–track crosses. They were found to have greater endurance and recuperative powers. Track dogs possess greater speed but are not bred to run several races in quick succession. Thirty years ago, in the United States, the Coursing Greyhound of the Year was the American show champion Strider; he was a show–track cross. Here there have long been links between bench, track and field, but with coursing no longer on the breed agenda, the racing dogs will be only ones judged on performance alone. This is a factor to be appreciated by all true Greyhound devotees. The field dogs always needed far greater agility than the track ones; that agility needs perpetuating.

The Great Hound

Frank Townend Barton MRCVS wrote in *Hounds* (1913):

> Speaking in an Irish kind of manner, a Greyhound is no Greyhound if it is not kept in constant training; both heart, lungs and muscular system must be maintained in the highest standard of vigour. If exercise is insufficient or irregularly given the muscles become soft, the heart becomes weak, and its power to respond to increased exertion fails; being a hollow muscular organ, there is a tendency for its fibres to degenerate when thrown into a state of comparative ease. When the muscles covering the skeleton are manipulated they should convey the sensation of being hard as boards, and the outlines of the individual muscles be plainly discernible; and the more vigorous the exercise, provided such is carried out with regularity, the better the muscular development.

An unfit, soft-muscled, unexercised Greyhound looks just that and reflects poorly on its owner. Of all breeds of dog, this one was meant for exercise

The Pinkneys out coursing, Samuel Spode, 1845.

and physical fitness. The Greyhound is the supreme canine athlete. Our Greyhounds have been exported all over the world because of their athletic excellence. If this deserved fame is to be retained, the show fraternity has a responsibility too, to respect those past sportsmen who strove to develop for us this 'great hound'. It should be a joy rather than a burden to respect this legacy.

VARIETIES OF THE MODERN GREYHOUND

The Newmarket Greyhound. This variety stands at the head of the list as the probable root of all our modern subdivisions ... the greyhounds running there, being eagerly sought after throughout the length and breadth of the land ... superior to all others ... the most racing-like dog ... yet possessed of as much stoutness as possible, in combination with great speed.

The Lancashire Greyhound ... must be large and strong ... possessed of tact and cleverness ... I am inclined to think that the Lancashire has the superiority in persistence.

The Yorkshire Greyhound is characterized by speed as great as that of Newmarket or Lancashire, coupled with a degree of cleverness rarely seen elsewhere.

The Wiltshire Greyhound was formerly bred exclusively for the extraordinary hares which are generally met with there ... These hares are generally fast, but they also have the power of throwing out even the best worker in a style quite different to the Lancashire and Yorkshire variety. Hence, the Wiltshire dog has been bred especially strong and stout-hearted...

J.H. Walsh, *The Pursuit of Wild Animals for Sport* (1856)

The Lancashire greyhounds ... were unbeatable on their own grounds at Altcar, their speed being outstanding, but they were less successful elsewhere. The Wiltshire hounds had untiring energy and great working powers and although small and compact, they possessed a wide chest and sturdy back and were able to turn at any angle on the run. But many weighed less than 35lbs., only half the weight of the Newmarket breed and of the modern stud dog and as coursing men consider that a good big one will almost always beat a good little one, it was desirable to cross the type with a dog of either the Lancashire or Newmarket strain.

Roy Genders, *The Greyhound and Greyhound Racing* (1975)

The energetic velocity of the greyhound, in pursuit of its game, has always been matter of admiration to the lovers of the sport; but more particularly so to the ruminative amateur when prompted by reflection to form comparisons. Various have been the opinions upon the difference of speed between a well-bred greyhound and a blood-horse of some celebrity, if opposed to each other for a mile, or for any greater or shorter distance. It has, by the best and most experienced judges, been thought, that upon a flat, a horse of this description would prove superior to the greyhound, for either an extended or a contracted distance; but that, in a hilly country, the greyhound would have an evident advantage.

The Sportsman's Cabinet (1803)

The Greyhound possesses an inherent right to occupy the highest place in the group of dogs hunting by keenness of sight and fleetness of foot ... the modern Greyhound (is) the most elegant of the canine race, the highest achievement of man's skill in manipulating the plastic nature of the dog, and forming it to his special requirements. In all his beauty of outline and wonderful development, not only of muscle, but of the hidden fire which gives dash, energy, and daring, stands revealed a manufactured article, the acme of perfection in beauty of outline and fitness of purpose.

Hugh Dalziel, *The Greyhound* (1887)

The training home at Brampton, Cumbria.

The Whirrying Whippet

Though it is not until recent years that the Whippet, or Snap-dog, has come into such prominence as to warrant its recognition by the Kennel Club as a variety, yet for many decades the animal has been known to the miners and other workers in the North of England. More than thirty years ago at least the name Whippet was bestowed upon a dog built very much on the lines that today find favour. It is, however, only some ten or twelve years since the effort to popularize the dog in the south of England was attempted. Somehow, straight-running, as the sport for which the Whippet is chiefly used is called, did not catch on in the South as it already had in the North …

W.D. Drury, *British Dogs* (1903)

The whippet affords a remarkable illustration of the talent, not to say genius, of the dog fancier, and his ability to manufacture new types of dogs. No one looking at the picture of Manorley May, which adorns this section, and bearing in mind her height, which is 17 inches, and her weight of 19lbs, could desire a more exquisitely proportioned four-legged creature, or one more instinct with the attributes of swiftness and virility made apparent … To all intents and purposes it represents a new species of dog…

Herbert Compton, *The Twentieth Century Dog* (1904)

'Real Whirryers'

Many years ago, when, as a young teenager, I worked as a kennel boy for my local vet, he had an apt term for Whippets: 'real whirryers', which I believe is an old Scottish expression for a fast flier. The Whippet can certainly run fast and is a type, both in conformation and function, which has long had appeal for man, as

Whippet racing. Top – Making ready. Below – Ready: waiting for the pistol shot.

Whippet racing - weighing in.

*Early show Whippets
Enterprise and Zuber.
W.E. Turner, 1894.*

many ancient depictions indicate, especially across the Mediterranean countries. There is an expensive book on the Whippet which goes to great lengths to try to prove that the Whippet has existed for centuries, using scores of old paintings and sculptures depicting small Greyhound-like dogs as evidence. Certainly, in the portraits painted by Oudry (his portrayal of Louis XV's Greyhounds of 1725) and Desportes (his 1699 self-portrait of himself as a hunter), smaller, more refined sighthounds are depicted. The dog shown in Richard Brompton's eighteenth-century portrait of

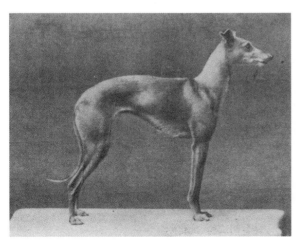

The 1904 Whippet Manorley May.

F.W. Blomberg. Richard Brompton, c. 1770.

Oudry's portrayal of Louis XV's Greyhounds, 1725.

Desportes's 1699 self-portrait of himself as a hunter.

Potsdam Greyhounds. Franz Krüger, 1837.

The Gamekeeper. John Pierson, 1800.

Italian Greyhound. L.R. Heyrault, 1851.

Frederick William Blomberg is remarkably Whippet-like, as is the bigger dog in John Pierson's depiction of a gamekeeper about the same time. Whippet-like small Greyhounds were favoured by the Prussian royalty and known as Potsdam Greyhounds, and could have been related to the Italian Greyhounds long patronized by the nobility.

Small Sighthounds

Apart from the fact that it is very unwise to talk of purebreeds before the nineteenth century, it is also unwise to claim that all smooth-haired small sighthounds have to be Whippets. By that measure the Cirneco dell'Etna of Sicily, the South African native hunting dogs, the Cretan Hound and the small podencos of the Mediterranean littoral would have to come under that name too. Throughout recorded history there have been accounts and depictions of small smooth-haired sighthounds. In England diminutive Greyhounds were long favoured as ladies' companion dogs, quite separately from the delicate Toy breed of Italian Greyhound. The latter appears remarkably similar to the small companion dogs depicted in statues and frescoes in the classical world.

Pointless Purity

Some will claim that the Whippet *must* have terrier blood to be a genuine Whippet, alleging that the Kennel Club show fraternity hijacked this type, made it into a pedigree breed with a closed gene pool, better named Miniature Greyhound than misappropriating the common name given to the rabbit-dog of the mining community of the northeast. It is too late now to undo this recognition but some find it hard to think of a Whippet as a purebreed. In *The Illustrated Book of the Dog* (1879), Vero Shaw wrote: 'The Whippet is undoubtedly a cross-bred dog which has been brought into existence to meet the exigencies of the sport with which it is associated'; he suggested the English White Terrier was its predecessor on the straight track. Before the days of kennel clubs in the world, purebreeding from a closed gene pool, whatever the quality of the progeny, would have been laughed off the face of the earth. Distinct breed types were prized, of course, but mainly because of their prowess, not their pedigree. The appearance of long-haired, so-called 'Wheeler' Whippets in purebred lines a few years back shows the deep-seated mixture

Whippet racing, 1900.

behind this breed and I regard that as a genetic plus, provided breed type is kept. Broken-haired Whippets were once favoured in mainland Europe.

In his monumental *Dogs: Their History and Development* (1927), Edward Ash refers to a Yorkshire strain of small Greyhound bred by a Mr Hodgson of Stamford Bridge in the East Riding of Yorkshire, who produced:

> ... a breed which, because of their exceptional merit, surprised the sportsmen of Yorkshire. This stud consisted of three bitches named 'The Dents' after family associations, greyhounds remarkable for their coursing. The Dents are described as having perfectly smooth skins and uncommonly fine and small ears. Their tails were short and curled and their appearance not unlike 'a very light smart rabbit-dog', which means, I presume, a whippet or Italian Greyhound. They had qualities which are not usually found together in the breed, for whilst they ran with remarkable fire and speed, yet they were able to turn with the hare, so that they always appeared to be upon their game, rendering their style of killing, we read, 'uncommonly great'. They were sold for large sums ...'

From such small sighthounds did the breed of Whippet emerge. A closed breed gene pool today could never reach out and claim such outstanding dogs, such is the show ring grip on breeding policy.

Field and Bench

These remarks are not intended as a criticism of show Whippets, many of whom are devastating hunters, or of their breeders, some of whom know a thing or two about breeding sporting dogs. The Laguna Whippets of Mrs D.U. McKay have a remarkable field and bench reputation; her Ch. Laguna Ligonier siring eleven champions. KC-registered Whippets were regularly coursed, with a determined bunch of knowledgeable devotees behind them. They rather shame the show Greyhound fanciers, who rarely test their breed in the field. I simply cannot see the point of admiring a hound that is designed to catch game using sheer speed if you never wish it to do so. The purpose and the build of such a dog is that of a

Rough-haired Whippet in Germany, 1924.

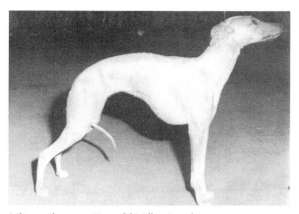

Whippet champion Nimrodel Willow Daughter, 1969.

Champion Laguna Ligonier.

sprinting machine. A Whippet was once recorded as covering 150yd in 8.6 seconds; such astounding pace is only achieved if the dog possesses the anatomy to facilitate such remarkable speed. Some Whippets have excelled in more than one activity. Ch. Nimrodel Willow Daughter won the Hound Group and reserve Best in Show at Birmingham National, two open bitch coursing titles and was awarded the Dutch medal for dual-purpose excellence. Handsome dogs can still run!

Eminent Kennels

The Laguna kennel is rightly respected in both the show and working dog field. In the 1996/7 edition of the National Whippet Coursing Club's results book, however, it states: 'The predominant kennels were BANATAY and LAGUNA. Sixteen Banatays ran in 91 stakes; 10 were finalists 20 times. Sixteen Lagunas ran in 92 stakes and again 10 were finalists but only 19 times.' Commenting in that admirable publication, *The Working Whippet Yearbook* (2007) the Banatay owner Andrea Barr added:

The Banatay kennel was established in June 1991, whereas the Lagunas were established in 1939, quite an achievement for a relatively 'new kennel'. When looking through the NWCC's owners' register I

Champion Laguna Lucky Lad.

Andrea Barr's coursing Whippet Banatay Bellwether – a highly successful coursing dog.

noted of the 33 Banatays running on the coursing field, 22 out of them were top dogs/puppies (triple finalists in one season) and good puppies (double finalists in their puppy season). Compared to the 98 Lagunas running, 33 of which were top dogs/puppies and good puppies.

This is some achievement in a highly competitive field. Breeding consistent winners is the real skill; in this arena too, the speed and agility of these little hounds is really tested and the soundness of their physiques utterly revealed.

Shedding Excess Heat

The horse is a 'single-flight' animal – that is, for most of its stride, some or all of its hooves are on the ground. All sighthounds are 'double-flight' creatures; they race in a series of leaps, so must therefore have extraordinary extension, fore and aft. This is permitted by the slope of the shoulders on the forehand and the pelvic slope in the hindhand. Long legs and a build like a radiator support this degree of extension. The radiator analogy is deliberate. Human beings are good at getting rid of excess heat but not good at storing it.

Dogs are just the opposite: very good at storing it, not very good at getting rid of it. Dogs give off excess heat rather as a radiator does, and they need adequate surface areas to achieve this. If a Whippet when racing or coursing cannot shed excess heat, it will suffer; if it reaches a temperature of over 108 degrees it could die.

Liver Role

Much is made in conformation shows of 'heart and lung' room in dogs that sprint as their function. The need for lung room I can understand but heart room? The heart stays the same size even during the greatest exertion. What is never mentioned is liver size. Sprinters run their whole race on sugar mobilized from the liver, liver glycogen. A big liver can store more sugar; sighthounds that run out of liver sugar collapse. It would be worthy research to do post-mortems on the great racing Whippets and Greyhounds and record the weights of their hearts and livers. I would be prepared to bet that these dogs were successful mainly because of their increased heart and liver size.

Physique

Shoulder Placement

Structure matters too, however. After a lack of sheer determination, the biggest fault for me in a sporting Whippet is upright shoulders, so often accompanied by short upper arms. The rearward extension determines the length of stride of the dog in the sprint; if you limit that extension you handicap the dog. The shoulder placement is the key to sound front movement; well-placed shoulders allow the full extension of forelimbs. Any Whippet with a hint of a Hackney-action, that high-stepping, prancing front action of the Toy breed, the Italian Greyhound, should never be bred from. The shoulder blades should not quite touch each other at the withers, at least one finger's width being desirable. I never see ring judges check this feature. Differences in topline are all too obvious in the lure-racing dogs; the correct Whippet back should be level at the shoulders and, from the shoulders, flow to a good arch over the loin; and, *at no time,* be roached, humped or wheel-backed. A flat back is incorrect; the arch should always be over the loin.

Sloping Croup

At the back, the falling away at the croup and low-set tail allows full forward reach of the powerhouse hindquarters, the source of running strength. Any lack of slope in the pelvis and the dog has limited forward reach in the rear legs, a terrible fault. Whippets carry their tails low because of this structural need in a running dog. Spitz breeds don't have to sprint for their keep, but have other needs, and they display a high tail set and little slope in the croup.

Feet

Function has long determined form. But just as the saying 'no hoof, no horse' is a perennial truth in that animal, 'no foot, no dog' is just as valid. I see far too many Whippets with poor feet, weak, not tight and the dog not 'standing up on them', usually a sign of unfitness through a lack of exercise. I have three books on the Whippet that do not have the words foot or feet in their index; yet feet are rather more important than that. In a show critique in the 1950s, the well-known Whippet expert and judge, C.H. Douglas-Todd, whose Ch. Wingedfoot Marksman of Allways sired ten champions, was writing that the pre-war faults such as thin feet and weak pasterns were rarely seen, but he did go on to state: 'Movement in some cases was literally so appalling that one shudders to think what the breed may descend to if this is not checked.' It was brave of him to be so outspoken in the pursuit of a better Whippet.

Judges' Views

Recent show judges' critiques make a number of points for me. Crufts 2001: 'Poor shoulder angulation with short upper arms is still a problem. This was often coupled with heavy shoulders and over-angulated hindquarters resulting in lack of hind power...' Crufts is the showcase for the purebred dog; it is depressing to think that dogs with such faults actually qualified for Crufts under Kennel Club-approved judges. An American specialist Whippet judge reported, after judging the breed here: 'Straight shoulders were practically endemic... Not nearly enough emphasis is placed on the standard's requirement for "muscular power and strength" combined with "elegance and grace of outline" ...' This judge also found 'exaggerated front action and no drive from behind'. For this experienced judge to find straight

Hunting Whippet.

shoulders practically endemic in a large entry of 212 is worrying.

The judge at the N Counties Club show of 2001 reported: 'Fronts seem to present the most problems', finding a lack of angulation. At that time, a Whippet Club show report stated that: 'Movement on the whole was not good', complaining once again about upright shoulders, resulting in some 'rather odd front movement'. Judges' comments ten years later

Racing Whippet.

included: 'Good front movement was the hardest to find'; 'Over-angulation is creeping in very quickly'; 'Movement, on some that I know have won well, was all over the place'; 'several dogs were just too short-stepping, mainly due to straight front construction and upright shoulders'; 'We seem to be losing toplines and that thrust and drive from behind, also the occasional lifting of the front legs thus losing the daisy-cutting movement'. A decade had passed and the faults appear ingrained.

In a long, well-argued and valuable critique, the judge at the Joint Whippet Club's autumn show in 2011 wrote:

> I must honestly say that in my more than 25 years of judging the breed, I have never judged a more variable entry of Whippets than this … the winners were outstanding … but on the other hand I was worried about the number of dogs shown that I would classify as downright poor Whippets … Frankly what a significant number of dogs were lacking was pure and simple type and quality.

This wonderfully honest judge went on to list as faults: oversized exhibits, massively round bone, enormous heads, woolly coats, thick skin, thick ears, untypical expressions and unbalanced movement. No doubt many of these poor-quality Whippets were bred from and this can only be bad news for the breed as a whole. To me, this situation indicates that there are many in this breed, on the show circuit, who just do not know what a quality dog should look like. Who but an ignorant exhibitor would show a poor-quality dog at all?

Importance of Balance

In his valuable book *The Whippet* (1985), Whippet expert Bo Bengtson writes:

> The important word is balance: maximum muscular power and strength balanced by maximum elegance. A little too much of one and you get a cart-horse, too much of the other and you get a wafer-thin cartoon caricature. The impression should be of long sweeping lines in a comparatively small package: anything abrupt, hard or broken-up is wrong. The hallmark of a top-class Whippet is the long, unbroken and gently curving line which starts behind the ears, sweeps into

the shoulders without any stop, continues in a perceptible but slight rise over the loin, then falls very gently away over the rather long croup and ends in a dramatic curve through the stifles down to the hocks …

He has captured the whole essence of the Whippet conformation in these descriptive and most illuminating words. He has gained a remarkable span of knowledge of the very best dogs, on the bench, in the field and on the track, over half a century.

Past Quality

I am old enough to remember Whippets in British show rings in the 1960s and 1970s (at a time when fewer than 2,000 were being registered each year, against over 3,500 in 2010), and I recall that firstly the quality was high and secondly show judges' critiques did not mention such disappointing fi ndings. The perpetuation of the instinct to hunt at speed and the anatomy that allows the dog to succeed, matter enormously in such a breed. The breed of Whippet should be 'whirrying' ahead of worrying. Breeding habits change gradually; in the show ring it is usually a matter of breeding rosette winner to rosette winner, appearance being the main criterion. In the racing world the consistently fastest is bred to 'promising speed'; the racing Whippet Blue Peter, owned by Joe Mather of Stockport, sired 1,042 puppies. Success at speed brings success at stud. Yet I have seen some racing Whippets with cow hocks, thin feet, far too fragile bone and weak, snipey jaws. Th is is a breed that must be based on the most power from the least body weight.

Speed and Work

The breed standard of the Whippet refers to this power in its general appearance section: 'Balanced combination of muscular power and strength with elegance and grace of outline. Built for speed and work.' I only wish some of the exhibitors at the shows whose critiques I quoted earlier would heed those key phrases. It is pleasing too to see in this breed standard under colour: 'Any colour or mixture of colours'. This not only gives the breed a rich variety of colours but prevents the absurd colour prejudices that exist in some other breeds. For some purebreed fanciers the colour is more important than structural soundness.

Shades of Colour

Colour of coat can, however, mislead judges, due to a trick of the human eyesight. Blacks and blues can appear smaller and more spindly. A dog with a black saddle can appear to have a dippy back. A black patch on the upper arm can give a different impression than a black patch over the withers and down to the brisket. A white underline on an otherwise black dog can make it look shelly. Foreface markings too can create illusions, sometimes shortening the muzzle. Heavy markings on the neck can make it look stuffy when it is not. Black stockings on a white dog can give a false picture of its gait. Lower-leg black markings affect the way the human eye sees leg movement. If you challenge a judge about such trompes d'oeil the usual response is, 'Oh, I can't get fooled like that!' I wonder.

Size Debate

Size is a long-standing debate in the world of the Whippet. A Durham miner once told me that sixty or seventy years ago, his grandfather favoured an 8lb Whippet, 'so's it could fit in y'overcoat pocket'. In the breed standard, a male Whippet can be from 18½ to 20in high. Such a dog might weigh around 21lb. The Whippet Club Racing Association height limit is 21in; coursing Whippets must go under the measure at 20in. Bigger dogs seem to be favoured in North America. No doubt in time we will see an American Whippet achieve recognition as a 22in specimen, rather as American Bulldogs are bigger than ours or the French variety. I have no problem with sportsmen seeking a hound to suit their terrain but this would be a Miniature Greyhound not a Whippet. It's of interest that the renowned Snowflake, weighing around 23lb, had sufficient power to twice win the Hillstown 32lb limit scratch race in 1969, the year when she did 10.16 seconds for 175yd.

Freak Progeny

The so-called 'bully whippets' that can occur in litters have been investigated by Professor Dana Mosher at the National Human Genome Research Institute, Bethesda, Maryland, USA. A recessive mutated gene means that a bully whippet pup grows up to have almost 20 per cent more muscle per cm of height than its litter mates. A protein called myostatin limits growth in normal Whippets but not in a flawed one. Dr Mosher's study revealed that having one copy of the rogue gene may increase the dog's speed over 200–300m sprints, the usual Whippet distance. Greyhounds have the same ancestors but in being bred for speed endurance, or sprint stamina for the longer distances, the mutated gene was probably bred out. Endurance was more vital in the Greyhound and as animals with more muscle burn more energy than less muscular animals, the desire for sprinting endurance led to the rejection from breeding stock of over-muscled dogs. Big, hugely muscled Whippets may excel over short sprints but, apart from threatening breed type, do not perform over longer stretches, as some lurcher breeders may require from whippet hybrids. This mutant gene also produces over-bites and a distinct cramping in the shoulders and thighs. Most bully whippets are not bred from.

Priorities

Some years ago, writing in the dog press, Ted Walsh, who knew a bit about Whippets, stated: 'A coursing dog should be judged on movement first, balance second, and make and shape last; if the first two are right, there shouldn't be much wrong with the third.' He also expressed his dismay at some of the dogs presented in the show ring, stating that they 'couldn't catch a cat in a kitchen'. There is rather more to a winning Whippet than a roach back, hyper-angulation in the hindlegs, a straight front and open feet, yet dogs with such features seem to be able to qualify for Crufts: I share Ted Walsh's dismay. In November 1993, one Whippet show judge's critique read:

> The lower classes of dogs cause me at least great concern. There were a few promising ones but the most prevalent construction on view was a combination of straight front assemblies, short ribbing back and loins, with exaggeratedly long hindlegs overstretch, thus accentuating the inadequate forequarters. This type of conformation was completed by an almost universal tendency to toe-in fore and aft. The battle, if there ever was one, to maintain size has been lost. The bitches, beautiful though many of them are, were also I regret to say, hefty.

These exhibits will have been bred from; I do hope that the working Whippet fraternity can demonstrate soundness ahead of beauty of form in this fine breed.

In the show dogs, I still see this 'exaggeratedly long hindlegs overstretch' and it seems to go unpunished by even highly experienced show ring judges. That is a worry!

Whippet Qualities

In an interview featuring Nigel Wallbank of the Working Whippet Club and Jeff Hutchings, co-founder of that club and co-editor of *The Working Whippet Yearbook*, published in *The Countryman's Weekly* in 2008, both were asked the describe the attributes of a good working Whippet. Nigel stated that for him they were: speed, stamina, durability, nose and brains, not necessarily in that order, adding that despite being purebred sighthounds, those from a working strain really do have superb noses. Jeff stated that for him it was gameness and nose, adding: 'Good nose is particularly marked in Mike Brown's "Lord of the Knight" strain … one of them, "Spears Rabbitcatcher of Pennymeadow" was a 19-inch, 25lb bitch owned by myself. Prior to the ban

Big powerful racing Whippet.

she took muntjac, fox and hare.' It was claimed in this interview that Nigel's 23in black dog Pennymeadow Black Jack was quite able to leap a five-bar gate with a rabbit in its mouth. These are words to gladden the heart of every Whippet admirer.

Jeff Hutchings's Elgedane Miss Ebony of Pennymeadow – superb working Whippet.

Renowned Breeder

In the 2007 edition of their excellent publication, *The Working Whippet Yearbook,* compilers Nigel Wallbank and Jeff Hutchings record an interview they had with renowned breeder Mike Brown in North Wales about the legendary dog Sooty Sam, the most famous working Whippet of modern times. They asked him how he started and he replied:

> All the dogs I started with came to me secondhand, dogs that were too big for the show ring or racing, but ideal for me – I was looking for something a bit different than your average Whippet … I've called my dogs working Whippets because that's what they do, you can be ready to call it a day out rabbiting, and they'll look at you as if to say – Going home already!! With lurchers you're lucky to get a few years of work out of them, my Whippets will run until they're 10 years old plus and give 110%, they are honest little dogs.

These are words worth remembering; successful working dogs in any breed come from genuine breed enthusiasts like Mike Brown. They emerge from performance, not appearance, but can still look good.

Whippet at Crufts, 1994.

Canine Athlete

Writing in the Whippet Club's Jubilee Show catalogue in 1950, W. Lewis Renwick declared that:

> Another important thing to remember is what the breed is bred for. Firstly, he is not a lady's pet dog, despite the fact that no more affectionate breed exists and no dog is happier than when living in the comfort of his master's home. He is first and last a Sporting Dog, his conformation being for great speed over short distances … anybody who has an eye for beauty of form and muscular development must admit there are few dogs so artistic to look upon.

These are important words for any Whippet breeder to have in his mind. The Whippet is a canine athlete or it is nothing. As the sporting dog comes under the threat from 'town-thinking' people over its use in the field, we should keep in mind that this breed was not evolved for the squires in their shires, but developed by hardworking miners in humble pit-villages. The Whippet is a breed of great charm and considerable distinction but it was never envisaged as a 'lounge lizard', with soft muscles, dull eyes, a bored expression, overlong claws and a timid demeanour. It is a hunting dog, by design and instinct. That should be prized.

> In one respect Whippet racing to my mind was superior to Greyhound racing for the simple reason that the owners, by training the dogs themselves, had a greater personal interest than if they had put them in charge of the officials of a track.
>
> A. Croxton Smith, *Dogs since 1900* (1950)

> My last but one bitch was bred in Norfolk by Janice Sheriden, an extremely powerful, quite long-backed blue specimen that worked in a time before the current hunting restrictions and laws were passed. She took fox, hare, rabbit and rat, day or night, and retrieved wildfowl off water. This dog was a joy to own…believe me it was a privilege working such a valiant and gutsy whippet.
>
> John Glover, writing in *The Working Whippet* 2009, compiled by Nigel Wallbank and Jeff Hutchings.

As an all round hunting dog the whippet is hard to better and its worth is probably only exceeded by that of a first class purpose-bred working lurcher. Most whippets will start work early and are usually quite dextrous at dealing with first rabbits ... Whippets appreciate socialising more than most breeds of sight hound and unlike greyhounds seldom thrive in kennels.

D. Brian Plummer, *The Complete Book of Sight Hounds, Long Dogs and Lurchers* (1991)

Not all open racers, by any means, come from famous parents; indeed, many hail from much more modest backgrounds...Often it happens that a bitch who is not too fast herself but whose brothers and sisters are open or good class, produces better pups than her more famous sisters. Because she carries the same blood as her faster littermates, even though she did not make the grade on the track, chances are high of a good litter.

Pauline Wilson, writing in her *Whippets: Rearing and Racing*, Faber & Faber, 1979.

All in all, in judging Whippets the golden rule should be: 'Check for soundness and symmetry and balance.' An exaggerated dog is not necessarily a good dog. An unbalanced dog is a poor dog. Cloddiness should never outweigh raciness, and there are far too many cloddy-type dogs winning today ... The Whippet is a 'speed king' not a 'shire horse' or a hunter.

C.H. Douglas-Todd FZS, *The Whippet* (revised by Kay Douglas-Todd, 1976)

The Deerhound – The Scottish Sighthound

The deerhounds were beautiful. The rough Highland greyhounds, swift and powerful, will pull down a stag sometimes single-handed, but the bravest always get killed in the end. This pure breed have keen noses as well as speed, and will follow the slot of a wounded deer perseveringly, if they find blood. Those most

Statue of the late Prince Consort at Balmoral, by W. Theed.

Pope's tribute to the Deerhound, 1858.

valued are not necessarily the most savage, for the reckless ones go in and get killed, but the more wary, who have taken the hint after a prog or two, are equally enduring, and will hold their bay for any indefinite time, which is a merit of the first importance.

Those words from the Earl of Tankerville's series of letters to *The Field* towards the end of the nineteenth century, following sporting visits to the Highlands, give the essential background to the breed as a sighthound of that time and in that employment.

Artist Admirers

Few breeds today draw the attention of both a nationally renowned artist and a writer, but the Deerhound once won the admiration of both Edwin Landseer and Sir Walter Scott, even the poetry of Pope and the affection of royalty. Commendably too, both the first-named demonstrated respect and affection for the hunted stag as well. Landseer produced any number of depictions

Sir Walter Scott and his dog. William Scoular, 1838.

of Deerhounds pursuing their quarry, managing to convey sympathy for the beleaguered stag and any severely wounded hounds. The hounds sketched by Landseer were Torrish and Morven, owned by Bateson of Cambusmere in Sutherlandshire. Scott's Deerhound cross, Maida, was regarded by him more as a friend than a pet, such was their relationship. It is comforting that a breed once so savage in the hunt can be such a gentle companion around the hearth; it is this combination of field persistence and utter determination, balanced by docility as a canine companion that characterizes so many sighthound breeds.

Outcrossings

Deer hunting, whether stalking, coursing or tracking, has embraced a number of different breeds and mixes of breeds. Collies and Foxhounds have been utilized, although never in the coursing role. In his *The Lady of the Lake* (1810), Scott refers to black St Huberts, but as par force hounds not just scenthounds. But when deer hunters wanted their quarry 'run down', the Deerhound was the choice. Writing in *The Field* magazine in 1890, but reminiscing on deerstalking some sixty years earlier, the Earl of Tankerville described the 'rough Highland greyhound': 'This pure breed have keen noses as well as speed and will follow the slot of a wounded deer perseveringly ...', going on to state: 'I saw there two of Mr Scrope's ... his notion was a half-breed between the bloodhound and the rough greyhound.' He described how committed such hounds were 'at the bay', sometimes holding a deer all night before the hunters reached them. That shows hound commitment combining the sighthound and

Deerstalking. Charles Hancock. c. 1850.

Mainly white Deerhound in stalking scene, 1885, from cast iron centre table after Landseer.

the scenthound talents. Few breed historians list such outcrossings to another breed, forever stating the purity of the Highland dogs!

'Idstone', in his *The Dog* (1880), writes: 'Many crosses have been adopted ... one of the Deerhound and Mastiff has been used by the proprietor of a deer-park in my immediate neighbourhood ... I also introduced a fine Morocco Deerhound, which has been used successfully ... A remote Bulldog cross has been used also ...' He noted that the Mastiff blood

produced a hound which went for the ear, the classic hunting mastiff mode of attack, rather than the hock. But the Deerhounds he really favoured, he described as having:

The racehorse points – the long neck, the clean head, the bright intellectual eye, the long sloping shoulder, the muscular arms, the straight legs, the close, well-knit feet, the wide, muscular, arched back and loin, the deep back-ribs, the large girth, the

Stalking scene with deerhounds, by Richard Ansdell (1815–85).

esprit, the life, the activity which, when controlled and schooled, is essential …

These are words worth revisiting by any Deerhound breeder of today.

Gillie with Deerhounds. R. Ansdell, 1874.

Valued Blood

The blood of the Deerhound has long been prized by knowledgeable lurcher men. The noted Deerhound and Deerhound-lurcher breeder, Bill Doherty, has written that 'My pure-bred deerhounds, although never possessing the ability to match the sheer versatility of their cross-bred relations, have also achieved a certain degree of all-round hunting success.' Many sportsmen are most impressed by their hunting skills and quite remarkable facility for detecting movement over huge distances. They can track as well as hunt by sight. Some breeds have changed in the hands of show breeders but this breed seems to have retained its essential type over several centuries. It is easy to overlook the value of hounds that could hunt red deer successfully before the wide use of long-range firearms. In a harsh winter the skill of such a dog could mean the difference between starvation and survival for the primitive hunters. Once this value diminished, however, these huge, shaggy, fast-running hounds fell on hard times, surviving only in some areas through the patronage of the nobility.

Deerhound blood has been utilized not just by lurcher men in Britain but by their opposite numbers hunting coyotes in America and kangaroo in Australia. Such breeders are seeking all-round hunting skills: a good nose, coursing ability and the keen determination to pursue a fast quarry over some distance. The use of Deerhound blood is a sincere compliment. In his *The Working Longdog* (1999),

Frank Sheardown writes:

> My own deerhound hybrids will hunt by sight and by getting their noses down. A great advantage as far as I am concerned … For hunting during the hours of daylight or at night without the aid of a lamp, deerhound hybrids take a lot of beating. All their senses are highly attuned and not only do they have good noses and superb hearing, but eyes like hawks in the daytime and like owls at night.

Highland Hound

In his little known book, *The History of the Dog* (1845), W.C.L. Martin has written:

> Three varieties of the greyhound, if not four, appear to have long existed – viz. the wire-haired greyhound, more or less rough in its coat, as that of Tartary and Eastern Russia; a silky-haired breed, as that of Natolia, Persia, and ancient Egypt; and a smooth-haired breed, now common in England, but which was first introduced into France …

He goes on to speculate about the Scoti originating from Scythia in southern Russia and bringing their hounds with them, via Gaul, into Ireland, then on into Argyle, the land of the Gael or Gaul. All the hounds which hunt using their speed have an ancient origin and have retained their phenotype, shaped by function, down the centuries. The first mention of Deerhounds is often alleged to be in Pitscottie's *History and Chronicles of Scotland,* which states that 'the king (AD1528) desired all gentlemen that had dogges that war guide to bring them to hunt … the Earls of Huntlie, Argyle and Athole, who brought their deirhoundis with thame …' But as Edward Ash has pointed out, the word 'deir' was added by Robert Lindesay in his *Chronicles of Scotland* of 1814. The often-quoted statement 'No one under the rank of Earl shall keep a Deerhound' is actually fiction, from Sir Walter Scott's *The Talisman* (1825). It was the antiquary Pennant who produced the first description of these 'true Highland greyhounds'.

Pennant recorded, when visiting Scotland in 1769, that he saw at Gordon Castle true Highland greyhounds, which had become very scarce. He described these hounds as being 'of large size, strong, deep-chested, and covered with very long and rough

hair', used 'in large numbers at the magnificent stag chases by the powerful chieftains'. Lurcher men, keepers and stalkers refer to them as staghounds to this day. The Earl de Folcoville had his noted Colonsay strain in the first half of the nineteenth century. MacNeile, in his chapter on Deerhounds, the first detailed write-up of the breed, in William Scrope's *Days of Deerstalking* (1838), described one of the purest specimens: 'This dog is of pale yellow, and appears to be remarkably pure in his breeding, not only from his shape and colour, but from the strength and wiry elasticity of his hair, which by Highlanders is thought to be a criterion of breeding.' MacNeile stated that the grey dogs appeared to be 'less lively and did not exhibit such a development of muscle, particularly on the back and loins, and have a tendency to cat hams'. But in this book MacNeile also wrote: 'In Scotland we know that very few, perhaps not above a dozen pure Deerhounds are to be met with. Should they once be lost it is difficult to imagine how any race of dogs can again be produced possessing such a combination of qualities.' Their loss today would be not just a huge loss to the canine race as a whole but a giant blow to Scotland's sporting heritage.

Size

Some of the early show specimens only came into the hands of show breeders and exhibitors because they were too tall for deer coursing. Now the breed standard asks for a minimum desirable height of 30in at the withers for dogs. The seeking of great size in dogs has little historical support and no functional advantage. No Greyhound reaching 30in at the withers has ever won the Waterloo Cup, once the most competitive match in the sighthound calendar. I would much rather have an overall sound dog of 28in at the withers than an oversized unsound dog. An inch or two in stature can never match the overall soundness so essential in a hunting dog.

Working Dimensions

It is interesting to note the height of past Deerhounds: M'Neill's Buscar (1836), a celebrated purebred worker, was 28in at the shoulder; Morse's Spey (1880) was 26in at the shoulder; Spencer Lucy's Morna (1879) was 26in high; the Duchess of Wellington's Lady Garry (1885) was 26in at the shoulder. In his valuable book of 1892 on the breed, E. Weston Bell wrote:

'Lady Garry', on left, was 26in at the shoulder. Sketch by D.B. Gray, 1892.

'... for the work this dog had to do, if we take his general appearance at over 30 inches, he would be almost too heavy and clumsy ...' And when considering 'the work this dog had to do', it is worth noting that in 1563, at a tainchell or deer-drive arranged by the Earl of Athol, 360 deer, five wolves and some roes were killed in one day, with 2,000 Highlanders employed in the drive. It is not easy to imagine hunting on such a scale but

Stag at Bay. G.D. Armour, c.1928.

likely that several hundred hounds were involved, some of which would have died. The sheer stamina of the hounds involved that day is truly awesome.

Show Dimensions
In 1872, the heights of the male Deerhounds at the Birmingham show consisted of: James Addie's 'Charlie' at 27½in, nine hounds at 28in and only three of 30in. The bitches averaged 26½in. It was therefore interesting to read the comments of the Deerhound judge at the Bath Dog Show in 2011:

> There are two noticeable problems. The fact that there is no longer a hare coursing section of the club seems to have released any constraints on size and this could become more of a problem. Size is fine if hounds are in proportion and still of correct type ... There are some around that you have to look at two or three times before you are sure it isn't a Wolfhound and this is clearly unacceptable ... remember that in the days when Deerhounds hunted their original quarry, the standard height was two inches less than it is now ... Like many large breeds, Deerhounds appear to be getting taller at the expense of angulation and this is really regrettable.

I attended this show and saw why this judge made such remarks. Such valuable words deserve to be heeded by all Deerhound fanciers if true type in this distinguished breed is to be protected. The working anatomy is the one that matters, not the fashion of the day.

Springy Step

The classic use of Deerhounds involved a brace running down their quarry. This demands not just speed, strength and stamina but superbly constructed dogs, whose limbs and, especially, feet, can cope with boulder-strewn terrain at great speed, whose joints can withstand fierce jarring and whose physique combines great power with lightness of build. The first point my eye seeks out in a moving Deerhound, even in a show ring, is a noticeable springiness of step and 'daisy-clipping' action in the feet; for me all other points are subordinate to this essential feature. It reveals soundness, as well as demonstrating show condition. There should never be anything heavy or clumsy about the Deerhound; it must always be a

Scotch Deerhound from Jesse's Anecdotes of Dogs, 1858.

balanced, symmetrical, light-footed hound, giving a lasting impression of speed with strength.

All sporting breeds need to be tested in the field. In the early 1950s Kenneth Cassels started to run meetings including deer work and coursing the blue hare on Dava Moor, Morayshire. Subsequently the Deerhound Club ran such meetings under National Coursing Club rules. Sadly, such trials for the hounds are no longer permitted. This breed does

Mr Morton Campbell's white deerhound 'Bosco'.

still need a field test to verify breeding soundness, however: Deerhounds are not stylish possessions but sporting hounds.

No Ornament

The Deerhound is described as a self-coloured or solid-coloured breed, but I have never seen a wholly white one. Morton Campbell's Bosco, of the late 1880s, came from the Highlands, had plenty of size and substance and was said to have an especially hard-textured pure white coat. I have not seen the attractive red coat colour for many, many years but I have seen some fine blue-grey specimens down the years. It is of interest that the portrayal of the breed in Jesse's *Anecdotes of Dogs* (1858) shows a pied dog, not a self-coloured one. I get depressed when I see Deerhounds in the show ring with woolly coats, poor feet and no spring in their gait, lacking leg muscle and girth of chest. This breed is descended from a primitive hunting dog, prized for its field prowess, famed for its strength and speed and essentially a functional animal, not an ornament. In his book on working Deerhounds, Bill Doherty writes: 'Exaggerated show points were bringing in faults at an alarming rate; shortcomings and structural faults that wouldn't get better or disappear with age and that would be found out in the field of work, even if deliberately ignored in the show ring.' Faults that persist can only be ones ignored or overlooked. It would be good to think of Deerhound fanciers putting the soundness of their dogs ahead of show ring preferences.

Against that background, it is of interest to note the comments made by the Deerhound judge at a 2011 championship show:

> Quite a few poor toplines with too steep a rise starting too far forward over ribbing, and not a slight rise over the loin drooping to tail, therefore this does not allow a good fallaway and makes the spine dip behind the withers. In my view this is the chassis of a galloping Deerhound, along with the carrier of the central nervous system; it is a structural fault which is both ugly and more importantly detrimental to sound movement; form follows function and a correct topline in my view is paramount to function. I would ask that we pay attention to this.

These are perceptive, constructive comments and I do hope that Deerhound breeders consider these words

Miss A. Doxfords's highland deerhound Champion Noel of Ruritania – 'a strong-loined dog of 1925'.

The Misses Loughrey's deerhound Champion 'Padraic of Ross'.

most carefully; there are a good number of committed breeders in this fine breed and there always have been.

Breeder Quality

It is likely that the Deerhound has retained its essential type because it seems to attract distinguished owners and breeders. Names like Miss Doxford of the Ruritania kennel, the Misses Loughrey of the Ross kennel, Miss Bell of the Enterkine kennels, Miss Linton (Geltsdale), Miss Hartley (Rotherwood) and Miss Noble (Ardkinglas) would grace any breed club register. But I do see, mainly over the last decade, far too many Deerhounds in a new mould: shelly, woolly-coated and light in bone, with sharp pointed heads and completely lacking the soft eye. Hounds like this are really without true type. It was good to read in *The*

Kennel Gazette of 1908: 'There is but little doubt that the best specimens of the breed have emanated from Scotland, as a glance at the pedigrees of the present-day hounds will show. Sir John McNeill, Lord Edward Bentinck, and the late Cameron of Lochiel owned hounds which, in their day, could not be beaten, either for sport or show.' As Scotland grows more aware of its heritage, it would be a great step forward if a talented patriotic Scottish breeder came forward and instigated a new interest in this outstanding breed 'north of the border'.

Ingrained Faults

Writing in his *Dogs of Scotland* (1891), Thomson Gray remarked that: 'Another great drawback in connection with deerhounds is that they become small and weedy through interbreeding … all breeders will acknowledge that it is a serious one.' Nobody wants the Deerhound to have the narrower head of the Borzoi or Greyhound, but if this pedigree breed does need an infusion of new blood there are some fine Deerhound-type lurchers around, although far too many of the latter are rather coarse-headed and often over-boned. The distinguished Deerhound breeder G.W. Hickman wrote in Drury's *British Dogs* (1903):

> Of late years many men have bred solely for size, and trusted to Providence for quality. The outcome of this has been that we have had on the show bench animals wanting in all the grace, elegance and symmetry which should characterise the Deerhound; with big heavy heads, bulging out at the eyes; with blunt muzzles, nearly as thick at the nose as just in front of the eyes; with big, heavy, dropping ears, often heavily coated and fringed in addition; and with a large but overgrown and weak-looking frame and coarse but doubtful-looking limbs.

The Kennel Gazette of August 1890 contains a report on a show in which for the challenge certificate only two Deerhounds were entered, which stated 'only Ben Bolt whose head is on the thick side and the shoulders heavy, put in an appearance, and consequently won'. No wonder that faults recur in this breed when the only exhibit wins, despite unacceptable flaws. In March 1891, the same magazine contained a show critique on Deerhounds by G.A. Graham, the Irish Wolfhound expert, which read:

It would be far more to the advantage of the breed if the correct type of head and coat could be insisted on. The abnormally wide skulled dogs should be eliminated, and a harder class of coat cultivated. The heavy ear also calls for condemnation. A long lean head, with ears in proportion, equal to those of a greyhound, should be strenuously aimed at.

Have such faults become ingrained in this breed's gene pool? The following November, when judging Barzois (sic), Graham commented:

The judge steadily aimed to select those which showed most muscular development, symmetry and fitness for work; combined with long narrow head, good ears, and plenty of quality. I would again impress on deerhound breeders the desirability of using crosses from those very suitable dogs, feeling sure the gain in quality, shape, and possibly speed, would be considerable, and well repay the trouble.

A Kennel Club show judge recommending cross-breeding, whatever next!

Recommended Outcross

As set out above, the judge of the breed at the Bath Dog Show in 2011 wrote a valuable critique on the entry, expressing concerns about size, a loss of type, coarseness of bone and head, lack of forechest and poor feet, the latter in a running dog being a serious disadvantage. Another judge in the same year commented on the large heavy heads in the entry, expressing concern about skull shape and eye-set. The Crufts judge for the breed in 2010 commented on skulls that were too broad and shorter than acceptable muzzles. At the Kennel Club show at Alexandra Palace in February 1889, adverse comments were made about coarse heads, skulls too wide behind the eyes, quality of coat texture and variations in size; and it was remarked that 'the continued absence of quality, thoroughbred looks, fine small ears and in a measure, symmetry of shape in this grand breed is much to be deplored'. He recommended an outcross to an outstanding Russian wolfhound adding that 'similar crosses were resorted to some forty years ago, and less frequently since, with enormous gain in both quality and symmetry, and with no appreciable alteration to character.' This reference is usually ignored by breed

purists today, but if there are long-standing faults in any breed, outcrossing can be beneficial, despite the contemporary unwise reverence for purebreeding.

The Deerhound in the United States has the highest percentage of dilated cardiomyopathy seen in breeds there. These dogs come from British stock. Although hip dysplasia is not a common problem in the breed, osteochondritis, and torsion of the stomach, spleen and lung have been recorded. Lurchermen utilizing Deerhound blood would be wise to obtain health checks before investing in breeding material.

Stature too in this breed should be based on the dogs' hunting feats and never on sheer size alone; this is a fine sporting breed, not an ornament. I agree with Bill Doherty when he writes: 'Gargantuan show specimens with their exaggerated points will rarely, if ever, emulate the soundness, health or working abilities of the various working deerhounds …' I do see some fine Deerhound lurchers at country shows; from a distance they look like impressive Deerhounds and could so easily provide fresh breeding stock.

Show Ring Faults

Critiques on Deerhounds in the show ring in 2007 included these faults: too many light eyes, large ears and upright fronts, weak pasterns, splayed fronts, weak quarters and a lack of muscle, lack of spring of rib, poorly knuckled feet, poor front assemblies – with elbows in front of chests and atypically wide behind. This is not encouraging. As reported above, I had a good look at the Deerhound entry at the Bath Dog Show of 2011 and found the subsequent judge's critique (as set out above) of interest; this report expressed concern about too many of the exhibits resembling the Irish Wolfhound, too many oversized, coarse bitches, a lack of forechest and, the worst fault – feet not fit for function, clumsy, sprawled and thin-padded (those are my words based on the judge's critique). There seem to be recurring faults in the breed and this is extremely worrying for the future of the breed. At the World Dog Show in Copenhagen, a highly experienced judge, Dr Goran Bodegard, was horrified to receive into his ring a long row of unworthy champions. He subsequently wrote: 'A Deerhound is not merely a wire-haired Greyhound – there are some important differences in outline – but I should nevertheless not hesitate to think in terms of introducing two or three unrelated Greyhound strains by cross-breeding self-coloured Greyhounds to Deerhounds to increase the gene pool.' Such a radical step has of course been taken before. Breeding the best means having vision *and* an open mind, not just making the best of a closed gene pool.

Challenge Ahead

In her valuable book on the breed, Nora Hartley, who bred the famous Rotherwood hounds, ends with these words: 'Stock-breeding is like a marathon – we take the torch from the hand of the past, do all that in us lies to carry it forward and pass it, still bravely flaring, into the grasp of the future. So let us do so for deerhounds.' Those wise words should be the leitmotiv for every Deerhound breeder during their time in the breed. Producing puppies is the task of the dam; producing sound typical Deerhounds is the task for the breeder, with any true devotee keeping the faith rather than lamely following the style of the day. All breeds are at the mercy of show ring whims but the ancient breeds merit our vigilance and care. In future this may well become more and more difficult, as owners increasingly seek dogs that have no function and merely satisfy their preferred appearance. There is a considerable challenge here.

Champion team of Mr Harry Rawson's deerhounds, Regius, Rhyme, Roderick and Ranger.

Rossie Ralph is the best bodied deerhound we have ever seen. He stands 30 and a quarter inches at the shoulder, measures round the chest 34 inches, has beautifully placed oblique shoulders, and stands so straight and true on his legs, together with his strong loin and well bent hocks, that as your eye rests upon him it tells you at once that this dog is possessed of great strength and speed. His head is thought by some to be a little thick; it may be if you judge him by a Barzoi standard, but a deerhound should not have a narrow, brainless skull, and therein he differs

Mr E. Weston Bell's deerhound 'Rossie Ralph' (K.C.S.B. 26,225). Sire, Lord Stalbridge's Brun; Dam, Clark's Fly III.

from the greyhound, as his calling calls for the use of brains. He must be possessed of courage, but he must have brains to use that courage discreetly.

D.J. Thomson Gray, *The Dogs of Scotland* (1891)

A good working deerhound should stand from 29 inches to 31 inches at shoulder, and in running condition WEIGH around 90lbs. A long, strong dog, his LOINS should be broad and slightly arched, very deep chest, and well sprung ribs. SHOULDERS laid back, to avoid the jarring action that quickly tires in rough going. Particular attention should be paid to FEET. A hard, thick pad and strong black nails are even more important than close-set TOES. Burnt heather and flinty rock will soon flay a thin sole. Long, well-bent THIGHS, upon which the MUSCLES should bulge, tough as rubber. A strong, not overlong NECK and punishing JAW, these perhaps are the salient points to look for in a working hound. But there is one more feature which calls for greater attention than in most breeds – his temperament. He is brave and trusting, but all too often it is forgotten that he is above all things courteous.

Miss M.F. Loughrey, writing on the Deerhound, in *Hounds & Dogs* (1932), in the Lonsdale Library series

If it had not been for shows, Deerhounds would have been in grave danger of extinction, but it cannot be said that they have ever enjoyed the abounding popularity to which appearance and sentiment, kindliness of disposition and good manners entitled them. I have no stupid prejudices about the importation of foreign breeds when they are worth while, but some of those that have become popular do not seem to me to have attractions in any way equal to those of Deerhounds.

A. Croxton Smith, *Dogs Since 1900* (1950)

The Irish Wolfhound

This Dog hath so himself Subdu'd
That Hunger cannot make him rude,
And his behaviour doth confess
True Courage dwells with Gentleness.
With sternest Wolves he does engage
And acts on them successful rage.

Livestock Protection

These words of Katherine Philips, written in 1664 on the Irish Greyhound, forerunner of the Irish Wolfhound, convey the timeless admiration for the noble nature of a huge, brave hound that is ferocious in the chase but gentle in repose. And a wolfhound had to produce a 'successful rage' to engage a wolf, a powerful potentially savage predator well able to defend itself and capable of weighing a hundredweight. Wherever wolves were found and livestock had to be protected, the big shepherd dogs like the shepherd's mastiff here and the German, Dutch and Belgian

Irish Wolfhounds at play.

varieties or the even bigger flock guardians, such as the Anatolian, the Pyrenean, the Tatra and Estrela Mountain Dogs and the Maremma, were utilized. Whenever an offensive had to be mounted, however, faster but similar-sized hounds were used, with the Russian wolfhounds inspiring Turgenev and Tolstoy with their heroic endeavours.

Wolf Threat

In medieval times, there were laws under which some court fines were assessed in terms of wolves' tongues. At one time, the yearly tax in Wales was established at 300 wolves' heads. France was one country particularly populated by wolves; as early as 1467, Louis XI created a special wolf-hunting office, whose top member was appointed from the highest families in the land. In the French province of Gevaudan in the 1760s, one wolf is alleged to have killed more than fifty people, the majority women and children. At the end of the French revolution in 1797, forty people were killed by wolves, tens of thousands of sheep, goats and horses slaughtered by them, and, in some remote districts not a single watchdog left alive. The dense forests led to the French hunting them mainly with packs of scenthounds rather than coursing them with faster hounds.

Celts' Role

Huge, shaggy-coated hunting dogs were used by the Celts in their central European homeland in the eighth century BC, and these accompanied them on their migrations to Britain, Ireland and Northern Spain from the fifth to the first century BC. In *The Gentleman's Recreation* (1674), Nicholas Cox writes:

> Although we have no wolves in England at the present, yet it is certain that heretofore we had routs of them, as they have to this very day in Ireland; and in that country are bred a race of greyhounds which are commonly called wolfdogs, which are strong,

Celtic Wolfdog of 1600.

Primitive Wolfdog depicted by Rubens, c. 1620.

Wolf-lurchers at work.

fleet and bear a natural enmity to the wolf. Now in these greyhounds of that nation there is an incredible force and boldness …

Differing Types

Behind the Irish Wolfhound there are at least three distinct types. Just over one hundred years ago, in *Der Hund* of 1876, Fitzinger identified:

> The Irish Greyhound, next to the Indian and Russian Greyhound, is the largest specimen of the greyhound type, combining the speed of the Greyhound with the size of the Mastiff. The second type is the Irish coursing dog, a cross between the Irish Greyhound and the Mastiff or bandogge. He is shorter in the neck, with a coarser skull, broader chest and heavily flewed lips.

The third variety he described as a cross between the Irish Greyhound and the shepherd dog, being low on the leg and having a shaggy coat. The latter sounds like a shepherd's mastiff or native flock guardian, a bigger version of the Irish Beardie or hirsel. In 1840, Colonel Hamilton Smith wrote, in his *Naturalists' Library*: 'Of the specimens we have seen, and the figures published of the Irish wolfdogs, no two

appear to be exactly alike in structure and colour, so that mastiff, staghound, and bloodhound, may have been crossed with the ancient species. This dog is the largest in Western Europe.' This is unsurprising; the Mastiff of England was recreated in that same century using far more mixed blood.

Old English wolf hunting.

Wolfdogs Owned

Lord Altamont wrote to the Linnaean Society in 1800 to state that:

> There were formerly in Ireland two kinds of wolfdogs – the greyhound and the mastiff. Till within these two years I was possessed of both kinds, perfectly distinct, and easily known from each other. The heads were not so sharp in the latter as the former; but there seemed a great similarity in temper and disposition, both being harmless and indolent.

Lord Altamont's Wolfdog from Linnaean Society's Transactions, 1788.

He stated that the painting held by the Society was of the mastiff wolfdog; it was 28in at the shoulder.

The Countess of Blessington in Ireland was presented with a giant Suliot Dog by the King of Naples. Lady Blessington was one of the Powers of Kilfane, who at one time were the only people who patronized the Irish Wolfhound. Suliot Dogs came from Epirus in Greece, location of the Molossian people, and were giant hounds, used as outpost sentries in the Austrian Army and as 'parade dogs' or mascots of German regiments. They were used to give added stature to German boarhounds (the hunting dogs being nearer to 26in at the shoulder than the 30in minimum of today's Great Danes). Lady Blessington's Suliot Dog is

Suliot dog of Countess Blessington by Landseer.

Tibetan Mastiff of Capt Graham's time.

Reinagle's Irish Wolfhound of 1879.

likely to have been used as a sire at Kilfane. This dog was the subject used by Edwin Landseer in his *Waiting for the Countess* sketch (1833).

Blended Revival

The Irish Wolfhound was all but lost to us in the latter half of the nineteenth century. Then, in 1863, an Englishman, Captain George Augustus Graham, a Deerhound breeder, noted that some of his stock threw back to the larger type of Irish Wolfhound. He obtained dogs of the Kilfane and Ballytobin strains, the only suitable blood available in Ireland at that time. He then interbred these with Glengarry Deerhounds, which had Irish Wolfhound blood in

their own ancestry. In due course he produced and then stabilized the type of Irish Wolfhound that he believed to be historically correct. Outcrossing continued, with Captain Graham using the blood of a 'great dog of Tibet', called Wolf, bought from a livestock dealer and of uncertain parentage, which was used at stud to Champion Sheelagh's daughter Tara. The resultant progeny, Nookoo and Vandal, can be found in the pedigree of every modern Irish Wolfhound. Then, between 1885 and 1900, seven Great Dane crosses were conducted, and Borzoi blood used several times in the 1890s.

In *The Twentieth Century Dog* (1904), Compton wrote that Graham obtained bitches from Power

Mr Graham's Irish wolfhound 'Scot'.

Keildar, born 1863, Graham's Deerhound. Used to recreate the Irish dog, he was one quarter Borzoi.

of Kilfane, Baker of Ballytobin and Mahoney of Dromore, adding '... from a cross between the deerhound and the Great Dane, with a dash of borzoi blood (the noted Karotai), and an outcross with a huge shaggy dog, stated to be a Thibetan mastiff (though I doubt the description being correct, having seen a photograph of the dog in question), the modern breed has been literally built up.' This is of course how all hounds were once bred, good dog to good dog, irrespective of breed titles. Closed gene pools are a modern phenomenon.

In *Dogs Since 1900* (1950), Croxton Smith writes:

> At the beginning of this century Mr IW Everett, whose Felixstowe Irish Wolfhounds obtained a dominant influence for many years, resorted to a cross with a brindle Great Dane. This alien blood was apparent for some time in the flatter skulls of the Felixstowe Wolfhounds, but it disappeared, and for a long time now the breed has been kept in its purity.

I have talked to Irish Wolfhound breeders of the present time who are still very anxious to avoid shaggier coats and the flatter skull because of this background to the breed. Those words of Croxton Smith about purity very much typify twentieth-century thinking about recognized breeds of dog, often placing purity ahead of soundness and health. In the twenty-first century slowly but surely attitudes are changing, so that coefficients of inbreeding and genetic health are to the fore. Fitness for function is becoming fashionable once more!

Respecting Function

Against that background, it is surely important for us to respect past function, which bequeathed us the wolfhound breeds, and breed to reflect that heritage. Russian Wolfhounds bred purely for beauty of form and Irish Wolfhounds bred mainly for shoulder height show little respect for their distinguished past service to man and little regard for historical honesty. It is sad to read, in show critiques on Irish Wolfhounds, such judges' comments as these: 'I was very shocked at the terrible soft condition of some of the hounds'; 'Movement should be a cause for concern, both for breeders and owners ... Many hounds lacked strength and muscle particularly in hindquarters'; 'the most prevalent fault in the entry was deviation from true in front action'. (And why do Irish Wolfhounds need legs like tree trunks when Russian ones do not?)

But in the Russian hounds too (covered in the next chapter) the critiques are worrying: 'The effortless power on the move seems to have disappeared', with another mentioning 'too much emphasis being placed on copious amounts of coat'. When hounds are bred without regard for their physical soundness and the coat becomes more important than the essential wolfhound anatomy, we are heading for the destruction of such remarkable breeds in the immediate future. Huge dogs need soundness of physique most of all; their ability to lead a fulfilling life is prejudiced when their anatomy itself is a handicap. Breeders and owners who rate the coat above structural soundness reveal at once their disrespect for their own breed.

Wolfhounds are extraordinary hounds; their past courage and athleticism deserves our respect. They were never intended to be ornaments or fashion accessories; they survived because they were superlative hunting dogs, and could still be. The breed came about because of the threat from wolves; now the threat is reversed and comes from human indifference.

Indian Wolfhounds

Where wolves threaten human lives or livestock, huge hounds are needed to meet that threat, and not just in the West. The Indian wolf has been hunted using similarly shaggy-coated hounds (*see* Chapter 3), like the Banjara or Vanjari, 28in high and grey mottled, and the 30in Rampur Hound, the smoother-coated Shikari dog of Kumaon, the Great Dane-like Sindh Hound, the beautiful ivory-coated Rajapalayam and the Dobermann-shaped Patti of Tamil Nadu.

Such types disappear when the threat from wolves recedes but their value to man was considerable. Our contemporary affection for the wolf would not have been shared by those living in remote villages in India or a number of European countries in the Middle Ages. Wolves, operating in packs, threatened livestock and sought human prey when desperate for food. Powerful dogs of the flock-guarding type were needed to protect livestock and strong-headed, very fast hounds were needed to course them. Hunting wolves for sport may not appeal to twenty-first-century sympathies, but that should not lessen our admiration for wolfhounds, their bravery and athleticism in the hunt, when wolf numbers required checking.

White Wolfhounds

European man has long utilized huge, white, rough-haired dogs in their age-old campaign to protect their livestock from wolf attacks, as the Pyrenean flock-guarding breeds illustrate. There are a number of depictions of such big white wolfhounds in antique art, in the work of Oudry, Desportes and Snyders, for example. It is rare nowadays to see a pure white Irish Wolfhound, however, despite this coat colour being permitted in the breed standard. In 1585, the Lord Deputy Perrott sent to Lord Walsingham 'a brace of good wolfdogs, one black and one white'. In 1623, the Duke of Buckingham asked the Earl of Cork for some white ones, claiming that this colour was the most in favour when given as presents to monarchs. Wholly white dogs can suffer from related problems, such as albinism, deafness and sometimes eye complaints too.

The pied colouration was shown in Lord Altamont's Irish 'wolfdogs' of the late eighteenth century but, like pure black, has perhaps been overwhelmed by the main coat colours: grey brindle, red, fawn, wheaten and steel grey. Perhaps the Deerhound, Great Dane and Tibetan Mastiff infusions have dwarfed those from the Greyhound and the Borzoi. 'Irish spotting' or white feet and throat on a solid colour is frowned on in this breed, whatever the merits of the carrier. A wide-ranging coat colour presentation in a breed must always be healthier than a restrictive one. Pure white Deerhounds are no longer wanted despite their appearance in Victorian paintings. Huge, pure white flock-guarding breeds are welcomed by kennel clubs,

Almost pure white Irish Wolfhound.

Solid black Irish Wolfhound.

featuring from Poland and Hungary in the north to Italy and Greece in the south.

Restoring Appeal

It is worth noting that in 1926 176 Irish Wolfhounds were registered with the KC; in 1980 it was 794; 601 in 2000; and down to a mere 352 in 2010. (For a comparable breed, like the Great Dane, the figures contrast: between the two World Wars, eighty-six quality Great Danes were imported into Britain to improve stock; in 1950 540 were registered with the KC, in 1970 the figure rose to 2,174, then fell in 2010 to 1,429.) In the 1950s, Irish Wolfhound registrations went into a trough: thirty-three in 1952 and only thirteen in 1954. The breed may have recovered from the dire days of the fifties, but does it have the 'essential greyhound' or sighthound characteristics to restore type and favour? A judge's critique in 2010 read:

> I last judged them at the Society's show in 2007 and many of the same failings are still in evidence and the breed is certainly not going through a purple patch at the moment. Once again it was rare to find 'great size and commanding appearance' and I tried where possible to go for the shapely sighthound look plus substance, movement and temperament, but it wasn't that easy to find all of those attributes in the same animal.

Greyhound Type

The judge of Irish Wolfhounds at the Crystal Palace show of 1890 made some interesting observations on the breed, which are still of value to the breeders of today:

> In conclusion I may perhaps be allowed to draw the attention of Irish Wolfhound breeders to a few points of practical importance. Size, and the power which usually accompanies it, is everything in this breed, for without it its existence would be unmeaning, and a really good muscular deerhound would not only possess all the principal characteristics, but also be in appearance, power, speed and utility, in every respect superior to a wolfhound of no greater size; for the comparative power of a dog of pure greyhound type exceeds that of every other breed, surpassing even that of the wolf itself. Size, however, has in a great measure been obtained, but the breed is still, I think,

deficient in character. The Irish wolfhound was, before everything, a greyhound, and it was the great nervous power and muscular energy peculiar to the greyhound which, with its size and the stately beauty also peculiar to the greyhound, made it of such remarkable value all over Europe both for ornament and for the destruction and capture of swift and powerful wild animals. Without the essential greyhound characteristics the breed is of little practical utility now, neither can it have the symmetry of form which accompanies those characteristics. Wanting these, it has no quality calculated to bring it into public favour which is not possessed in an equal or superior degree by other large breeds.

Those last few words make a point about essential breed type in the Irish Wolfhound.

Maintaining Size

In his wide-ranging book, *How to Breed Dogs* (1947), the American vet and experienced dog breeder Leon F. Whitney writes:

> Suppose you are a breeder of Irish Wolfhounds. You have been breeding within your own strain now for twenty years. You have tried all methods of feeding and have never been able to produce a dog weighing over 146 pounds. You would breed to dogs belonging to another breeder whose dogs get to weigh 190 pounds, and size is what you really desire, but your dogs have been of such fine quality with the exception of size, that you intensely dislike breaking your charm and going outside to breed. But how else can you get greater size in your strain? That strain is to you what a pure line is to the geneticist to all intents and purposes. You have come up against a barrier … if you are wise you will breed to some giant dog outside of your own strain, and be sure that this dog comes from a strain the members of which are all very large.

It is vital to keep in mind, however, that unsoundness is much more apparent in huge dogs than small ones. Size, for its own sake, is no substitute for quality in the bigger breeds. Selecting the soundest breeding stock, wherever from, will always be paramount.

In his *Animated Nature* (1770), Oliver Goldsmith writes:

The last variety, and the most wonderful of all that I shall mention is the great Irish wolfdog … bred up in the houses of the great, or such gentlemen as choose to keep him as a curiosity, being neither good for hunting the hare, the fox, nor the stag … The largest of those I have seen … was made extremely like a greyhound, but rather more robust … his nature seemed heavy and phlegmatic. This I ascribe to his having been bred up to a size beyond his nature … The greatest pains have been taken with these to enlarge the breed, both by food and matching. This end was effectually obtained, indeed, for the size was enormous; but, as it seemed to me, at the expense of the animal's fierceness, vigilance and sagacity.

Three and a half centuries later, we are surely wise enough, and better scientifically advised, not to repeat Goldsmith's concerns. Breeding giant dogs demands knowledge and skill.

Inbreeding Dilemma

When attending World Dog Shows in places like Helsinki and Vienna, I do see some outstanding Irish Wolfhounds. In Slovakia, for example, Petra Tomasovicova has some excellent stock, with her dog Ch. Absolut Roan Inish Tullamore Good Stuff rightly winning well, becoming an international champion of champions. Just as the importation of quality Great Danes between the wars set up that breed here for half a century, do we now need an infusion of blood from overseas to resuscitate this superb breed here? Or would this just recycle old genes? At last, both in Britain and in Ireland, we are taking more interest in the future of our native breeds. Perhaps this new emphasis will inspire Irish Wolfhound breeders to greater heights. It would be such a joy to witness that.

In North America, Dr Urfer has conducted studies into the genotype of this breed and concluded that it is extremely inbred. (According to Professors Ostrander and Kruglyak of the Cancer Research Center in Seattle, the modern breed of Irish Wolfhound probably arose from just six animals.) Dogs born after 1980 were found to have a significant decrease in mean lifespan compared to those born in the 1960s. Dr Urfer found four distinct genetic bottlenecks in the breed that need to be remedied. It would be so uplifting if that remedial work could be launched in the British Isles, with outcrossing to

Ch. Absolut Roan Inish Tullamore Good Stuff.

other breeds not ruled out by unsupportive kennel clubs. In the end it is this outstanding breed that has to survive, not its show fanciers. To be fair, the three breed clubs in the UK have formed a Health Group to look at inherited defects, including the shortening lifespan, and I commend them for this.

That we have in the Deerhound the modern representative of the old Irish Wolfdog is patent. Of less stature, less robust, and of slimmer form, the main characteristics of the breed remain; and in very exceptional instances specimens occur which throw back to and resemble in a marked manner the old stock from which they have sprung. It is not probable that our remote ancestors arrived at any very high standard as to quality or looks. Strength, stature, and fleetness were the points most carefully cultivated – at any rate, as regards those breeds used in the capture of large and fierce game. It is somewhat remarkable that whilst we have accounts of all the noticeable breeds from a remote period, including

the Irish Wolfdog, we do not find any allusion to the Deerhound, save in the writings of a comparatively recent date, which would in a measure justify us in supposing that the Deerhound is the modern representative of that superb animal.

George A. Graham, writing in Vero Shaw's *The Illustrated Book of the Dog* (1879–81). Captain Graham wrote similarly in Sidney Turner's *The Kennel Encyclopaedia* (Vol. 2, 1908) and without enlarging on what he meant by 'comparatively recent date', it is hard to think that such a knowledgeable man was so unfamiliar with Deerhound references of the seventeenth and early eighteenth centuries (*see above*, under Deerhounds). But the loose nomenclature used by writers in past centuries to refer to types of hounds used on deer and wolf is very confusing for even the most diligent researcher.

> Surely Captain Graham, with all your experience, is it not high time you gave up breeding (or at least exhibiting) such things as these? I at least cannot say anything in their favour, so I must leave it in your hands to sing their praise.
>
> Critique on the Irish Wolfhounds shown at the Birmingham Dog Show, 30 November–4 December 1889, by the judge, Arthur Maxwell, as reported in *The Kennel Gazette* (December 1889)

About two or three generations of hounds after Graham's experiments, Mr IW Everett obtained a cross of a golden brindle Great Dane dog and a blue deerhound bitch. They had a bitch puppy whom he named 'FELIXSTOWE SHEELAH', and he mated her with the best Irish Wolfhounds he could find at the time. She had some puppies by a hound called KENMARE … KENMARE'S dam also had some Dane blood. The Dane type occasionally crops out a little even now in some lines, though the most recent infusion of Dane blood is by now at least eight generations into the background, and was never bred in to as the borzoi and Tibetan crosses were. But of course there were several different infusions of Dane, as against only one of these other breeds.

Phyllis Gardner, *The Irish Wolfhound* (1928)

Irish Wolfhound.

The Irish Wolfhounds, judging from the classes, have made a decided advance in point of character, and show distinct type of their own. The Great Dane or Deerhound types are disappearing, and the mongrel element was entirely absent in the exhibits. I may here state that this breed of dogs is very much enquired after for their original use – wolf and coyote hunting in different parts of North America and Canada, especially in the Rocky Mountains.

Judge's critique on the entry at the Kennel Club's 34th show, at the Agricultural Hall, in April 1890.

DECLARATION AGAINST TRANSPORTING WOLF DOGS.

For as much as we are credibly informed that wolves do much increase, and that some of the enemy's party, who have laid down arms and have liberty to go beyond sea, and others, do attempt to carry away several such great dogs as are commonly called wolf-dogs, whereby the breed of them, which is useful for the destroying of wolves, would if not prevented speedily decay. These are, therefore, to prohibit all persons from exporting any of the said dogs out of this kingdom, and searchers and other officers of the Customs in the several ports and creeks of this dominion are strictly required to seize and make stop of all such dogs, and deliver them either to the common huntsman appointed for the precinct where they are seized upon, or to the governor of the said precinct.

Dated at Kilkenny, 27 April 1652

The Hybrid Sighthound: the Lurcher

A number of the sighthound breeds can rightly claim an ancient origin and a long record as a distinct type. But every hunting dog was developed from varied sources – the hybrid was the foundation stock – with anatomical features being rooted in function rather than any desire for cosmetic appeal. Our Mastiff was once revered all over northern Europe as a hunting dog: the Englische Dogge. It was a powerful, strong-headed, active, agile, heavy *hound*, used to close with quarry and seize it for the accompanying hunters. The German Mastiff, or Deutsche Dogge, became the Great Dane, but both came from huge, functional boar-lurchers, a type perpetuated today in some bull-lurchers. Brindle mastiffs were used in the nineteenth-century deer hunt in Scotland, used towards the end of the chase to pull down the quarry. In his *Hunting and Hunting Reserves in Medieval Scotland* (1979), John Gilbert writes of references to mastiffs in the Scottish Forest Laws – capable of attacking and pulling down deer; they wore spiked collars when they were used on wolves and boar, when they hunted to the horn. These dogs were nothing like the contemporary breed of Mastiff, but athletic muscular hunting dogs, showing tuck-up and signs of sighthound blood, very much in the mould of today's bull-lurcher.

English Hunting Mastiff. Lithograph, 1850.

Mastiff cross Greyhounds used in Deer Hunt.

'Poachers' in 1824 with their lurcher.

The lurcher is supposed to have been originally a cross between the greyhound and the shepherd's dog, recrossed with the terrier; hence the quickness of his scent, his speed, and intelligence. The habits of this dog lead him to concealment and cunning, and he is seldom found in the possession of honourable sportsmen. He is often employed by poachers in killing hares and rabbits in the obscurity of night …

Edward Jesse, *Anecdotes of Dogs* (1858)

With respect to the lurcher, it appears to us to be a mongrel breed between the rough greyhound and the shepherd's dog. Bewick, who figures and describes it, says, that it is less and shorter than the greyhound, with stronger limbs; its body is covered with a coat of rough hair, commonly of a pale yellow colour; its aspect is sullen, and its habits, whence it derives its name, are cunning and insidious. At the same time it must be confessed that this dog is very attached to its master, displays most extraordinary intelligence, and is trained with great facility. As it possesses the advantage of a fine scent, it is often nefariously employed during the night-time in the capture of game; the more especially as it works silently, never giving tongue.

W.C.L. Martin, *The History of the Dog* (1845)

Gypsies and Greyhounds. Sir Alfred Munnings, 1913.

Coarsely bred Greyhound with kennel mates, 17th century.

Lurcher of 600 years ago. Lombardy, c. 1400.

One of the chief auxiliaries of the poacher is that clever rascal, the Lurcher, a compound of Sheepdog and Greyhound, with the brains of one and the speed of the other. Many imagine that the term Lurcher is of comparatively modern derivation. It is as old as Queen Anne, and no doubt was in use before that queen. 'He who keeps Greyhounds, Lurchers, Setting-Dogs, to kill the game, being not qualified, forfeits £5, a Moiety to the Informer, the other to the poor.' So runs a statute of Queen Anne. If it were not for his disreputable associations the Lurcher might very well become a favourite companion on account of his cleverness and teachability.

A. Croxton Smith, *British Dogs* (1945)

Hunting Excellence

For a thousand years in Britain, the humbler hunters have had their own hybrid sighthound, with pride in its performance rather than its purity of breeding, yet purpose-bred in the pursuit of hunting excellence just as shrewdly as any Foxhound or gundog. Forever associated with gypsies, poachers and country characters, the lowly lurcher has survived the campaigns of rural police forces, watchful gamekeepers and wary landowners, and to this day still keeps the pot filled for many a working-class household. Yet nowadays the lurcher fancier is classless; Barbours and bespoke boots feature as much at lurcher shows as moleskin and mufflers. The extraordinary rise in lurcher shows in the last half-century demonstrates the awareness of interest in these remarkable hunting dogs of mixed parentage. But it has also brought, at times, a tendency to breed a type that will win 'on the

flags' rather than a 'chase, catch and kill' champion. The showier dog, often carrying the exaggerated angulation favoured in the official show rings, sadly appears at the shows close to a big town.

A Function not a Breed

But what is a lurcher? Writing in 1803, William Taplin considered the lurcher was a cross between:

> the shepherd's dog and the greyhound, which from breeding *in and in* with the latter, has so refined upon the first change, that very little of the shepherd's dog seems now to be retained in the stock; its patience, docility, and fidelity excepted. The lurcher, if thus bred, without any farther collateral crosses, is about three fourths the height and size of a full grown greyhound, and of a yellowish or sandy-red colour, rough and wiry-haired with ears naturally erect, but dropping a little at the point, of great speed, courage, sagacity and fidelity.

Yet if you look around at a lurcher show today it is soon apparent that the event would be better labelled 'any variety, sporting dog', for the height, weight, coat and colour are essentially anything but uniform. For a lurcher must be a cross-bred dog – fast enough to take all legal quarry, crafty enough not to get detected when used by the poacher, and able to withstand the cold and the wet, as well as the odd encounter with barbed wire. Purists might say it should really be a Collie cross Greyhound to be truly a lurcher; but Deerhound, Whippet, Saluki, Bedlington Terrier and Beardie blood have all been used over the years to

Real Hybrid: Whippet × Bedlington × Deerhound × Greyhound.

Superb Greyhound cross Whippet.

Kelpie × Whippet.

Saluki Lurcher.

Bedlington Lurcher.

Collie cross Greyhound hybrid.

*Second cross ¼ Bulldog
¾ Greyhound.*

instil dash, greater stamina or a more protective coat. Such an infusion, however, does need to be related both to quarry and country.

The word 'lurcher' describes a function, not a breed of dog, just as the word 'gundog' describes the various breeds of dog working to the gun. Historically, the lurcher was the 'stealer' or 'the thievishe dog', the 'look-dog' of East Anglia, utilized by the humbler hunter, often hunting unlawfully. Like gundogs, lurchers vary in size, coat, head structure and precise function, with Deerhound, Smithfield and Bedlington lurchers being quite distinct from the Bull, Whippet and Bearded Collie types. Dogs portrayed in antique art, displaying the sighthound phenotype, are usually described as belonging to the nearest similar contemporary breed, rather than as lurchers, despite hunters of the past placing performance well ahead of purity of breeding. Today, any mongrel with the sighthound silhouette can attract the loosely applied title of 'lurcher' but the automatic association with unlawful hunting no longer penalizes the dogs. They are now part of what has been dubbed 'country-chic'.

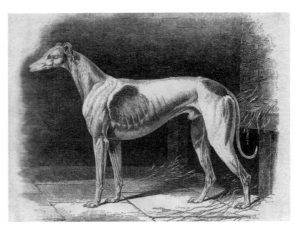

King Cob – Bulldog-blooded Greyhound.

'Half-and-half' – first cross from the Bulldog.

Penalties of Purity

The twenty-first century is exposing, for all dog fanciers to see, the penalties of breeding for purity of blood rather than performance. A dog that can do absolutely nothing can be more highly prized than one able to fill the pot. Appearance and human whim decide on breeds, not their capability. Uninformed purebreeding and ignoring the inbreeding coefficients are threatening the lives and ease of life of so many purebred dogs. But lurchermen breed for performance still, and are proud of their dogs' hunting skills. Honest breed historians know too that no breed of dog was actually kept pure before the late nineteenth century and the advent of dog shows. If you take the Greyhound, for example, Lord Orford of Houghton Hall in Norfolk, to improve his Greyhounds introduced lurcher blood, then that of the Italian Greyhound, then the Foxhound and even that of the Bulldog. Lord Rivers did something similar, breeding from a half bull and half Greyhound bitch, whose progeny he recrossed for six or seven generations with his own Greyhounds. The Bulldog-blooded King Cob is behind every racing Greyhound of today. Sporting dog breeders, sighthound breeders especially, need an open mind if performance is rated above breed points.

Thevishe Dog

It is common to find the less diligent researchers linking the 'tumbler', quaintly described by a number of sixteenth-century writers, with the lurcher. Correspondents contributing to country sports magazines on the subject of lurchers often sign themselves 'Tumbler'. But the tumbler was the decoy dog, a very different animal. Dr Caius, for all his learning, knew little about dogs, and yet has over the years become much quoted as some form of authority. But even he mentioned the 'Thevishe Dog or Stealer, that is a poaching dog'. His lengthy and extraordinary description of the 'tumbler' is in effect an exaggerated account of the antics of the decoy dog. I know of no lurcher that hunts by 'dissembling friendship and pretending favour', as he describes.

Nondescript Dogs

From the ranks of dogs without a modern use, we have lost the decoy dog of England but the blood lives on in the Nova Scotia Duck Tolling Retriever and the Kooikerhondje of Holland. The first named lures the inquisitive ducks to within range of the hunters' rifles; the second entices them along ever-narrowing little waterways until they are netted. We have lost the ginger 'coy dog' of East Anglia, referred to by such rural affairs writers as James Wentworth Day. But whereas the red decoy dog is perpetuated in distinct breeds, the lurcher was and ever shall be a nondescript dog. As 'Stonehenge' described them a century and a half ago: 'A poacher possessing such an animal seldom keeps him long, every keeper being on the look out, and putting a charge of shot into him on the first opportunity … the poacher does not often attempt to rear the dog which would suit him best, but contents himself with one which will not so much attract the notice of those who watch him.'

Favoured Blends

A farm labourer's dog is not so easily researched as that of the squire, but 'Stonehenge' has managed to convey the vital ordinariness, the essential anonymity and the fundamental disregard for type in what has long been a cross-bred, purely functional hound, used for illegal hunting. This variation in type still manifests itself in today's lurcher shows, with classes for dogs over and under 26in at the withers, rough-haired or smooth-haired. Some breeders swear by the long-haired Saluki cross and others by Bedlington blood; some fanciers favour a stiff-coated dog and others the smooth-coated variety. A small minority still prize the Smithfield blood from the old drovers' dogs and there are usually the more bizarre crosses, such as Airedale cross Whippet or Bearded Collie

Afghan Hound cross Deerhound.

Cretan Hound. Lavrys.

cross Dobermann Pinscher. The normal combination, however, is that of sighthound with herding dog, with more recently, Kelpie and Malinois blood utilized. Sir Walter Scott's much-loved 'Deerhound', Maida, was actually a Deerhound-Pyrenean Mountain Dog cross, bred by Macdonell of Glengarry.

Non-Conformists

Judges at Kennel Club dog shows have scoffed at the whole business of even attempting to judge such a wide variation of type in one lurcher ring, but, of course, that is exactly what they do when judging 'Best in Show', when all the winners in each breed, then group, competition come together to compete with one another. Lurcher show judges are not conformist anyway, having once included such diverse characters as Moses Aaron-Smith, a gamekeeper from Derbyshire, born in a gypsy wagon of pure Romany stock; Ted Walsh, a retired army colonel and expert on coursing; and Martin Knoweldon, a commercial artist specializing in the depiction of sighthounds in full stride.

The most popular breed of dog in the United Kingdom is the Labrador Retriever, with nearly 35,000 registrations with the Kennel Club each year. By contrast, it is estimated that around 50,000 lurchers are newly born each year but registered with nobody. There are around 100 lurcher shows a year, some featuring lure-chasing and high-jumping, but the lurcher has no breed standard and no breed clubs as such.

The Association of Lurcher Clubs (ALC) was formed in 1995, with the idea of uniting the various small lurcher and coursing clubs in a joint purpose. It offers support to lurcher owners and helps fight for the restoration of hunting and coursing with lurchers. The ALC is a full voting member of the Council of Hunting Associations. In conjunction with the National Working Terrier Federation, the ALC aims to promote and support all kinds of hunting with lurchers and terriers, working to a code of good practice and with the permission and goodwill of landowners, farmers and the police. Such an organization deserves the support of lurchermen across the home countries; a united voice can achieve so much more than individual ones, which are so often used only when difficulties arise.

Overseas Dogs

Overseas, a number of breed types act as lurchers: the Banjara Greyhound, the Cretan Hound, the Portuguese Podengo and the Ibizan Hound. But our lurchers can possess a wide range of skills, being not just fast running dogs, but able to use ground and air scent and track quarry as well as course it. The lurcher of Britain can be a combination of coursing Greyhound, retriever, tracker, pointer and watchdog. It would be more correct to describe the word lurcher itself as indicating a role, rather than a distinct type of dog. For it does not matter if a lurcher is 20in or 26in at the shoulder, rough-coated or smooth, black and tan or buckskin, prick-eared or drop-eared, provided it is biddable and can run. Uniformity of conformation matters little, but composition matters a great deal: good feet with strong toes, plenty of lung room, a flexible back, well-angled shoulders and immense power from the hindquarters are essential. Now that the type is not immediately under suspicion of illegal hunting the lurcher can afford to actually *look* like a hunting dog.

Value of the Hybrid

The lurcher world, despite the establishment of the Association of Lurcher Clubs, or ALC, and the National Lurcher Racing Club, with regional branches, has never needed an infrastructure, a tight organizational body. Still, it would be good to see a modern nonconformist like Lord Orford, who more than two hundred years ago made use of Bulldog blood to increase the 'heart' and gameness of his Greyhounds. His line was perpetuated by Colonel

Thornton, who bought all his stock. We perpetuate closed gene pools at our peril; we very much need a new and very nonconformist approach today.

I strongly support the view expressed twenty five years ago by four veterinary scientists at the Ontario Veterinary College, which read: 'The advantages of hybrid vigour in a pure-bred line could be realized in a carefully controlled breeding program making use of outcrosses.' The American veterinary surgeon Leon Whitney found fifty years ago better disease resistance in his crosses between two pedigree breeds. Also in North America, a study by Scott and Fuller (*Genetics and the Social Behaviour of Dogs*, University of Chicago Press, 1965) indicated that the high puppy mortality characteristic of matings within a breed was greatly reduced when two different breeds were crossed. Another study by Rehfeld (*Studies in a Closed Beagle Colony*, Argonne National Laboratory, 1970) showed that the frequency of neonatal death in purebred Beagles increased with the degree of inbreeding. Most pedigree dog breeders resort to close line-breeding when they realize that such a programme is more likely to produce uniform animals of predictable merit. Then, to their dismay, a few animals with recessive disorders begin appearing in the line-bred progeny. When the first abnormal puppy is born, the initial reaction is to deny that anything heritable is at fault in their line. It is regarded as a freak and the puppy disposed of. When further abnormal births occur, the cover-up continues. Some sighthound breeds have coefficients of inbreeding that give cause for anxiety.

Conserving Healthy Breeds

The veterinary profession and geneticists know well that inbreeding is usually accompanied by an increase in defects: smaller litter sizes, increased post-natal mortality, general lessening of body size, lower reproductive performance, less robustness and behavioural problems. It is not inbreeding per se that brings about these defects but the presence of deleterious recessive genes that are being carried in the stock. Yet it is consistently argued by pedigree dog breeders, and regrettably even by some with veterinary qualifications, that our pedigree breeds of dog are just as healthy, virile and robust as any crossbred dog, mongrel or mutt. This is in spite of the weight of empirical evidence, especially from North

America, over the last fifty years in particular. There are, of course, plenty of perfectly healthy pedigree dogs and far too many ill-kept mongrels and pitiful pi-dogs in the world. It is in the area of planned dog breeding where action can and must be taken to conserve the famous sighthound breeds handed down to us. Hybrids such as the lurcher show the way; seeking the purity of blood rather than a healthier, longer-living dog is not a compassionate act.

No dog in Britain ever drew more fire than the lurcher, not even the sheep-worrier. The gamekeeper hero of a novel by G Christopher Davies, Peter Penniless, lies in wait for some poachers who are about to gate-net a field, having stopped the meuses. As the poachers approach, accompanied by their lurcher dog, which has been trained to drive the hares directly towards the gates … Peter asks his employer what he should do if the dog scents them. The employer, elderly gamekeeper Quadling, replies, 'Shoot it. That's why I brought my gun. The men may be too quick for us, but I thought we might have a shot at the dog.'
Carson Ritchie, *The British Dog* (1981)

The Lurcher is by no means the ugly brute he is sometimes described to be. True, they vary greatly, and the name more properly describes the peculiar duties of the dog, and his manner of performing them, than distinctiveness of type.
Hugh Dalziel, *British Dogs* (1888)

To the mind of many, the most intelligent of all [sighthounds] is the Lurcher, rather blown upon as to his reputation through his association with the Romany, but a creature of singular parts. He, I suppose, approximates to the hunting dog employed by our remote ancestors in that he can still be relied on to catch, kill and deliver one's dinner wherever game is to be found.
Brian Vesey-Fitzgerald, *The Book of the Dog* (1948)

With respect to the lurcher … When taken to the warren, it steals along with the utmost caution, creeps upon the rabbits while feeding, and darts upon them in an instant; it waylays them as they return to their burrow, where it is ready to seize them, and then brings its booty to its master. Bewick knew a man who kept a pair of these dogs, and who confessed that

Impressive Bull Lurcher.

at any time he could procure in an evening as many rabbits as he could carry home. This dog is equally expert at taking hares, partly by speed, but more by cunning wiles. It will drive partridges to the net with the utmost circumspection and address; and will even seize and pull down a fallow deer, and, leaving it disabled, return to its master and guide him to the scene of its exploits. The true lurcher is not so often to be seen as formerly; it is essentially a poacher's dog, so that any person known to possess one becomes a suspected character.

W.C.L. Martin, *The History of the Dog* (1845)

RABBIT-COURSING: ... THE DOGS are a cross of the terrier and greyhound, and are usually limited in weight, 25lbs. being that which is generally adopted. They are very fast for their size, but would of course be beaten by even an inferior thorough-bred greyhound; hence, the stipulation is generally made as to breed and weight. They have great power of turning and stopping themselves, which is required by the short running and quick turning of the rabbits, which spurt about more sharply than hares.

J.H. Walsh, *Manual of British Rural Sports – The Pursuit of Wild Animals for Sport* (1856)

Breeding 'in-and-in' – a practice which the deerhound has proved singularly capable of without immediate detriment – took place to an extent that brought back with multiplied force the old complaints of infertility, degeneracy, and 'distemper' of the most inveterate type. To this latter ailment some kennels were particularly subject (such as the Duke of Leeds's, and afterwards, as we have been especially told, Lord Dalhousie's at Invermark). All were notorious for it, although the fact seemed chiefly to come out in detached specimens that were obtained elsewhere, while the disease was almost unknown in forests where the cross-breeds prevailed.

George Cupples, *Scotch Deer-hounds and Their Masters* (1894)

As to breeding, we used an English greyhound bitch with courage, speed and a special hatred for a wolf, crossed with an English fox hound with all the qualities necessary, except the speed. We then picked the bitch with the most good qualities and crossed her with another fox hound whose ancestry is perfect. Here we get the dog we are using now and with which we have made the most satisfactory of catches ... Where this dog has the advantage over the fox hound is in speed and the fact that it is ever on the watch ahead for the game.

A.R. Harding, *Wolf and Coyote Trapping* (1909)

CHAPTER 3

THE WIDER SIGHTHOUND DIASPORA

The Long Reach of the Longdog

A longdog is a hybrid between two sighthounds, between two dogs of similar type, both bred essentially for speed but also specifically 'tailored' for a particular task ... Lurchers were bred as all-purpose hunting dogs and are the result of ameliorating purebred sighthounds with the blood of other breeds, breeds other than sighthounds, that is – namely collies, Bedlington Terriers, and occasionally, gun dog breeds.

Brian Plummer, *The Complete Book of Sight Hounds, Long Dogs and Lurchers* (1991)

A longdog is either a purebred greyhound, whippet, deerhound, wolfhound, borzoi, saluki, Afghan or the less familiar Pharaoh hound, Ibizan hound and sloughi, or a cross between two such purebreds, or the offspring of such until herding blood is introduced ... A longdog takes its quarry in a different way from the lurcher. There is a good deal less of the reflex action about them and more of the hunting.

Frank Sheardown, *The Working Longdog* (1999)

It could be argued that of all types of sporting dog the longdog has the longest reach, appearing from the American prairies to the Asiatic steppes and from Northern Europe to Central Africa. You may not find

Smooth Saluki cross Greyhound.

Saluki Lurcher.

them in the densely wooded areas of Scandinavia or South America, but where there are open spaces, and especially where deer abound, you will find the canine speedsters. As human settlements change their nature and urban living increases remorselessly, we may gradually lose them, as the demise of such types

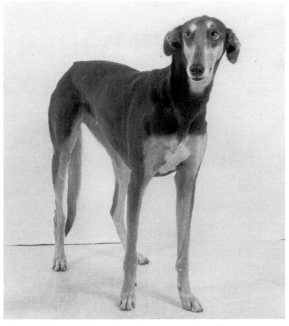

Chart Polski – Polish Greyhound. Courtesy of Royal Canin, France.

Russian Long dogs 1853. Gilbert Collection.

Model of Rampur Hound, c. 1900.

Magyar Agar – Hungarian Greyhound.

as the Mahratta Hound of India and the Circassian Hound of the steppes indicate, but the Rampur Hound of India, the Chart Polski and Magyar Agar of Eastern Europe still have their devotees. In Russia, the Borzoi once embraced a host of longdog variations. In days of Empire, the big game hunters, like Baker in Ceylon, used huge longdogs when hunting the local deer. Colonists too introduced longdogs to North America and Australia, where they quickly adjusted to quite different quarry.

Boar Hunting in Ceylon, 1870.

American Hounds

The longdog function in the United States was first carried out there by what they call staghounds, big rough-haired hunting dogs, crossbred in pursuit of function not whim, although hunters' preferences do manifest themselves in their anatomies. In his *Hunting Dogs* (1909), Oliver Hartley refers to a Minnesota wolfer who averaged thirty-five wolves a year and who pinned his faith on the long-eared variety of hounds, with features of strength, endurance, good tonguers and stayers. He had been advised that the best dogs for coyotes were part English blue (that is, Greyhounds), and Russian stag (that is, Borzois). He wrote that the English blue are very fast and the stag are long-winded, with the grit to make a good fight.

Effective Blends

He also wrote that another admired and capable dog is the half Scotch stag hound (that is, Scottish Deerhound) and half Greyhound. He recorded that a Wisconsin hunter believed that the best breed for catching and killing coyotes is made by half shepherd (our working collie) and half hound, being quicker than a hound and trailing just as well on a hot trail. He wrote too that another fast breed for coyotes is a quarter English bull, a quarter Bloodhound and one half Foxhound. Here is a classic example of blending blood in pursuit of performance, the hunter's endless challenge. Nowadays so many sighthound breeders seem unconcerned by performance, seeking flashy show points ahead of soundness and function. Sadly,

too, you can see longdogs at country shows with alarming physical faults.

Prairie Hunters

Freeman Lloyd, writing in *The Kennel Encyclopaedia* (1908), states that 'It is the "Long Dog" of the Prairie, a breed that has been produced to suit the requirements of the climate, the plains and the particular style of hunting, that is engaged in running down and killing the Prairie Wolf'. He writes that 'all the best "Long Dogs" are about three-quarters Deerhound' and that he had seen 'some very good dogs the result of a first cross with a Borzoi and Greyhound … they had good backs, grand ribs and a good deal of the depth of the Muscovite … sound animals with a lot of sense'. But he did question the stamina of the pure Borzoi in the long pursuits on the plains. Lurcher breeders will identify with his words 'with a lot of sense'; a fast dog with no brains is not an ideal hunting companion.

'Cold Blood Greyhounds'

Leon V. Almirall, in his 1941 book *Canines and Coyotes*, describes a lifetime spent hunting coyotes on the prairies with a variety of hounds, from purebred registered Greyhounds, Deerhounds and Russian Wolfhounds to assorted longdogs from this base stock. He also utilized what is known in the US as 'cold blood Greyhounds', big smooth-coated longdogs from Greyhound ancestry. He again and again emphasizes the crucial importance of early pace in hunting coyotes. He claims that if the coyote was not taken in the first mile of the course then it was not going to be taken at all. Almirall writes that one of the greatest

Coursing on the plains.

Coursing greyhound.

Lord Butte – an American Waterloo Cup winner, and a first prize winner at Denver, 1903. Property of L.F. Bartel, Denver, Col.

Champion Lansdowne Hall Stream – property of Mr B.F. Lewis, Lansdowne, Pa.

coyote hounds ever seen there was imported from Leeds in Yorkshire, a purebred registered Greyhound called Top Gear, 85lb in weight and possessed of 'burning pace, backed by a sturdy heart and lungs, and marvellous coordination'. He favoured the bigger, stronger sighthound, needing shoulder height to allow the hound to see over scrub yet not burdened with 'an ounce of superfluous poundage'.

The Wolf Hunt

In his *Wolf and Coyote Trapping* (1909), A.R. Harding gives an enlightening description of wolf hunting:

On the open plains of the west, wolves are often hunted with large swift running dogs, grey hounds, stag or wolf hounds or their crosses. The hunters go on horseback and the wolves are usually roused out of some coulee or draw … Wolf, dogs and horsemen, race across the often rough and dangerous ground at breakneck speed … The lighter and swifter grey hounds, as a rule, are the first to overtake the wolf and by coming up alongside and snapping at his flanks, force him to turn and face them, thus giving the heavier and fiercer wolf hounds a chance to close in and grapple with and kill the wolf. Unless the dogs

North Dakota wolf hounds.

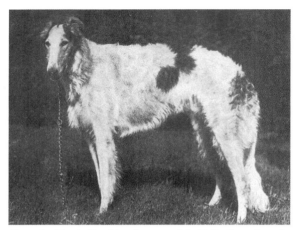

Champion Bistri of Perchina. Property of the Valley Farm Kennels, Simsbury, Conn.

Mr John E. Thayer's deerhound, 'Hillside Romola'.

are well trained and very courageous, a large timber wolf often proves more than a match for the bunch of four or five dogs.

The blend of suitable breeding material, backed by courage and sound training, has long been behind the successful longdog.

Imported Stock

In the United States, the importation of sighthound stock, mainly from Britain, but from Russia too, laid the basis of both the show stock and the coursing dogs, as well as providing the breeding material for the creation of the American Staghound or longdog. Joseph Thomas, with his famous Valley Farm kennel and its renowned Borzoi Bistri, was also a keen coursing man. John Thayer had some

high-quality Deerhounds, whilst Greyhounds like Lansdowne Hall Stream shone in the show ring, and Lord Butte won the American Waterloo Cup in 1902. From the blood of fine sighthounds such as these was the longdog that became known as the American Staghound, perfected by Western 'wolfers', founded. The renowned General George Custer usually travelled with around a dozen Greyhounds, Deerhounds and Foxhounds; on the eve of his sad end at the battle of Little Big Horn he held a coursing meet with forty longdogs.

Importance of Conformation

Longdog enthusiasts have long been aware of the need to blend blood to retain field prowess. In his *Gazehounds & Coursing* (1999), M.H. Dutch Salmon, a great longdog fan, writes:

A mixed pack in Western America and their trophies.

A western wolfer and his Borzoi.

I believe conformation to be more important to hounds, both sight and scent, than to any other type of hunting dog. An exception to this might be the big-going pointers and setters of southern field trial fame. But the average hunting bird dog is simply not put to the physical test of the average hound. You might consider that some degree of hip dysplasia is now present in an alarmingly high percentage of bird dogs, especially retrievers … Hip dysplasia is virtually non-existent in hounds. Why? Because a working hound (and almost all hounds work) with any evidence of hip dysplasia simply can't cut it in the field. Such traits of unsoundness are culled out straight away and as long as hounds are worked will remain rare.

Culling in the pursuit of the very best dogs used to be commonplace but modern attitudes have led to it falling out of favour.

'Horses for Courses'

In his book *Lurchers and Longdogs* (1977), Ted Walsh mentions the Nebraska coyote hound, 29½in at the shoulder and weighing 90lb. He quotes from a Minnesota report on the American houndman, which states:

> He merely breeds one good hound to another regardless of background … the basis of the American lurcher is the greyhound crossed first with the Scottish deerhound; secondarily with the Irish Wolfhound and Borzoi; rarely with the whippet or saluki. This breeding pattern may be explained by considering the game coursed in North America, the hare (jack rabbit), red fox and coyote.

This account sets out the use of 'cold blood' or coursing greyhound on hare, a rougher-coated hound on red fox and the emergence of an American

The Staghound type favoured on the Plains.

Coyote Hound, 75–100lb, with a Deerhound coat. But it stresses that no kennel there was raising either Deerhounds or Borzois primarily for hunting. The Whippet was recommended for the cotton-tail rabbit, lacking the stamina for the jack rabbit.

Outback Hunters

In Australia, lurcher-like running dogs are a type described either as Staghounds, Kangaroo Dogs or Bush Greyhounds. Their similarity illustrates how function dictates form. Freeman Lloyd likened a day's coyote hunting with antelope coursing in Africa and an open 'go as you please' coursing match in Australia. He mentioned the 'Strathdoon Dingo Killer', a blend of Borzoi and Deerhound with the tried and tested Kangaroo Hound. The latter was described by him as 'a large Greyhound, having in many cases the coat of the Deerhound'. The kangaroo can be a formidable quarry, capable of disembowelling a hound with

Maggie the 'Roo Dog (from Wheatbelt line).

Australian Wheatbelt Staghound.

its immensely powerful hindfeet. Lloyd's words emphasize the endless need to consider terrain, climate and quarry in developing an efficient hunting dog, especially a longdog, even from a blend of well-tried types.

Imported Blood

Australian hunters have made good use of imported longdog blood, blending the blood of Salukis, Borzois and Scottish Deerhounds with the long-utilized

Kangaroo hunt in Victorian Australia.

Greyhound source. Kangaroo Dogs from the famous Wheatbelt line have strong Greyhound blood; Staghounds from the same line have clear Saluki blood, intended to improve their heat tolerance and long-distance sprinting capability. The Wheatbelt Kangaroo Dogs remind me of the outstanding longdogs once bred by Nuttall of Clitheroe, who, I believe, used a purebred Deerhound sire to a retired track or coursing Greyhound dam. Brian Plummer has described them as 'truly magnificent animals … leg weakness, a common fault in deerhounds and in first-cross deerhound hybrids was practically unknown in these kennels, partly due to the judicious selection of both sire and dam by Nuttall and partly due to careful feeding of the whelps at his kennels'. Those words sum up the key ingredients for the successful breeding of any longdog: the selection of breeding stock and wise rearing. May the future be kind to them, wherever in the world they are favoured.

Selection the Key
In his *The Modern Lurcher* (1984), Michael Shaw makes some valid points about longdogs, writing:

> In 1948 Anastasia Noble, in an attempt to put right faults which were manifesting themselves in the deerhound due to injudicious inbreeding, introduced coursing greyhound blood to improve type and structure in her dogs, but no one used the fourth generation pure deerhounds derived from this cross … Another criticism levied at this longdog is that the first cross deerhound/greyhound males are invariably too big for coursing. EG Walsh, who judged the Lowther Lurcher Show in 1983, stated in a letter to *Shooting News* that the exhibits in the larger lurcher class were invariably deerhound/greyhound hybrids and the majority of these were ungainly oversized dogs bred from poor greyhounds and very badly proportioned deerhounds. Thus it can be stated that while the majority of winners at lurcher shows are deerhound bred, many of the very worse specimens – incongruous brutes neither elegant nor useful – also came about from this breeding.

As always in the breeding of sporting dogs, it is never the *blend of breeds* that leads to success, but the selection of the material used for breeding the longdog or lurcher. Mating two sighthound breeds together might technically provide you with a longdog but it can produce only a poor one if the stock is not chosen with knowledge and skill. Every sighthound, purebred or crossbred, *has* to perform!

A Newly Created Longdog breed – The Silken Windhound
The desire of the dog-owning public to have a small sighthound-type dog has been met in some way by the Italian Greyhound and in the sporting field by the Bedlington-Whippet lurcher and, more recently,

Silken Windhound, Gill Grist's Blake. Grist.

Silken Windhound, Gill Grist's Firefly, the first of the breed in Britain. Gill, with Lorraine Marchant, has founded the breed here. Grist.

by the Cirneco dell'Etna. But a small, long-haired sighthound has been missing. In the early 1980s, however, a Texan geneticist, Francie Stull (who had bred over 200 champion Borzois from her Kristull kennel), started crossing Borzois and Whippet-types to produce what she termed a Silken Windhound. After years of selected breeding, this new breed seems to be devoid of health issues, have an easily managed coat, lives to die of old age rather than acquired disease and looks like a diminutive Borzoi. They are fast gaining ground in North America and in some European countries, with kennel club recognition likely. These small longdogs are 18–24in tall, with a wide range of coat colours. Dr Stull has founded The International Silken Windhound Society to further the new breed's worldwide ambitions. I do hope their sporting needs are being met; whatever their size, they are still sighthounds and they carry the hunting genes.

Sighthounds of the Deserts

Roughly one third of the Earth's surface is desert. Low-latitude deserts such as the Sahara are hot and dry; mid-latitude deserts such as the Gobi are cold and dry, being related to mountain barriers sealing them off from moist maritime winds. These types of terrain demanded hunting dogs of different types,

Sloughis in the Egyptian Desert.

but always cursorial. The steppe is the extensive grassland, treeless region of Eurasia, extending from the Ukraine through southeastern Europe and central Asian Russia to the Manchurian plains. A different but essentially similar type of sighthound was developed there. The prairie is the extensive grassland and treeless region of the northern USA and Canada, rather like the pampas in South America and the Great Plains between the Mississippi river and the Rocky Mountains in the north. As soon as European settlers encountered them, and the outback in Australia, they introduced longdogs to hunt there, as described above. How differently the native Indians and aboriginal Australians might have developed had they had the help of sighthounds.

Hunting with sighthounds in India.

Antelope hunting in India.

In native surroundings – a Bedouin in the Desert of Saliha with two of his favourite breed.

Two Arabs on foot kept pace with us, leading the hounds on leashes. For a mile we walked, not a word being said. Then the sheik motioned us to a standstill with a wave of his hand, walked his horse gently up the side of the valley, and stood below the crest of the rise, looking intently before him. Without turning his head he waved one of the footmen to approach him. The man stole up, his pair of hounds sliding obediently at his heels. They looked the picture of grace and beauty, their long, silky, sandy-coloured coats blending almost imperceptibly with the sand.

James Wentworth Day, The Dog in Sport (1938), capturing in a few sentences the whole essence of sighthound work in the desert.

Pot-Fillers

Find a desert and a sighthound will not be far away. For a hound that hunts by speed and capitalizes on superb eyesight, the desert is the hunting ground to excel in. The Saluki, the Sloughi, the Azawakh and the Africanis much further south all exploit their remarkable sprinting ability and capability to detect animal movement at long range. The desert sighthounds of the world are true lurchers; most are unrecognized and unregistered, but they have been carefully bred to function. They should never be underestimated as highly effective hunting dogs,

Saudi Arabia. 1965: Arab children with Saluki.

surviving hard times in tough places. They are pot-fillers where other predators do not succeed; they are canine hunters where other sporting dogs cannot

Sloughi of Northern Africa. Ch. Kalbi. Property of Herr Michel La Fontijn.

hunt. Only the cheetah rivals their success, with perhaps the Abyssinian wolf a contender.

The Saluki is easily the best-known desert sighthound, with the feathered variety well established in Europe. Commendably, some of the Saluki owners in Britain have coursed their hounds and now use them for lure-chasing. Some real devotees go to Spain for old-time coursing. These superb hunting dogs were bred to exacting standards by expert huntsmen over many centuries; the very least we can do in these constricted times is to let them stretch their legs – really fly; let their instinctive behaviour manifest itself; give them spiritual contentment.

Research Confusion

Anyone researching the desert sighthounds can be forgiven for becoming confused by the loose use of names of types across North Africa and into Arabia. In Robert Leighton's hefty tome *The New Book of the Dog* (1912), the words on 'Oriental Greyhounds' are supplied by the Hon. Florence Amherst, an early importer of these hounds. She writes:

The Slughi (Tazi) is to be found in Arabia (including the Hedjaz), Syria, Mesopotamia, Valleys of the Euphrates and Tigris, Kurdistan, Persia, Turkestan, Sinai Peninsula, Egypt, the Nile Valley, Abyssinia, and Northern Africa. By examining the extent and position of the deserts inhabited by the great nomadic Arab tribes connected by pilgrim ways and caravan routes, the distribution of the Gazelle Hound can be easily followed. The different types of the Slughi are known by the distinctive names of the Shami, Yamani, Omani, and Nejdi. The Yemen and Oman breeds have not much feathering on ears or tail. The Nejdi has shorter hair than any of the above varieties. Native experts can tell them apart.

European would-be experts of today try to separate Sloughis from smooth and feathered Salukis and identify the Tasy as a quite separate breed, rightly or wrongly. But one certainty endures: those who use these desert hounds value them, whatever the breed title, from Morocco right across to the Indian subcontinent.

Indian Hounds

The deserts of the Indian subcontinent have proved good hunting grounds for sighthounds. The Sindh Hound is found in the deserts of Sindh and Rajasthan and is famous as a boar-lurcher, being Great Dane size: 28–30in and around 100lb in weight. Lighter and more Sloughi-like is the Rampur Hound, the Greyhound of Northern India, the Maharajah of Baria having once had a famous kennel. Around 28in at the shoulder and weighing around 75lb, they have been used on stag and boar and for hunting jackal. A century ago, some were brought to Britain and exhibited at the Dublin show. I believe some were recently imported into North America, relocated from Ontario to New Jersey, and are now being seriously promoted. The lurcher of Maharashtra is the Mudhol Hound, between the Greyhound and the Whippet in size. More Saluki-like is the lurcher of the Banjara, a nomadic tribe with gypsy connections. The Banjara, or Vanjari, is famed for its stamina and nose and its ability to pull down deer, always going for the hindquarters, not the throat, as many Deerhounds do instinctively. There is also a Kanni Hound, bred and favoured in Tamil Nadu state, very similar in appearance to the Mudhol and Rampur hounds.

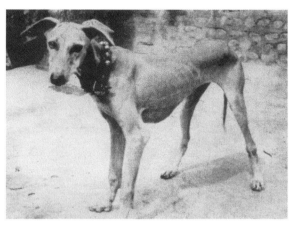

The Maratha, Mudhol or Pashmi Hound.

In *The Kennel Encyclopaedia* (1908), H.W. Bush writes:

A breed which is also, as some suppose, a descendant of the Arab or Persian Greyhound, is the Banjara, so called because it is *the* dog of the Banjaras, a wandering tribe, once the sole carriers of merchandise in India, but whose occupation is practically now gone, since railways run everywhere … The true Banjara is a fine, upstanding hound about 28 inches high, generally black, mottled with grey or blue, with a rough but silky coat, a high-bred, hound-like head, and well-feathered on ears, legs and tail. He shows a good deal of resemblance to the Persian Greyhound, but

Rampur Hound. The above illustration shows a very typical specimen of this breed.

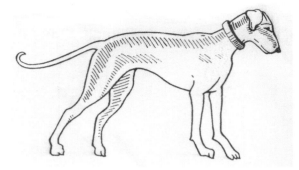

The Poligar.

Chippiparai dog.

is stouter built, and with a squarer muzzle. Probably this wandering race of gypsies may have brought the originals with them from Western Asia, the subsequent modification being due to a cross with some of the indigenous breeds. The Banjara breed possesses indomitable pluck, can go about as fast as a Foxhound, and will run all day. His nose is superior to that of any other domestic breed in a hot climate, but he wants better speed for coursing deer, and attachment to Europeans.

There is a hint in these words of the European hunters in India seeking a sighthound rather than an all-round hunting dog or lurcher-type hound.

Long-Distance Runners
The Chippiparai, the lurcher of the south, mainly the Thanjavor area, is described as being Dobermann-

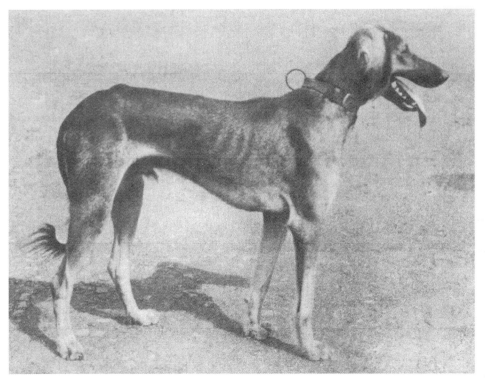

Mahratta Hound.

The Vaghari Hound.

like in outline, but usually white in colour and used mainly for hare-hunting. Very hardy, reputed to be very much a one-man dog, they are regarded as the most intelligent and biddable Indian breed, being used as police dogs in some areas. The Poligar (or Pertabgarh) Hound is the Greyhound of Southern India; it has been called the lurcher of India, used on fox, deer, jackal, and, in packs, on boar. For generations this breed was used for pig-hunting on foot with spears, rather as the ancient Greeks hunted them. Around 26in at the shoulder and weighing between 40 and 45lb, they are thin-coated but the coat has a stiff wiry texture, harsh to the hand when back-brushed. They are famous long-distance runners but sadly have a delicate constitution, needing careful rearing. Writing as 'The Old Shekarry' in the early 1890s, Major Leveson described his hunting dogs as:

'two couple, immensely powerful – crosses between a big Polygar dog and a rough Brinjarree bitch – standing over 30 inches in height, and possessing indomitable pluck, but little amenability to discipline'.

Pig and Panther Hound

In *The Kennel Encyclopaedia* there is also mention of the Mahratta Hound, illustrated by a photograph of a sighthound resembling the Saluki. Scepticism was expressed about this hound's claimed ability to pull down a black buck, but it was praised for its prowess on pig and panther, both formidable adversaries. This hound was described as blue and tan in colour, 22in

Levrier Persian 'Masjed' from Les Races des Chiens, 1905.

A Persian Greyhound, by Harrison Weir. 19th Century.

high, and 'evidently of Persian or Arab origin', being used both in the hills and on the plains and able to 'go through a tremendous amount of work in the hot weather'. It was described as being exceedingly rare, even then. Such dogs were often owned by nomadic tribes wandering seasonally across huge tracts of land, without heed of – to them – notional national boundaries. *The Kennel Encyclopaedia* also contains an account by H.W. Bush that reads: 'For its peculiar breeds, India is undoubtedly indebted to the Banjara carriers, who in the early days probably brought down with their caravans hounds from Arabia and Persia. These dogs were crossed with some indigenous breeds, and climatic influences helped to work further changes, but through all, the Arab blood is traceable.' In every continent in every century, useful dogs have moved with their owners across what are now national boundaries. Breeds have always been developed by people according to the demands of the local terrain and quarry.

Caravan Hounds

The hunting dogs of the nomadic Indian peoples today fall into two types: the lighter-boned, smooth-coated Mudhol or Karvani dogs and the stronger-boned, silky-feathered Pashmi or Pisouris, which can range from 20in to 28in. They are used on a wide variety of quarry, from chinkara and blackbuck, fox and rabbit to civet and mongoose, even black-faced monkeys, a local pest. The Mudhol, Pashmi and Rampur hounds have become known collectively as the Caravan Hounds and, with the backing of the Indian National Kennel Club, a group of dedicated breeders is reviving them.

Their group name comes from their early associations with itinerant Indian gypsy tribes. As with all wandering peoples, gypsies draw on the most efficient hunting dogs they encounter and so, not surprisingly, a consistent type in such dogs is elusive. Pariah dog blood has given them great robustness, they are famed for the toughness of their feet, strong but fine bone and a light frame. No doubt when they are bred 'for type' their gene pool will be reduced and inbreeding deficiencies encountered. But these remarkable hounds are well worth conserving; their blood, however diverse in origin, has been proved in the toughest school – surviving extreme climate, restricted nutrition, harsh hunting terrain and

casually conducted breeding; yet that alone could prove their saviour. Breeding good hunting dog to good hunting dog has long produced a better product than handsome dog to another handsome dog and the desert sighthounds demonstrate this to this day.

Salukis: Arabian Sighthounds

In close country, hunters can ambush or trap their prey; not so in the wide open spaces of the Middle Eastern countries and Persia, as is now examined. Philip Browning's (of Rabia Salukis) presentation to the Saluki or Gazelle Hound Club's teaching seminar, on 29 November 1998, included the following words:

> There is no other hound which has taken such a wide range of game from jerboa, hare, gazelle, oryx, even wild ass, as well as fox, jackal, wolf and even hyena not to mention chukar, the desert partridge. That hunt alone calls for the scenting ability of a pointer or setter to locate; its acute eyesight to identify and

18th century Mughal India; hawking with sighthounds.

Akbar the Great hunting, c. 1700.

A Typical Sloughi (Shami). Bred in England by the Hon. F. Amherst.

lock on like radar; stalking ability of a cat to close the distance; a burst of speed like a greyhound to take it under the low take-off flight and a final flying leap to catch the bird feet into the air.

Performance Ahead of Purity

It is of course possible that the Saluqi of times past was used in a much wider role than is customary today. In Central Asia for example it seems it is indeed a much more versatile hound using scent as well as sight to locate its prey. However in desert conditions there is not much scope for scenting game; whereas the open terrain is conducive to hunting by sight : ... It is a well-known phenomenon that faculties atrophy if they are not exercised. So it is just possible that in earlier times the Saluqi hunted both by scent and by sight.

Those words of Terence Clark and Muawiya Derhalli in *Al-Mansur's Book on Hunting* (2001), tell you a lot about desert sighthounds. Writers on Salukis will assure you that their breed is the oldest purebred

Arab Greyhound. The property of an Arab Sheikh. (1908 depiction).

Arab Greyhound. The property of an Arab Sheikh.(1908 depiction).

Persian Greyhound, 'Zillah'.

dog, but their desert owners have always placed performance ahead of purity of blood. In many ways, using scent as well as sight, they are fast hunting dogs without a registration as a pedigree, a lurcher in effect. Fast hunting dogs have been traded between Asia and North Africa for centuries and the Saluki/Sloughi type can be detected from Morocco in the west, right across to northern and central India in the east. The sighthound silhouette is unmistakeable in these hounds, the cursorial hound physique being essential for their wide-ranging hunting role. Speed is the basis of their talent, but they have an enviable physical toughness, remarkable resilience, and immense agility, backed by good scenting powers and great perseverance. The wide open spaces are their natural hunting grounds.

Various Types

There is no single type of Saluki. Most of the hounds I have seen in Middle Eastern countries have been smooth-haired (the Nejdi type), not feathered (the Shami or Syrian type). The smooth coat is dominant. In the pedigree world we have smooth and feathered hounds registered as Salukis, with the smooth-coated Sloughi (from North Africa) listed as a separate breed. The Arabs there, however, referred to them as *mogrebi,* or western. The Tuareg Sloughi, sometimes

known as the 'oska', is classified separately in some countries as the Azawakh Sloughi, from the valley of that name in Mali and Niger. Both the Azawakh and the Sloughi have been found to possess an additional allele on the glucose-phosphate-isomerase gene locus, not found in other sighthounds but also featuring in the jackal, suggesting a separate origin. Circassia, in the Caucasus, was once famous for its sighthounds; but Circassian people can be found in Syria, Iraq, Jordan and Turkey too. East African hounds like the Shilluk greyhound from the plains of the White Nile in Southern Sudan are more Saluki-like than Greyhound-like. Asiatic hounds, like the Poligar and the Vaghari of India, also have a distinct smooth-haired Saluki look to them.

Lurchers of the Desert

The famed areas for the best Salukis as hunting dogs have long been the Wadi Sirhan in Syria and Rutba on the Jordan/Iraq border. The Saluki type manifests itself from West Africa, through North Africa and what was Mesopotamia, to the Iran/Afghanistan border. Some are used to track game; others to slow game down for the hawk and others to catch desert partridges before they can take off. If anything, they are the lurchers of the desert – versatile hunting dogs, not just fast runners. This shows once again

Brig. Gen. F.F. Lance with his Salukis (Ch. Sarona Kelb is on the right).

the understatement and inadequacy of the generic term 'sighthound' for this group of cursorial hounds. They may present a challenge to the impatient but, from their distinguished heritage, have genes worth having. When used to infuse stamina in the chase to lurchers, they certainly produce a handsomer dog.

Britain's Salukis

In 1835, Zillah, a black and tan Persian Greyhound (the first name of the Saluki here), was on show at the Regents Park Zoological Gardens. Forty years later a light fawn bitch called Tierma won a prize at a Kennel Club show. But it was not until half a century later that the first breed club held their founding meeting, leading to the breed becoming recognized in 1923. The first challenge certificate winner in the breed here was Sarona Kelb, bred in Damascus and owned by Brigadier General Lance. He also bred the first champion, Orchard Shahin, daughter of Sarona Kelb. He and his wife also organized coursing for the new breed in 1925. They were concerned that the Saluki might become purely a show dog; they strove to preserve its original function, and it was noticeable, in its early years, that all the show winners looked as though they could run. I give the Saluki or Gazelle Hound Club's members full marks for their work in striving to retain a sporting hound throughout most of the twentieth century.

Exasperating Salukis

I have known men famed for their skill at training hunting dogs of all kinds regularly reduced to the hair-tearing stage when faced with an independently minded Saluki. Is it perversity, wilfulness, lack of concentration, periodic deafness or just straight-forward stubbornness which makes this breed so trying? My abiding memory of hare-coursing in Jordan is of the need for a jeep with a well-filled tank and powerful binoculars, not to find the game, but to recover the hounds! But for the patient, the stoical and the long-suffering, the rewards, in the end, of seeing a once-exasperating Saluki mature into a good, reliable hunting dog are manifold (perhaps understood best, in different fields, by Basset Hound and Clumber Spaniel owners!). What a sight a Saluki is at full stretch, seeming to fly across ground that a human being could not jog over.

Bedouin Advice

The advice I received from the Bedouin about the criteria for a sighthound to run fast for extended periods over difficult terrain boils down to just two points: girth of chest and girth of loin. Heart and lung room and power of propulsion would be another way of putting it. The users of gazelle hounds in the desert looked for, in say a 26in hound, a girth of chest of 26–31in and a girth of loin of 18–24in. The Bedouin do not bother with breed descriptions Kennel Club-style, with flowery accounts of anatomical beauty. From al-Mutawakkili, writing in the ninth century, we can however learn that a long body with a short

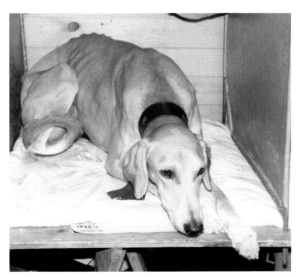

Smooth Saluki at Crufts, 1991.

back, powerful loins, deep chests, fleshy shoulders and powerful flanks were valued by the hunters of those times.

Two Coats

At first glance it is easy to mis-identify a smooth Saluki as a Sloughi. The two Saluki coats can crop up in the same litter. In a letter of July 1977, Gwen Angel of Mazuri Salukis reported 'Nanajan Sharoon was imported, a deer grizzle and quite well feathered. Strangely enough, mated to Mazuri Haj Khalid (feathered) she produced four smooths and four feathered in her first litter. She came from the Baghdad area where most of the Arabs kept smooths.' Deborah Copperthwaite's smooth line is believed to have come from seventeen generations of all-feathered breeding. I am glad that the Saluki fraternity have kept the two coats as one breed and not, as so many other bi- or multi-coated breeds have done, created separate breeds – and much more worryingly, separate, closed gene pools, under the rules of pedigree dog breeding.

Valued Blood

Lurcher men were slow to appreciate the value of Saluki blood for some years. Even now, however, show-bred Salukis with shelly bodies and few hunting instincts are being utilized by lurcher breeders in the forlorn hope that some good Saluki features will be inherited in their breeding programmes. With coursing now illegal, I am not surprised that really keen sportsmen have stopped importing *real* hunting Salukis from the Middle East, hounds with a known field performance. Lurcher men would be the first to admit, however, that the Salukis once deployed to the field by the admirable Saluki Coursing Club are fine hounds. Amena Viceroy of Anasazi won the Scottish thirty-two-dog three-day stake three years in succession, the only hound to achieve this in the thirty years of the event. Salukis like this deserve all the praise we can muster.

KC Failure

For those who seek pedigree status and need registration for their imported stock, the Kennel

Club has not been particularly cooperative. Sir Terence Clark KBE CMG CVO, once our ambassador in Oman and a keen coursing man, who knows and appreciates hunting Salukis, once raised this issue with the KC. Not a show-ring fancier, Sir Terence was anxious that Saluki breeders here should benefit from the fine hunting stock, often crop-eared and lacking the breed points of the KC pedigree Saluki, available in countries like Iraq; these were real Salukis, but they could not be registered by those who would wish to do so. Perhaps the time has passed for proven hunting lines to be attracted here.

In replying to Sir Terence's letter, the then secretary of the Kennel Club, General Sinnatt, wrote: 'it would be difficult to believe that breeding patterns within desert tribes would be as strictly controlled as those under the aegis of the Kennel Club'. This, despite the fact that every Saluki in Britain originated from the 'breeding patterns within desert tribes' so patronizingly referred to by the then chief executive of the KC. How can real sporting men take such an organization seriously? Can the lofty KC pedestal be justified when so many breeds desperately need their leadership?

The Saluki judge at Crufts 2007 recorded: 'I wondered where the breed is heading ... Hindquarters were a particular worry with lack of length and substance to upper thighs.' The KC tells us that these are 'the best of the very best': what must the non-qualifiers be like! At the Saluki or Gazelle Hound Club show of 2006, the judge reported: 'I was shocked at how poorly many dogs move.' At two other shows that year criticisms ranged from a lack of quality in depth and lack of forward reach to plaiting and close movement behind.

The Arabs could send some improving blood, if only our KC would let them! As with so many ancient breeds, the Saluki has a relatively clean genotype and the breed club is active in dealing with health issues, working with the Animal Health Trust to maintain a database. So far, no hereditary diseases with known DNA-based tests have been identified in the breed. That is unusual and most encouraging.

Tracking Skills

In her book *Sighthounds Afield* (2004), Denise Como includes a chapter by Dr John Burchard, PhD, who describes the tracking prowess of the Saluki:

> Coursing hares in Arabia is rather different from the 'walk-up' method commonly used in the USA ...

Superb coursing Saluki. Wilmott.

Waters's Burydown Palymyra. Wilmott.

Hares in Arabia are scarcer … Once you know a hare is hiding in the immediate vicinity, you may bring up one or two Salukis, who will then find it by scent, or you may try to flush it by walking about, and slip the hounds only when the hare is actually sighted. A falcon is also very helpful at this stage, since it will spot the slightest movement on the part of the hare … Falcon and hounds quickly learn to make the most of this kind of cooperative hunting, which soon becomes an active partnership.

This is of course the timeless partnership between Salukis and hawks over much of southern Asia and north Africa.

Versatile Hunters

In his most absorbing book, *The Dog in Sport* (1938), James Wentworth Day has captured the immense versatility in the hunting field of the Saluki:

Apart from the fact that on a long trek the Bedouin carry their Salukis, particularly the puppies, on cam-el-back, they are unsparing of them when it comes to real hunting. Not only four-footed game but winged game are caught by the really well-trained Saluki. He will stalk a desert partridge or even a bustard, startle

it into sudden flight, and, quite surprisingly, often catch it in the air, leaping from the ground at full gallop to a height of several feet. I have not the slightest doubt that they could be taught to catch English partridges in the same way.

I recall this versatility when I see wildlife conservationists striving to catch ground-nesting birds for research, clumsily using huge nets at some risk of damage to the birds. Well-intentioned scientists have still not grasped the value of sporting dogs to their work, seeing them sometimes as a threat to their work rather than a benefit.

Israeli Salukis

Joshua Tamaria, past controller of the Israel Kennel Club, has claimed that the Saluki arose in the Sinai Peninsula and was moved across to Egypt and North Africa from there. During the Israeli occupation of the Sinai, Salukis were purchased from the Sinai Bedouin with the intention of breeding a unique semi-wild form of the breed. Dr Rita Trainin, one-time breeding advisor to the Israel Windhound Club, visited the Sinai in 1968 to study the hounds there. She found smooth-haired not feathered hounds, with wider, flatter skulls, thicker necks and less height at the shoulder, around 25in. She realized that here was a separate strain of the breed, called them the Negev Saluki, and tried to start a breeding programme to develop this strain. The International Kennel Club, the FCI, showed interest but the American Kennel Club refused to recognize the strain. Israeli breeders

Israeli Salukis, 1988.

Sinai Salukis, 1968.

tried to persuade the Israeli Bedouin to keep the strain going after Israel's withdrawal from Sinai. This did not happen and sadly the project failed – a missed opportunity for the breed to benefit from new blood.

Crosses Used
There is nothing unique to Britain in the use by hunters of Saluki cross sheepdogs as versatile hunting dogs, which use speed, scent and stamina to catch their quarry. In Iraq, the *luqi* or Saluki crossed with a local sheepdog has long been used as a 'thinking' sighthound. The quarry would be gazelle, fox or hare; the ground mostly rocky but very muddy in the rainy season and the going extremely testing, especially to the feet. The *luqi* is prized for its superior nose, in conditions where scenting is surprisingly difficult. Perhaps too this sheepdog blood made the *luqi* more biddable, something many lurcher men here seek in their Saluki cross dogs. The Kurds produced the *khilasi,* a cross between their Saluqi and a Kurdish sheepdog, to improve scenting ability and response to training. In south Syria, the Arabs bred the *zaghuri,* allegedly from an outcross to a *zeiger,* Old High German for a pointer, said to have been introduced by the Crusaders, to enhance scenting power. Hunters seek performance ahead of purity of blood.

Appalling Movement
With that in mind, it was sad to read the 2010 Crufts critique on Salukis: 'Having judged for 27 years and been fortunate enough to have assessed over 2,500 Salukis, I feel that I have the experience to see that our breed is not in a good state. I saw far too many cat feet, level toplines, short ear leathers, short tails and the most appalling movement …' The last few words for me being the most worrying. The desert Salukis move quite beautifully, their effortless grace being a distinct feature of the breed wherever it is seen. I understand that the Bedu of the Negev Desert have timed their

The 'Iraq' Salukis of Miss Kerrison.

Miss Barr with a group of feathered Salukis.

hounds (using the speedometer of a cross-country vehicle), at around 50mph and expect their hounds to course for at least a mile on occasions.

They stress three key physical features in a good Saluki: a four-fingers' wide croup, well-muscled; a deep chest yet less deep than our show specimens exhibit; and long feet with well-arched toes. They do not seek a fine head, but a wide skull and a powerful underjaw. I wonder how they would view our Crufts entry. Have we 'improved' their hounds? Have we kept faith, not just with Bedu breeders who gave us the breed, but early pioneers of the breed here, the Amhersts, the Lances, Mrs J.H. Barr and Miss S. Kerrison and her 'Iraq' kennel?

The legendary Ch. Sarona Kelb (Seleughi ex Baalbek), born in June 1919, sire of five Champion sons and five Champion daughters.

Salukis. Young Salukis 'Of Ruritania' belonging to Miss Doxford.

The Saluki is a breed of great antiquity and has been bred in its native lands for thousands of years as a functional hunting hound. It would seem that changing the standard to fit the current crop of show dogs is clearly a setback for those who are trying to preserve the breed as it was originally developed ... As the Saluki has one of the oldest documented histories of any breed, perhaps one should rely on history and function rather than current fancy.

> Ann Chamberlain, *Saluki* (2001), commenting on proposals to alter the word picture of the breed to suit contemporary exhibits.

I once clocked with my pickup two salukis and a greyhound chasing a jackrabbit down a dirt road for nearly a quarter mile, till the hare broke off the road and went cross-country. By the speedometer they were never running at less than 40mph at any time and were often pushing 45! ... By my experience, the field greyhound is the fastest of the sighthounds on live game up to about 1000 yards. Beyond that no breed can stay with the saluki.

> M.H. Dutch Salmon, *Gazehounds and Coursing* (1977)

What we must acknowledge is that the Saluki is first and foremost a remarkable hunter, dare I say,

the Premier Hound. As such, its beauty comes from function, and fitness to perform that function, which is enduring beauty; without that, any beauty is fashion and fantasy and that has no enduring quality!

> Philip Browning, of Rabia Salukis, in a presentation to the Saluki or Gazelle Hound Club's teaching seminar, 29 November 1998

The characteristics that set the Saluki complex [that is, this type of sighthound] apart from the true herding and working breeds was their independence and ability to work without human intervention. They are all 'coursing' hounds, whatever their prey. A coursing hound is distinguished from the other hounds by several characteristics. First of all, they are built to run long distances at great speed. Secondly, they have enough length of muzzle to grab and hold prey, either by the leg or by the throat. Thirdly, they rely on their remarkable eyesight to course the prey, never taking their eyes off the target animal. Of course, they come equipped with noses, too, and they use them!

> Ann Chamberlain, *Saluki* (2001)

Sloughis: African Sighthounds
Sizing up the Sloughi

A magnificent sloughui arrived a few days ago from Algeria, as a present to the Emperor Louis Napoleon

Algerian Greyhound (Sloughi). Barye, 1868.

from Marshal de Macmahon the Governor. This splendid animal is the size of a small calf, its colour jet black, marked on the flanks and front with yellow spots; only the Arab chiefs possess them. They are used for hunting, their speed being extraordinary, and the sheiks refuse the most brilliant offers for these beautiful animals.

Those words of obvious admiration come from what the author George Cupples termed 'a modern newspaper account' in his remarkably widely researched *Scotch Deer-hounds and Their Masters* (1894).

Sounding the Same

For the name of one sighthound breed to sound almost the same as a sister breed does not exactly help discussions about the two breeds. And they are now two distinct breeds: in the pedigree world we have smooth and feathered hounds registered as Salukis, with the smooth-coated Sloughi (from North Africa) listed as a separate breed. The Arabs there, however, referred to them as *mogrebi* (magreb) or western. The Tuareg Sloughi, sometimes known as

the 'oska', is classified separately in some countries as the Azawakh Sloughi, from the valley of that name in Mali and Niger. This can lead to further confusion as the Azawakh and the Sloughi are separate breeds too. Some historians believe that the sighthounds in Eastern Arabia came from Asia originally, possibly with the invading Hyksos. The Sighthound Club of Germany had DNA tests conducted in 1993 which showed that, of the Afghan Hound, the Saluki and the Sloughi, the biggest genetic difference is between the Saluki and the Sloughi. The Sloughi was genetically closer to the Afghan Hound. The Sloughi is much more than a smooth Saluki look-alike.

True Sloughi

The Moroccan Sahara may well be the last refuge of the true Sloughi, conserved by the nomadic tribesmen of those areas yet unaffected by the remorseless spread of the desert and commercial gazelle-hunting using motorized methods. In the settlements they have been crossed with herding or watchdog types to prevent the ravages of wild pig or jackals. Kennel Clubs separate the breed into two types: the desert type, slender, lightly-built, graceful and elegant; and the mountain type, bigger, stronger, more compact. This has led to a wide height range, from 22in to 28in, although since the breed itself exists in the more remote parts of three sizeable countries – Algeria, Tunisia and Morocco – this is hardly surprising. I

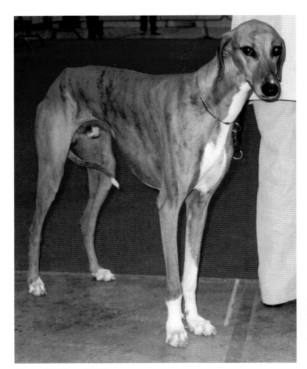

Azawakh (from Mali).

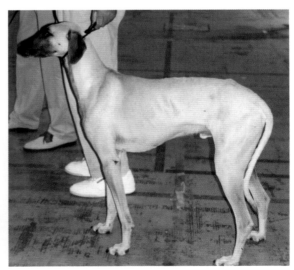

Sloughi (from Morocco).

Sloughi. Courtesy of Royal Canin, France.

Sloughi. Courtesy of Royal Canin, France.

have to admit that the first time I saw one, admittedly from a distance, I thought I was seeing a coarsely bred Greyhound. Then on closer inspection, and after a long, most instructive lecture from the handler, I realized that there was in front of me a remarkable canine survivor.

Distinctive Features
As with all hunting dogs bred by primitive people, only the very best were bred from, and to become the very best they had to cope with a climate and terrain which could not have been more testing. Now they will have to face 'urban improvement', veterinary 'care' and its annual inoculations, modern convenience dog food and being bred wholly on appearance – each factor an apparent kindness, every one a potential threat. Thankfully, the breed has attracted some sensible, level-headed fanciers, keen to perpetuate what is a distinctive and admirable breed of sporting

dog. I soon realized the essential differences between this breed and its sister sighthound breeds, the Saluki and more importantly the Azawakh, so similar at a glance, so dissimilar in key details. All three breeds have to run fast – for quite a long time, against their most sought-after quarry – the gazelle family.

A distinctive feature of the North African sighthounds is the prominent haunch bones. Many Arab hunters will automatically place three or four fingers on the four vertebrae between the hook (hip) and pin-bones to assess the hound's potential for speed in the chase. Sloughis always look shorter-bodied than their Saluki cousins and lack the extremely prominent pin-bones of the Azawakh. The Sloughi has an almost level topline and moderate angulation in the hindquarters, with flatter, less-bunched muscles than, say, the Greyhound. Magreb Sloughis tend to move with their heads low, causing some show ring judges, more familiar with the flashier breeds, questioning the reason for this. For me, it is a more workmanlike gait. The desert-bred Sloughis can feature more than one type of foot, with a wider cat-foot, unusual for a sighthound breed, now being favoured, with well-arched toes and thick pads. The hocks are set low, and, unlike the Azawakh, the tail is carried low on the move. Their gait looks effortless, harmonious and economical.

Our Kennel Club recognizes the breed, describing it as having a dignified bearing, a 'noble haughtiness' and an extremely expressive face. Thankfully, it also looks for a racy and strong breed without coarseness and asks for the elongated hare-foot and a long well-developed second thigh, predictably in a sighthound breed. I saw a striking red Sloughi at a World Dog Show a few years ago, with sooty markings on the feet, under the tail and along the tips of the ears, the 'charbon' or charcoal coat, strangely being lost in their native country.

Not surprisingly, the sandy dogs are favoured in the desert areas and the brindles, often with a black mantle, in the mountains, where they hunt wild pig, the bigger deer and even jackals. I believe some continental enthusiasts have tested their stock at non-commercial racing tracks, as well as using them in lure-coursing. This may not please the purists seeking to preserve a hunting dog but, for me, some use is always better than no use.

Value of a Bat-ear
I have read accounts linking these impressive hounds with the Phoenicians, who settled in Carthage in North Africa, opposite Sicily, and were *the* great trading people in the Mediterranean of their time. Whilst they may have brought their Saluki-like hounds with them from the Syria-Lebanon region, I suspect that the Berbers were hunting with hounds way before then, inhabiting the mountains and deserts of North Africa since prehistoric times. I am not suggesting a separate origin for the Sloughi but arguing a history for this type of hunting dog before the Phoenician wanderings. It is, however, of interest to students of fast hunting dogs that those found in North Africa were drop-eared whilst those

Study of a 'Barbary' Dog.
Pieter Boel, c. 1669.

Bedouin Greyhound of Akkaba from Jardine's Naturalist's Library, 1841.

Hunting Sloughi.

on the opposite side of the Mediterranean, from the Spanish islands in the west to the Greek islands in the east, were prick-eared. It could be that the African dogs needed covered ears as protection against sand storms, whereas the southern European hounds used sound much more in the hunting field and benefited from sound-catching, bat-like ears in their particular terrain. The latter were rather more than sighthounds, not just relying on sheer speed and an astonishing ability to spot distant movement, to hunt successfully.

Victim of Urban Sprawl
The Sloughi is in Britain but not in favour; twenty were registered in 1981, twenty-one in 2001 but only eight in 2010. They look out of place here, with their fine skin, thin, smooth coats and spare build; they perhaps belong within sight of the Atlas Mountains rather than the Cairngorms. I find much to admire in the breed and especially their survival into modern times. They thoroughly deserve devoted patronage and their long-term future may reside in the south of France, where Moroccans now live in some numbers and seem anxious to conserve their national heritage. Like the Azawakh of Mali, the Sloughi is a victim of the advance of urban living in the region where it evolved; pastoral communities are under threat and nomads losing their ancestral lands.

Versatility Prized
For lurchermen, this breed is of interest; in their homeland, they are expected to locate, stalk, pursue surreptitiously, then chase and seize their prey, rather than just race after it once sprung. They are never

expected to kill their quarry, wounded game often being kept alive to retain its food value over time in a hot, demanding climate. Slower than a Greyhound and looking less muscular, the Sloughi has greater stamina and certainly greater robustness in extreme heat. Compared to a Greyhound, the Sloughi is built more on a square than a rectangle and the ears are longer and droopier; white Sloughis are not favoured, but, unlike the Saluki, brindle is. The Saluki has been dubbed the Persian sighthound and the Sloughi the Arab sighthound; despite their obvious similarities, when you see the two breeds side by side, you soon see the two distinct breeds. Sadly, many of these

Show Sloughi.

A strong bond between the Muslim nomads and their Sloughis exists even to this day. A registration is underway at a Moroccan dog show.

ancient hunting dog breeds will no doubt be lost to us in the coming years and with them will go part of us too.

The people of the Sahara (of Northern Africa) have great love for the slougui or greyhound ... A Saharene will go twenty or thirty leagues to couple a handsome greyhound bitch with a dog of established reputation; for one that is really famous will run down a gazelle ... The greyhound of the Sahara is far superior to that of the Tell. He is of tawny colour, and tall, with a sharp snout, broad forehead, short ears, and muscular neck; the muscles of the hind-quarters being also very prominent. He has no belly, clean limbs, well detached sinews, the hock near the ground, the under part of the paw small and dry, the palate and the tongue black, and the hair very soft: between the two ilia there should be the breadth of four fingers, and the tip of the tail should be able to pass under the thigh and reach the hip-bone. Both the forearms are generally fired in five lines to harden the muscles.
      William John Burchell, *Travels in the Interior of Southern Africa* (quoted in George R. Jesse's *Researches into the History of the British Dog*, 1866)

The Arabs hunt both on foot and on horseback. A horseman who would chase the hare must take with him a greyhound, which is called slougui, from Slouguia, a spot where they were originally produced from the coupling of she-wolves with dogs. The male

slougui lives twenty years, the female twelve. Greyhounds that are able to run a gazelle down are rare.
      General E. Daumas, *Horses of the Sahara* (quoted in George R. Jesse's *Researches into the History of the British Dog*, 1866)

Assessing the Azawakh

This hunting and pastoral dog from the Azawakh (meaning land of the north) Valley, sometimes called the Tuareg Sloughi, has been described by one breed advocate as 'fleet-footed enough to catch gazelles, hares and the European mouflon (wild sheep), courageous enough to ward off big predators, untiring like a camel and as beautiful as an Arab horse'. The Azawakh is not used on gazelle until it is fully mature, and was once carried across the saddle of its master's horse until the game was sighted for a chase that could last more than an hour. Their nomadic breeders culled their canine stock ruthlessly, often retaining one male pup for hunting and a female for reproduction purposes. They were the treasured breed of the Oullimiden Tuareg, living in what is now Mali, Upper Volta, northern Nigeria and Mauritania.

Enhanced Response

A primitive breed, many of the bitches coming into season once rather than twice a year, the Azawakh has survived harsh conditions, living in the Sahel region of Mali, south of the Sahara, an area the size of France, amongst the once nomadic Tuareg and Berber people

Azawakh.

for a millennium or so. Alleged to lack the intense prey-drive of the Saluki, they have however the enhanced biddability of the herding breeds, acting as flock protectors for their pastoral owners. Although the breed can display variety of type, the gene pool is small yet apparently free of inheritable defects. Some historians believe that, before spreading south and west, the sighthounds of Eastern Arabia came from Asia originally, probably the steppes, real sighthound country. Studies on the blood of the Azawakh and the Sloughi showed that both have an additional allele on the glucose-phosphate-isomerase gene locus not found in other sighthounds and dogs but present in the coyote, fox and jackal. These two breeds, however,

Proud owner with two Azawakhs.

have distinct differences, both from one another and from their sister breed the Saluki. Azawakhs are claimed to be the most 'feline' of all dog breeds – aloof, independent, responding only to their masters – and not always to them!

Breed Characteristics
I believe there are now well over 2,000 Azawakhs in Europe, mostly in France and Germany, but they are not yet established here. At World Dog Shows they are soon identified by their lack of hindquarter

angulation, unusual in a sighthound breed, and by their distinctive range of coat colour. I am told that the Mali hunters often dye their hounds' tails so that they can spot them in the hunt. The shoulder blades are quite prominent and the pin bones, the upper boney protuberance of the pelvis, often higher than the withers; the tuck-up is pronounced, the brisket deep but not always reaching to the elbows. Their gait is springy, almost flashy, with both the head and tail held high, giving an impression of suppleness and elasticity. Often strikingly coated, from sandy to rich red, sometimes with a black mask, usually with white markings, on the throat, chest, blaze, toes and tail tip, they can also come in a highly distinctive red brindle.

The high pin bones or haunch, which have been claimed as a 'unique' feature of the breed, are also present in the Cretan Hound, the Rampur Hound and other sighthound-type hunting dogs that have no links to the Mali breed. Some Waterloo Cup winners of the late nineteenth century also featured the high rump and prominent pin bones seen in this breed. Modern show ring judges might claim that a dog higher at the haunch than the withers could display a lack of coordination on the move and too straight a stifle. Yet they themselves so often reward exhibits that have excessive angulation in the hindquarters, with the dog's hindfeet far, far beyond the body when standing. No Waterloo Cup winner ever carried such

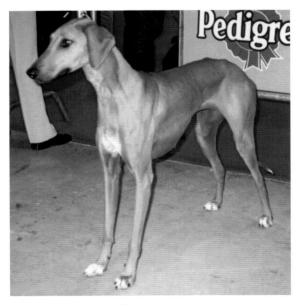

Azawakh at a World Dog Show.

African boy with his Azawakh.

a terrible fault; it may be 'showy' but it can never be sound. If you study the anatomy of a highly successful racing Greyhound like Local Interprize, winner of three classic events in 1948, you soon spot the hind-feet immediately below the set of tail with no sign of hindquarter exaggeration. With well let-down hocks and great length of ribcage, this dog is a model for any sighthound exponent.

Sadly, I can visualize the exaggerators being attracted to this breed rather as have to the Borzoi. The ears are very large and wide, the eyes almost feline, the sternum is very prominent and the tuck-up almost extreme. Cartoonists depicting ladies of leisure promenading with their elegant sighthounds in past decades would have a field day with this breed! They could in time become huge 'Italian Greyhounds', prized for their sheer elegance and daintiness, rather than their basic hunting dog phenotype. This would insult those Saharan hunters who have conserved these distinctive hounds for well over a thousand years, but it is unfortunately a well-worn path for a sporting breed of dog. It seems too, quite illogical to admire a primitive hunting dog and then disrespectfully strive to alter its type and even its shape to suit a mainly urban fad.

I do hope this remarkable breed doesn't become the latest show breed 'must-have', rather as the Borzoi, the Afghan Hound and the Saluki once were. They were never equipped for our climes, didn't evolve for our expectations of a companion dog and are not built for our hunting country. They do provide, however, a sighthound gene pool resource for those breeders wishing to improve their coefficients of inbreeding, to reduce incidences of heritable defects and to correct anatomical faults in overbred sighthound breeds. Some lurchermen might admire their independent nature but find their rather individual approach to performance in the field slightly bewildering!

American Breeder
In America, the leading breeder is David Moore, who favours the more primitive types he has imported from Africa to the more 'showy' ones preferred in France. He is anxious that when the breed is registered here, it should be bred to his type and the French standard overlooked. As the former colonial power in Mali, the French may win this one, but lurcher breeders would back David Moore in his declared preference for the hunting type ahead of the more extrovert exhibition hound. Breed characteristics should never become victim to show ring bias, as has happened in so many sporting breeds, and not to their advantage as sporting dogs. The French standard, for example, bans all-white dogs and discourages white patches on the body, both found in their country of origin. Moore's hounds have these white markings, are considered 'rustic' and 'less refined' than those bred in Europe, yet are better-natured and better hunting material. I know which type I would go for!

Hounds Traded
It is foolish, too, to attempt to claim an ancient origin or a supposed link to other more distant sighthound breeds merely on shared or similar physical features. Mali was a medieval state controlling the trade routes between savannah and Sahara, reaching its peak in the fourteenth century, later governed by France and independent in 1960, after a brief partnership with Senegal to the west. Around 5 per cent of its people are Tuareg and Moor, both subgroups of the Berber people. It shares a long northern border with Algeria, which is 25 per cent Berber, and a northern border with Mauritania, the homeland of the Moors. Mali's location gave it significant trading importance, with Timbuktu known to every schoolboy.

This means it was open to outside influences, not cut off from them. The hunting dogs of Mali would soon become known from Morocco to the northwest and Egypt to the northeast. Similarly, valuable hunting dogs from both north and south were moved southwards along the ancient trade routes. It is unwise to think of the Azawakh developing in isolation and somehow retaining ancient purity of blood. The similarities between the Sloughi and the Azawakh are, not surprisingly, greater than the differences.

South African Hounds
The deserts of South Africa understandably saw the development of cursorial hounds. The Khoi were reported as long ago as 1719 as having dogs about 18in at the shoulder, with a sharp muzzle, pointed ears, with a body like a jackal's and a ridge, or mane, of hair turned forward on the spine and neck. The original Khoi dogs of Namibia, like the Kalahari Tswana dogs, had the appearance of medium-sized

South African native hunting dogs. Gallant.

Greyhounds and some sported ridges. One hundred years ago, the Khoi were reported as having a dozen ridged dogs near Naauwpoort, from where, in 1901, a Scots Guards officer is said to have had two ridged dogs in his 'bobbery' hunting pack. Boer settlers had a 'Steekbaard' hunting dog, a staghound type, ridged and a blend of indigenous dogs and imported hounds, like the Scottish Deerhound.

Bush Dogs

The Venda dog, like the I-Twina, possesses a tall, slender, lightly boned physique and relatively large, 'bat' ears, much like the hunting dogs depicted on ancient Egyptian artefacts, and may have a north African origin. Stayt, quoted in Helgesen, *The Definitive Rhodesian Ridgeback* (2nd edition, 1984), described these hounds as 'excellent and trusty bush

So-called 'African Bloodhounds' – sighthound hybrids.

Bush hunting dog. Gallant.

Tribal hunting dog in South Africa. Gallant.

dogs'; they were used to bay lions, guard cattle and hunt buck. The I-Maku is more Basenji-like, with replicas in the Luangwa Valley in Zambia and the Basenji of Zaire. The I-Baku have been linked with Arabian dogs, perhaps through Islamic trade routes on the eastern coast of Africa. These remarkable dogs deserve our admiration for their survival alone. They represent a triumph of natural selection over fickle human whim; we should value their genes and assist their conservation. No doubt before they could be brought into Britain they would have to be vaccinated, something they never needed in their native country. Veterinary scientists would be wise to study such dogs and be humbled by them.

Sighthounds of the Mediterranean Littoral

The Podengo

In his *The New Book of the Dog* (1912), Robert Leighton writes:

> Turning again to the south of Europe one may include a reference to the hound known in Spain and Portugal as the **Podengo**. This dog, with its racy limbs, its pointed muzzle, erect ears, and keen, obliquely set eyes, reminds one at once of its probable ancestor, the jackal, and the resemblance is rendered yet more close when the coat happens to be red. In build it is of Greyhound type, and it is frequently used for coursing rabbit and hare; but in the Peninsula, and more especially in La Mancha, Andalusia and Estramadura, it is slipped to the stag and the bear, and is also employed as a gundog.

Such a wide range of employment would demand not just a wide spread of hunting skills but also hounds of varying size. Horowitz, writing in *Hutchinson's Dog Encyclopaedia* (1934), gave the view that these dogs came to Iberia with the Moors, likening them to similar hunting dogs found in North Africa. He gave details of variations in size, coat and colour in

Hare-hunt in Spain, mid-12th century.

the Portuguese dogs not found there today. Even before that, van Bylandt, in his monumental work *Dogs of All Nations* (1904), referred to the Podengo or Portuguese Greyhound, but in one size only, and the Charnique or Balearic Greyhound, our Ibizan Hound of today. He did not mention the similar dogs found in Malta, Sicily and Crete.

Likely Breeder Material
Despite much holidaying there, British sportsmen seem to know little of the hunting dogs of the Mediterranean littoral. You are unlikely to find the blood of, say, an Ibizan Hound, a Pharaoh Hound, a Portuguese

Podengo or a Greek Hound featuring in the lurcher blends of Britain. This is a loss, for these breeds are robust, breed true to type, have superb feet, good noses, lightning reactions to quarry and proven prowess on rabbit, a more difficult catch than many realize. These Mediterranean hounds hunt by sight, scent and their acute hearing and should not be pigeonholed as either scent- or sighthounds. This alone should attract the interest of lurcher men looking beyond outcrosses to pastoral breeds, however clever and biddable the latter

Charnique – known here as the Ibizan Hound.

Hunting with Podencos in mainland Spain – Manuael Benedito, painter. 'The return from a Monteria', c. 1910 (Banco De Urquilo collection, Madrid).

may be. But as the range of quarry here is legally limited and rabbit or rat hunting an easily available sport, a look at these all-round sporting dogs makes some sense.

Rabbit Hunters

With fewer of us having to hunt for our food, it is understandable for hunting dogs to decline. Already the old Grecian Greyhound and the Old Bosnian Sighthound have disappeared. The Old Croatian Sighthound may just have been saved but ten years ago only two dozen or so remained. Britons holidaying in the Canaries may underrate the sporting potential there; but the Podencos Canarios, or hunting dogs, find plenty of sport on rabbit there, even in Lanzarote. This type of sporting dog is found too in Mallorca and Ibiza. The rabbits there do not live underground but in crevices, piles of rocks or in crumbling stone walls.

Podengo of Portugal. Grande.

Canaan Dog.

As both the late Brian Plummer and Ted Walsh frequently pointed out, catching rabbits above ground is never easy. They may be classed as vermin and sneered at by the more privileged hunter but they can make a good hare-dog look stupid. The Sicilians pride their rabbit-dog, the Cirneco dell'Etna, on its scenting skill just as much as its speed and agility. Dry stone walls and rocky hillsides really test a dog's hunting ability. Volcanic lava really tests a dog's feet. The rabbit is worthy prey; Ibizan Hounds would be better in open ground, Cretan Hounds, Portuguese Podengos and Cirnechi dell'Etna in hedgerows, quarries, deserted mines or abandoned industrial sites.

Warren Hounds

At the start of the last century, one enthusiast here imported a Portuguese Warren Hound, one of the Podengo breeds of all-round sporting dogs from southern Europe. It did not gain supporters; if it had been imported under its proper title, Portuguese Rabbit Dog, it might have done better, as there's a lot to a name. In the last few years, Betty Judge has brought in a number of the small variety of the Portuguese Podengo. They look a little like Cairn Terriers, but are commendably nondescript, with no fancy coats, special heads or breed features for the exaggerators to get excited about. They are alert, robust, keen-eyed and determined little sporting dogs. When I was in Portugal fairly regularly some thirty years ago, I was impressed by both the medium-sized and the small-sized Portuguese Rabbit Dogs; they were brilliant at hunting rabbits in trying conditions, such as cork farms, where there are dry stone walls and terraces, which provide enormous scope for agile rabbits.

These Portuguese hunting dogs come in three sizes: the Podengo Grande is 21–28in at the withers, the Podengo Medio is 16–21in and the Podengo Pequeno is 8–12in. I never saw the biggest variety but the medium-sized one reminded me of the Canaan Dog of Israel, another extremely versatile breed. These *podengos* may not be sighthounds in the strictest sense, but over short distances their speed and agility in the hunt is the envy of many sighthound fanciers.

The Hunting Dog of Sicily

Newcomer to Britain

A specialist on rabbit and hare, but so silent a hunter it can catch unwary feathered game too, this 18in,

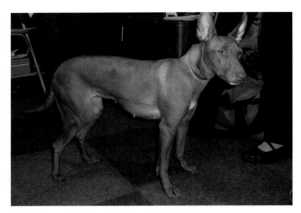

The Cirneco dell'Etna of Sicily at Crufts 2012.

23lb Sicilian Greyhound is largely unknown to British sportsmen, yet now has a small, enthusiastic bunch of around fifty supporters here. Officially recognized as the Cirneco dell'Etna, it has been linked with the foothills of Mount Etna in Sicily for many centuries. Resembling a reduced Pharaoh Hound, being fawn, in all shades, with white markings permissible, it reminds me more of the Cretan Hound, but is much like the other *podencos* of the Mediterranean littoral. I have seen similar hunting dogs in Corsica, with the smallest variety of the Portuguese Podengo also being utilized by hunters in a comparable fashion. Rather like its sister breeds from that part of the world, the Cirneco dell'Etna has superb hearing, aided no doubt by the bat-ears, and really durable feet, a basic feature so overlooked by many lurcher breeders here.

Cretan Hound. Lavrys.

They are used to working with ferrets and at 18–20in lack the legginess of the 22–29in Ibizan Hound, but display a squarer torso than the similar Pharaoh Hound. Like the Cretan Hound they use an effortless energy-conserving trot in the hunt, relying more on their remarkable agility, superb hearing, keen sense of smell and lightning-fast reactions than sheer speed. Crossed with a Whippet, their blood would have much to contribute to our hunting dog scene, although I am not sure that their bat-ears would not cause problems in a climate famous for cold winds.

Field Trials

Talking to an enthusiastic Italian breeder at a World Dog Show about the breed, he described them in his fractured English as a Trotting Sleuth Hound, meaning not an active Bloodhound but a tracking dog with an effortless trotting gait in the hunting field, backed by 'infinite versatility'. He stressed their remarkable hearing, based on extremely sensitive, highly mobile ears, which can act independently, each one responding separately to the noise most acute on that side. He was proud of their field capability ahead of their appearance, waxing eloquent about the field trials available in the breed. Perhaps fanciers like him have ensured that the breed is still very much a sporting one, not mainly an exhibitor's dog.

These Sicilian hounds have their own field trial regulations, covering shooting over game and trials without guns. Around 150 hounds are newly registered there each year. It is worth noting that their field trial regulations stipulate that: dogs that do not make a tenacious effort in their work; that hesitate on a scent trail; that are distracted and do not cover the ground designated for their turn within the first five minutes will be eliminated.

Cyrenaican Hound

Dutch hound expert Leo Bosman links this breed with historic references to the Cane Cireneico, the dog of Cyrenaica, or eastern Libya of today, hinting at a desert origin. Others have held that the breed title comes from the Latin, *cernere*, to sift or separate (as in our word discern), or seek out or 'sniff out' its prey. Cyrenaica was based on the ancient Greek and then Roman city of Cyrene, with close trading links between Greece, Rome and the North African littoral. Sicily would be the closest part of Italy to Africa. Our word gazehound, using the original meaning of the word 'gaze', means a par force hound, showing how a name alone can indicate the function of hunting *at force* in a pack – as opposed to sighthounds, which hunted by speed either singly or as a brace. The two words gazehound and sighthound are not synonymous. The Cirneco dell'Etna could have been 'the hunting dog from the Etna area that fastened on to its prey using sight and scent'. Old breed names can usually be linked with function, as pointers, setters, terriers, bouviers and retrievers all demonstrate.

Sicilian Lurcher

It is of interest that in *Hutchinson's Dog Encyclopaedia* (1934), a three-volume summary of dog knowledge at that time, reference is made to the breed: 'The Cernecchi are undoubtedly the Sicilian Segugi' – the latter being the racy, long-eared and drop-eared, 22in, 50lb hunting dogs, used on rabbit, hare and even boar, of mainland Italy. The book goes on to state, 'They are not coursing dogs, like Greyhounds, neither are they retrievers, or dogs going to ground, although many sportsmen use them for hunting rabbits.' This coverage points out that Sicilian sportsmen made use of a hybrid between the Cernecco and a pointing dog, used with ferrets and hunting with guile rather than speed. Sounds like a Sicilian lurcher to me! Today the purebred Sicilian hunting dog is worth a glance by sportsmen here.

Testing Terrain

Rigorously selected over centuries to hunt on terrain formed by volcanic lava, in extreme heat and in pursuit of an often underrated quarry, the humble rabbit, this breed is robust mentally, physically hardy and relatively free from inherited defects. I have concerns about them being bred by non-hunting owners to resemble Italian Greyhounds – with the dreaded hackney front action favoured – or being bred bigger by some show-ring fanciers – to resemble small Pharaoh Hounds, spoiling breed type. Abroad the breed is recognized as a 'primitive type', not as a sighthound. They are much more than sighthounds in the hunting field, sheer speed alone being of limited value in their hunting grounds. You could argue too that our lazy division of hounds into just two categories, sight and scent-hounds, is in itself somewhat 'primitive'. We should always recognize

diverse talents in hunting dogs, and this little breed has talent in abundance. The early imports into Britain appear to be in good hands and that is very good news indeed. This is a hunting breed that really deserves to prosper.

The Italian Greyhound

Despite its name, and the depictions of small sighthound-like dogs on Roman statues, this breed was developed in Britain and was probably originally just a miniature Greyhound. Many breeds can throw a small variety and they often become more popular as pets than their standard size sporting or working equivalents. The breed is allocated in Britain to the Toy Group but in some places in North America and continental Europe their fanciers try to satisfy any latent sighthound abilities.

It is, I believe, entirely fair to state that just as British breeders developed the breed they also have to take the blame for its deterioration. In her authoritative book *Toy Dogs* (1907), Lillian Raymond-Mallock writes:

> The original Italian seems to have been a much larger dog than is now in vogue, and weighed in the neighbourhood of fourteen pounds, while the present-day specimens must not exceed seven and one-half pounds, and the smaller they are the better. Reducing their size has also greatly reduced their stamina, and the inbreeding found in most purebred dogs, does not tend to improve their constitutions. Great difficulty is

Italian Greyhound.

experienced in producing very small yet typical animals, without impairing their health, and unfortunately a toy terrier cross is sometimes used, which though it has the effect of producing diminutiveness, brings serious defects, notably the bulging eye, and the apple head, both of which are most difficult to eradicate. In appearance the Italian greyhound should resemble his 'cousin of the leash', in miniature ...

Those final words should provide any breeder with a clear mandate. Yet at shows I see some almost handicapped specimens of this little breed: often it seems bred to be fawn-like rather than small sighthound-like.

Need for Field Use

In at least two places in North America – Michigan in the USA and Ontario in Canada – Italian Greyhounds take part in lure-racing, many of them show champions. The top hound in the breed in 2006 in Canada's competitions was described as having 'the prey drive, tenacity and enthusiasm of any good running sighthound'. Thinking of the breed as it is here, I would fear serious injury, but I am assured that no Italian Greyhound has ever been severely injured while lure-coursing, with the only minor injury being, quite predictably, pad burns. Most of these trials are run on hay or horse pastures and not on specially prepared surfaces.

I was pleased but not surprised to read the critique of the Crufts 2010 judge for this breed, which contained the important words: 'I just feel we must not overdo the hind angulation any further.' Already this feature looks harmful but seems not to bother many in the breed. Having been at the show, I could see what the breed judge at the 2010 Bath Dog Show meant when writing: 'Why did I come home feeling worried about the future of the breed? ... Rear movement is often disappointing ... there is a lack of forechest, straight upper arms and consequently appearing out at elbow.'

The breed in Britain desperately needs an elementary field test; any breed with Greyhound in its title really needs to honour that word. For me, too, it is most unwise for our Kennel Club to label its smaller companion dog breeds Toy breeds and collect them into a Toy group. This can encourage some owners to regard their dogs as ornaments and treat them as toys for insensitive self-indulgence, rather than as sentient creatures with the distinct needs of respected pets.

Italian Sporting Greyhound. del Bianco, c. 1630.

Turkish Dog.

The Turkish Greyhound

In his 1887 edition of *The Dog*, the Victorian dog expert 'Stonehenge' gave this description of The Turkish Greyhound: 'This little dog approaches the Italian greyhound in size, but is considerably stouter in his proportions. He is very thinly coated with hair, and is seldom met with in a state of purity, being generally crossed with some of the many varieties which are supposed to be scavengers of all Turkish cities.' An illustration of a 'Turkish Dog' around that time shows a small dog resembling his description but which may well have been lost to us as a distinct type. It is worth noting that the Pharaonic Empire stretched from Turkey in the north, down through Syria and across into Libya, with valuable hunting dogs being traded throughout this territory. Cleopatra, the last Pharaoh, was a Macedonian Greek and so links to mainland Greece were assured. It is not surprising that similar-looking hounds were found right across this empire.

The Albanian Greyhound/Wolfhound

Two of the main Victorian writers on dogs, William Youatt and 'Stonehenge' mention the Albanian Greyhound or Wolfhound, as do several sporting visitors there. Pliny wrote that Alexander the Great was presented by the King of Albania with a dog of unusual size, the common reference to a dog used to deter wolves from livestock. In his 1854 book, *The Dog*, Youatt writes: 'The Albanian Dog can be traced to a remote period of history … He is almost as large as a mastiff, with long and silky hair, the legs being shorter and stronger than those of the greyhound …' In his book, also entitled *The Dog*, of thirty years later, 'Stonehenge' writes:

> A very large and magnificent animal of the greyhound or deerhound type is met with in Albania, coarser in shape and in the hair of his tail than the Grecian greyhound, but with a finer coat on the body. He is especially used as a guard against wolves, but also for hunting them. The varieties are too great to allow of any very definite description of this dog.

As my illustration from the 1930s shows, this is a sighthound type but one that may have been lost to us.

The Albanian Wolfhound, 1930.

Bat-eared sighthounds are found all around the Mediterranean.

Gozo, 1956: local 'rabbit dogs'.

The Pharaoh Hound

If somebody hears the term 'Pharaoh Hound' for the first time, he might be tempted to think this breed is an old Egyptian luxury dog or a new breed, created to get a dog which looks like the drawings from ancient Egypt. But both issues are wrong: The breed we call by the name 'Pharaoh Hound' is a dog similar to sighthounds used on the Maltese Islands as a rabbit hunter since time immemorial. It was the British, who…gave the breed its unfounded name 'Pharaoh Hound'.

Jan Scotland and Peter Gatt, writing in Denise Como's *Sighthounds Afield*, AuthorHouse, 2004.

Unearned Title

Just over half a century ago I was based in Malta and had the chance to go rabbiting on the small neighbouring island of Gozo. The local hunters there used small, bat-eared sighthounds, like small Ibizan Hounds, but in the pack was a red Whippet left behind by a departing British officer and a self-coloured rich tan Manchester Terrier. They seemed to operate as a bitch and dog brace called a 'mizzewgin'. The speed and agility of these dogs was simply breathtaking, as they negotiated dry stone walls, rocky outcrops and boulders at pace. I do not recall seeing any kept purely as pets.

Years later I was told that dogs like these had been imported into Britain and christened Pharaoh Hounds. The Mediterranean littoral abounds with bat-eared sighthounds resembling those on ancient Egyptian artefacts, as the *podencos* of the Spanish islands – like the Ibizan Hound, the Cretan Hound, the Portuguese Podengo (in three sizes) and the Cirneco dell'Etna of Sicily – demonstrate. Each of these breeds or types exemplify the similar hunting dogs used at the time of the pharaohs and long before then. It is difficult to fathom how the bat-eared hunting dog from Malta earned this title. The Maltese call them Kelp tal-Fenech or rabbit dogs. Some were imported in the late 1920s but did not make their

Maltese rabbit dog imported in the 1920s.

The Kelp tal-Fenech.

Pharaoh Hound (on a loose lead).

Pharaoh Hound (on a tight lead).

mark. The similar breed from Portugal, then named the Portuguese Warren Hound, now the Portuguese Podengo, had a comparable fate but unlike the Pharaoh Hound did not gain a foothold here until the small variety came here quite recently.

The popularity of the Pharaoh Hound here, however, actually declined, from thirty-seven registered in 1979 down to a mere nine in 2007, and then up to thirty-eight in 2010. Despite their obvious handsomeness and lack of any exaggeration, the breed has just not gained ground here as their early backers had hoped; perhaps a breed title of Maltese Warren Hound would have sounded more genuine. When I made this point in a magazine article a decade or so ago, I promptly received quite vitriolic letters, separately, from two outraged female fanciers, claiming, quite seriously, that this breed had developed in Malta in total isolation from any other, a relic of ancient Egyptian landings. I merely pointed out that Maltese fanciers held a similar view to mine. I am actually a fan of the breed! The Maltese breeders who down the centuries have conserved this attractive breed have every reason to resent the Pharaonic or Egyptian claims, which incidentally deprive such bat-eared hounds of a thousand years of their history *before* the title of Pharaoh was actually bestowed in ancient Egypt!

It is also more than foolish to ascribe a two-thousand-year unbroken lineage to any breed of dog, especially in the Middle East. The journal Science published in 2004 the findings of an enquiry into the antiquity of dog breeds, with the conclusion that a number of breeds commonly believed to have an ancient origin, such as the Pharaoh Hound and the Ibizan Hound, are often considered to be the oldest of all dog breeds and descending directly from the ancient Egyptian dogs depicted on tomb walls over 5000 years ago. But the findings of their enquiry indicated that these two breeds were recreated in much more recent times, through combinations of other breeds. So, although they resemble depictions of ancient Egyptian sighthounds, their genes do not. Perhaps a copy of that enquiry should be read by my two angry lady correspondents!

Maltese Claim

The hound developed by Maltese hunters to catch rabbits is strikingly like its Sicilian equivalent, the Cirneco dell'Etna, now recognized here under that breed name. It would very sensible if the Pharaoh Hound were to be re-registered as the Kelb tal-Fenech and the Maltese given due credit for their handsome breed. The Portuguese Podengo, the small variety, not bearing an invented breed title, attracted twice as many registrations here as the Pharaoh Hound in 2010. It is worth noting that the Ibizan Hound, despite being long established here, only registered around 100 in total in the whole of the last decade, a sad sign of lack of popularity. Yet our sportsmen are quite willing nowadays to make use of foreign breeds, as the HPRs show in the gundog world; the scenthound breeders have long valued overseas blood, but only on merit. What can Pharaoh Hounds bring to our sporting table?

My memory of the Malta/Gozo hounds is of a smaller (around 20in at the withers), leaner, finer-boned, less substantial, stronger-headed, sturdier, less elegant, much more workmanlike little hound, with amazing agility. It is understandable for dogs bred here to grow bigger and become more refined, once an elegant appearance is sought for show ring presence, but if breed type is precious, then the model of the Maltese Rabbit Dog, as perceived and shaped by its pioneer native breeders must surely count. An elegant sighthound-like anatomy may be eye-catching but this hound is rather more than a sighthound – it is a much more versatile hunting dog with great staying power. There is also a mistaken tendency to ape the Egyptian portrayals of bat-eared hounds in the seeking of a reshaped Pharaoh Hound. I believe the Canadian Pharaoh Hound Club's magazine is actually called *The Anubis News*!

Hunting by Ear

The hunting dogs on Gozo had superb feet, able to cope with stony terrain, dry stone walls and cliff tops. They were much more all-round hunting dogs than sighthounds. They had quite remarkable hearing, with their wide upstanding ears acting like radio receivers and supporting the search for air scent. Dogs have better hearing than we do, can locate fainter sounds and detect more high-pitched ones. I have seen lurchers here with bat-ears but in a colder climate they are a liability. Prick-eared terriers have been claimed by some to have enhanced hearing as a direct result of their ear-construction. A study in America a few years back found that terriers hunted more by ear than the nose, although they are superior to humans in both these senses.

Lurcher breeders, however, would be wise to note the very limited availability of breeding stock, stock that has had firm words of criticism at recent dog shows. A judge in 2009 reported finding narrow fronts and flat feet in the breed. Three years earlier, a judge reported: 'There were few that had the combination of elegance and power so essential in a sighthound and some tended to be cloddy, lacking breed type, but equally there is a lack of strength in fronts particularly in width of chest, and through the pasterns, so essential in a working hound.'

Primitive Types Grouping

I understand that the FCI, the International Kennel Club, which was responsible for the breed title of Pharaoh Hound, has now moved the breed's grouping away from sighthounds and across to 'primitive types', which hardly helps their perpetuation as hounds. I believe that our own KC couldn't accept the breed being described as rabbit dogs, despite that being the translation of their long-held Maltese title. How is it that you can register deerhounds, foxhounds, wolfhounds and badger-dogs but not rabbit dogs? The Kennel Club's sighthound list contains such exotics as Afghan Hounds, Borzois, Salukis, Sloughis and Ibizan Hounds, why not Maltese Hounds or even Gozoan Hounds! Breed titles can contribute to the confusion of breeds, as the allocation of the Spanish Water Dog to the Gundog Group, but the Portuguese Water Dog to the Utility Group, illustrates. If the Portuguese Podengo can have 'warren hound' in brackets after its accepted KC title, perhaps the Kelb tal-Fenech could have 'Maltese Warren Hound' in brackets after its correct name.

Where Has It All Gone Wrong?

A decade ago, an enlightened judge wrote, after assessing the entry at the club's summer show: 'Breeders, what have you done to this lovely breed? The heads are awful … Briskets seem to be a thing of the past … Where has it all gone wrong?' Sadly, those heartfelt words could be applied to quite a number of pedigree sporting breed show exhibits. The new emphasis on function in the exhibition world can only do good and I hope it is sternly seen through. The moans about losing breed type usually come from the lazier, less honest breeders; the hunters on Gozo all those years ago did not mention it, being perhaps keener on the performance of their excellent hounds.

The Ibizan Hound – the Pedigree Lurcher

We holiday a great deal in the Mediterranean yet most British sportsmen seem to know little of the hunting dogs of that region. As a result you are unlikely to find the blood of, say, an Ibizan Hound, a Pharaoh Hound, a Portuguese Podengo or a Greek Hound featuring in the lurcher blends of Britain. This is a loss, for these breeds are hardy, have superb feet, good noses,

Hunting with a Cretan Hound. Lavrys.

The Podenco of Ibiza.

remarkable hearing and lightning reactions to quarry and proven prowess on rabbit, a more difficult catch than many realize. These Mediterranean hounds hunt by sight and scent and cannot be pigeon-holed as either scent or sighthounds. This alone should attract the interest of lurcher men looking beyond outcrosses to pastoral breeds, however clever and biddable the latter may be.

Common Ancestor

German scientist Max Hilsheimer has linked all these hounds to a common ancestor, the Tesem, writing: 'This breed has died out in modern Egypt, but still exists in Crete, the Balearic Islands and Pityusa … The island of Ibiza is the chief breeding centre …' (*Antiquity*, vol VI no.24). Long-time Ibizan Hound breeder, Rafael Serra of Vinebre in northern Spain, has written that: 'The Ibizan Hound is a farmer's hunting dog … which hunts rabbits in packs over rough rocky terrain, mainly at a ground-covering trot, but which needs repeated short bursts of speed involving extreme agility and high jumps.' There is, unusually for this type of hound, a rough-coated variant, believed to come from an outcross to hounds from further north. Ibizans will retrieve live game to hand, having soft mouths despite their sharp muzzles. They are distinctive, with their pink noses, large mobile ears, amber eyes and a wrinkled frown. They are renowned for their 'suspended trot', an effortless, economical 'hover-stride', of value in a hot, dusty, energy-sapping terrain.

Difficult to Train

Not every lurcher expert has written to recommend these Mediterranean breeds, however. Brian Plummer, in his *Secrets of Dog Training* (1992) states:

> Not only do these hounds possess the rather remote disposition of the typical Middle Eastern sighthound, but they also have excellent olfactory senses and a tendency to run head down on the scent of game … In the hands of an experienced and competent trainer, the pharaoh hound and the Ibizan hound can be versatile and useful hunting dogs – in Malta and the Balearic Islands they occupy the same role as the lurcher in Britain – though they are infinitely more difficult to train … when I specialised in training recalcitrant sighthounds, owners of Ibizan and pharaoh hounds were the most frequent clients.

Not the best recommendation, and from an informed source.

Lurcher Potential

But the blood of the Ibizan Hound brings with it well above average hearing, a priceless attribute in an all-round hunting dog like the lurcher. Breeders here may not favour the bat-ear but its shape and position acts like a radio receiver, enhancing sound considerably. We talk of sight- and scent-hounds, but hunting dogs, terriers especially, rely on their hearing much more than we admit. If you ally this benefit to keen

Ibizan Hounds – early imports.

Ibizan Hound retrieving to the saddle. Diana Berry.

Levrier des Baleares (Podenco ou Mallorquin).

A good specimen of the smooth-haired variety of Balearic Eivissenc.

eyesight, discerning scenting powers, astonishing agility for a tall dog and impressively quick reflexes, you have some very desirable lurcher ingredients. The Ibizan Hound may not be making great progress here as a breed, for although twenty-five were entered for Crufts in 1980, only eight were registered with the Kennel Club in 2010, but that does not mean they do not have value by way of introducing fresh blood.

Known throughout the Balearic Isles and across into Valencia and Barcelona, with a Catalan name of Ca Eivissenc, known as the Charnique in the south of France and the Balearen Laufhund in Germany, its hunting sequence has been graphically described as: find and flush, pursue at 40mph, kill with a neck-break, then retrieve to hand. Not a bad write-up for the lurcher role. They have been utilized here by mounted hunters, retrieving well to saddle. The Spanish hunting strain

seems as strong, vigorous, robust and uncomplicated today as it must have been centuries ago and the Balearic devotees have taken their job seriously, culling unwanted specimens and only breeding from the best-performing stock. Lithe and elegant, remarkably deer-like and even-tempered companion dogs, they may fade from view here in time, and that will be a loss to British sportsmen; for me, they offer more than the current fondness for bull blood.

At Crufts in 2010, I was greatly impressed by the Best of Breed winner, Ch. Fineza del Paran, a beautifully proportioned hound, and the Best Opposite Sex winner, Necronomicon Ishaq from Finland – where they breed so many really impressive sporting breeds – a distinctive hound, so typical of the hunting type. Show-ring fanciers are a fickle lot, so often following a breed whilst it has novelty value only to move on to the

Ibizan Hound in the hunting field.

Ibizan Hound at Crufts, 2006.

next favoured import, drawn by the allure of the exotic perhaps, to the detriment of the breed concerned. Breeders of the purebred Ibizan Hound will not like my recommending their breed for lurcher breeding, but for me it is a tribute to the breed, not a sullying.

Show Ring Comments
The judge of Ibizan Hounds at Crufts in 2011 made some worrying observations:

> Movement caused me to shudder once or twice, extravagant, high stepping forehands (which would look better between the shafts of a governess cart) are not what the breed standard calls for when it uses the word 'hover'. The action at the trot is low, light, almost ground skimming and most importantly, long. Too many Ibizans here today displayed a 'snapping upward' from upper arm down to the pastern, creating a heightened trot rather than a forward one … endeavour to breed your next generation to conform not only to the breed Standard but to also heed the breed's function, for if we lose the Ibizan Hound's ability to function, we lose the Ibizan Hound.

These words have importance for the very future of this attractive sporting sighthound and I pray that they are heeded. If the show ring is the only test ground for this breed and its future as a sporting hound, then these observations at the top show deserve careful consideration by the breed's fanciers.

Remarkable Success
The physique of this hound is a challenge to sighthound breeders; with upright shoulders, relatively short upper arms and lacking the deep brisket, it seems to defy accepted wisdom for hounds that rely on speed. The Greyhound is expected to have a deep and capacious chest, allegedly to allow 'heart room', even though the heart does not actually require space around it; the Ibizan Hound apparently needs a long, flat ribcage, with space between the elbow and the brisket.

Its function demands far greater agility than that usually shown by the Greyhound. Half a century ago, when driving to Gibraltar, I stopped at Sitges near Barcelona, where a parade of *podencos* was being held; the hunting demonstration involved a small pack of hounds from Mallorca working a small ravine

for rabbit. The hounds worked as a natural team, the smaller ones flushing, the bigger ones chasing, with remarkable success. The terrain was testing and shoulder flexibility essential. It was easy to see why the forequarters were needed the way they were; hounds the world over have to succeed in *their* country, not fit a template. They have to function!

The Spanish Galgo
Moorish Connections
A Spanish writer on dogs, Carlos Salas Melero, editor of *Revista del Perro* (*Dog Review*), has written:

> Spain has been considered a paradise for different hunting species as is proven by the etymological sense of the word 'Spain' which comes from Span – Hispania, which means 'the land of rabbits' … As far as we know hare hunting with Greyhounds is a procedure introduced into this country from French Gaul, although later the Arabs imported their Sloughis. Out of the cross of both types the Spanish Galgo also emerged – a tough, resistant, tenacious animal and also the fastest racer.

Such a dog was mentioned by Cervantes when he wrote of Don Quixote being accompanied by a '*rocin flaco y galgo corredor*' – a skinny horse and the fastest dog. A sighthound with a likely Asiatic origin, it is undoubtedly the result of an admixture of hounds brought into Spain by the Gauls, hence its name, and those brought in during the long occupation of Spain by the Moors.

Latecomer to Show Ring
This sporting sighthound owes little to the show ring for its survival. In a breed feature in *Chiens de France* in 1984, veterinary doctor Christian Bougerol wrote: 'That the Galgo has survived to the present is because essentially it has been modelled by a harsh environment and conserved by a traditional society which has held it in high esteem.' Rather like our lurcher, poor shepherds and peasants used them to supplement their daily fare, and, unlike our Greyhound, the Galgo was never the preserve of the aristocracy. To respond to the demands of the track in Spain they have been crossed in more recent times with our racing Greyhounds. Males stand 24–28in at the withers, bitches 23–27in; the hunting type is

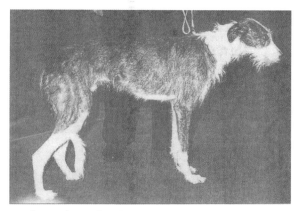

Rough-coated Spanish Galgo.

renowned for its long, strong, elastic trot, giving it great stamina in the field. Brindle is the favoured colour. Quite a number of the hunting variety strongly resemble a Greyhound lurcher.

Saving the Sporting Breed

Some Spanish patriots have even claimed their sighthound breed as an ancestor of our Greyhound, quoting accounts of the trading in dogs between the two countries throughout the sixteenth, seventeenth and eighteenth centuries. There are marked physical similarities between the two breeds, although the Galgo can feature the rough coat too. Dr Bougerol ended his article by stating that the Galgo has nothing to gain by becoming exclusively a companion dog or 'beauty hound', writing: 'If it merits attention, it is by reason of its ability to catch the hare under the most difficult conditions. What is feared is that it finally loses its identity, classified with the rare, misunderstood breeds, breeds to be reconstituted or preserved and to become a breed bred for its beauty.' In the quarter century since he wrote those words, so many sighthound breeds have gone that way and more will surely and sadly follow, without coordinated efforts by breed devotees across national boundaries.

Welfare Issues

Sadly, the Galgo has been described as the 'most brutally abused dog' in Spain, due to its high rate of abandonment by hard-hearted hunters, its poor-quality breeding establishments and misuse by misguided owners unable to cope with a hunting dog in urban areas. Every year more than 350 are rehomed by worthy rescue organizations, but it is estimated that twice that number are put down each year, some without much compassion from their recent owners. At least one of the leading rescue organizations is run by British expatriates who are appalled by the casual attitude of local so-called sportsmen towards the welfare of their dogs, which are discarded after three years of age, their coursing life behind them, together, it seems, with their actual life. There is evidence from time to time of their lives ending in quite horrifying ways, acts which disgrace the name of sport and the reputation of sighthound owners everywhere. The Spanish government has now been persuaded to act over such callous animal cruelty.

Smooth-coated Spanish Galgo.

Rough-haired Galgo-like Ibizan Hound.

The Eurasian Sighthounds

Sighthounds of the Steppes

In his informative *Observations on Borzois* (1912), American Joseph B. Thomas states:

> It seems sure that all breeds of Russian Borzoi came from one common root, namely, from the crossing of the Asiatic or Eastern Borzoi, which penetrated into Russia some hundreds of years ago, with the Northern wolflike dogs, or even perhaps with the wolf itself. This is proved by the ears and by the long hair on the neck. The Courland Borzoi seems also to have added its blood to the breed and given to it the long, curly hair.

He referred to *The Hunter's Calendar and Reference Book* of 1892, which listed a dozen Asiatic Borzoi types, ranging from Caucasian or mountain and Turkomenian to Crimean and Kirghiz Borzois. The list included the Moldavian Borzoi and, under the Hortoy type, the Polish Borzoi. The Chart Polski or Polish Greyhound and the Magyar Agar or Hungarian Greyhound are still with us and the new meritocracy in Russia seems to be reviving the hunting Borzoi. We know little of the Chortaj or West Russian Coursing Hound or Eastern Greyhound and the Steppe Borzoi or South Russian Steppe Hound, both smooth-coated 26in sighthounds. The latter is the sighthound of the Rostovskaya area, lacks the heavier Borzoi coat and is known locally as the Stepnaya Barzaya.

Eastern European Sighthounds

It is understandable for countries with wide, open spaces, like the prairies, the steppes and the plains of the puszta, as well as the desert, to have coursing hounds. In the more heavily wooded terrain of Western Europe the preference for scenthounds is logical. The Magyar Agar of Hungary may have been introduced by the invading Magyars, from the steppes of Russia, in the ninth century. Coursing hounds were also brought into both Hungary and Poland at the time of the Kievan Russian empire, which by AD1030 had formed the largest federation in Europe. The Mongols reached both Hungary and Poland in 1206–59 invasions, no doubt bringing their hunting dogs with them. Ottoman armies passing through Hungary towards Vienna on the various invasions

Kirghiz Greyhounds (Ahk-taz-eet).

of that area in the period 1328–1683 would have been accompanied by their hunting dogs. Trading in valuable hunting dogs, and parading them, especially by nomads or migrants, is timeless. An Englishman, William Blaine, attended a hunting expedition of the Grand Vizier of the Mongol Empire in India in 1785, and listed 300 'Greyhounds' and well over 200 hawks as part of the entourage.

Hungarian and Polish Greyhounds

The Magyar Agar, or Magyarorszag, is around 55lb and 26in high, coming in all the sighthound colours, with a short, coarse coat. They are used on hare and foxes, sometimes kept as pot-fillers by shepherds. Racing Greyhounds have also been imported for track racing there in recent years and crossed with local coursing hounds. Stronger-headed

Chart Polski Polish Greyhounds.

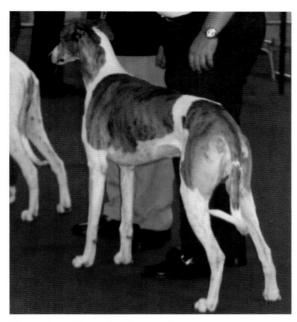

Magyar Agar – Hungarian Greyhounds.

than our greyhound, resembling our Greyhound lurchers, interest in the breed in its native land led to recognition as a breed internationally in 1966. I have seen them at World Dog Shows, such as Vienna and Budapest, becoming more uniform but sadly judged purely on appearance. The Polish sighthound or Chart Polski almost died out in the last century but a group of breed enthusiasts revived it and it now appears to be thriving. The ones I have seen sported the coarser tail, hinting at a link with the Saluki, but more likely from past Borzoi influence.

I believe that the Polish community in the United States is now taking an interest in their mother country's sighthound. First described in Poland in 1600, they have been depicted in Polish paintings, with a detailed description of them appearing in *The Hunter's Catalogue* of 1891. They have been used on wolf, fox, deer, rabbit and occasionally in certain areas on wildfowl too. Renowned for their persistence in the chase, famed for their robustness and avoidance of injury, there is also a long-coated variety, less coated than a Borzoi, more like a steppe sighthound.

Borzoi Background

In his *Hunting Dogs: Borzoi and Hounds* (1899), Russian biologist and breed historian Leonid

Sabaneev describes how Eastern Borzoi were brought into Russia from Persia and bred to sharp-eared, wolf-like northern dogs, then, a century later, outcrossed to the English Greyhound, the Polish Khorty and finally the bearded Borzoi of Assyria. Eventually, still seeking improvement, further crossings were made to the mountain Borzoi, a more robust, far hardier hound. Writing in *Borzoi International Magazine* in 1990, P.M. Semchenkov wrote: 'For almost 50 years the blood of mountain and Crimean Borzois has been added to the Russian Borzois, and for still longer time, Khorty (Polish) blood has been added … to improve the strength and racing endurance of the Russian Borzois.' He added in the 1993 issue: 'Every expert and devoted breeder should be aware of the fact that the Russian Borzoi breed never had and never will have the uniformity that is characteristic of many European breeds. A characteristic feature of all Russia's aboriginal breeds is a great number of interbreed types.' For me, that is a genetic plus.

Borzoi Types

The longer-haired Russian Wolfhound or Borzoi, championed by the Tsars and lionized by writers such as Turgenev and Tolstoy, was patronized here initially by the nobility and has maintained popularity without finding a field use. (I did once learn of one being used,

Perchino Borzois ready to hunt.

Korotai, Zarladai and Kassatka from the Woronzova Hunt.

sian dogs stand thirty-two inches at the shoulder, are enormously deep through the girth …

To be fair to Scottish Deerhounds, a different technique is required on deer, resulting in a different method of seizing.

Coat Texture
In *The Twentieth Century Dog* (1904), Herbert Compton writes:

> Contrary to popular belief, it is the smooth coated borzoi which is the most common in England. The Duchess of Newcastle is my authority for saying that the rough borzoi (Goustopsovy), even in Russia, is scarcer than the smooth (Psovy); both come in the same litter at times. A *real* rough coat, as seen on the imported hound Kaissack, is almost an unknown thing in England, and those who did not see this specimen cannot realize in the least what it was like. The imported hound Korotai also had a very heavy coat, but it was not so good in mixture, being coarser … The heaviest coated specimens that have been bred in this country have been sired by Kaissack or Korotai or their descendants.

Have we long bred selectively for the heavier coat and then claimed it as 'typical'?

devastatingly, on fox in Scotland, however.) Behind the modern single breed of Russian Borzoi, there are barrel-chested Caucasian Borzoi, huge curly-haired Courland Borzoi and bigger-boned Crimean dogs. This type was found as far west as Albania too. The Kennel Club Borzoi is now confined by a closed gene pool, in the rigid pursuit of purity rather than performance, but the lesser-known Borzoi types are really South Russian lurchers both in employment and in breeding method. Hungry peasants and level-headed kulaks did not keep hounds because they were pretty! A writer in *The Field* magazine of 7 February 1891 stated:

> The wolfdog in the south of Russia, near Jassy, is much larger than the borzoi. A perfect wolfdog must run up to a wolf, collar him by the neck just under the ear, and, with the two animals rolling over, must never lose his hold, or the wolf would snap him through the leg. Three such dogs hold the wolf powerless so that he can be muzzled and taken alive. The biggest Scotch deerhounds have been tried and found wanting, as they will not hold long enough. The Rus-

Wolfhunt with Borzois.

'The Hunting Party with Tsar Alexander III and Tsarina Maria Fedorovna' by Nikolai Semenovich Samokish (1860–1944) showing a fox hunt with Borzois and scent hounds.

Admiration Attracted

Deservedly, the graceful athletic build of the Russian wolfhound has long drawn widespread admiration: Charles Darwin described it as an 'embodiment of symmetry and beauty'. Undoubtedly the attractive silky coat of the modern pedigree Borzoi enhances its physical appearance. But as with the Saluki and the Ibizan hound, of this type of swift hound, there were varieties of coat in the Borzoi too. In *The Hunter's Calendar and Reference Book,* published in Moscow in 1892, Sabaneev divided the Borzoi into four groups: first, Russian or Psovoy Borzoi, more or less long-coated; second, Asiatic, with pendant ears; third, Hortoy, smooth-coated; and fourth, the Brudastoy, stiff-coated or wire-haired. But whether the hounds were sleek or bristle-haired, wolf coursing in Russia

Hunt picnic in 19th-century Russia.

before the Revolution was what fox-hunting was to Britain and par force hunting was to France. Brindle Borzois were known in the Perchino hunt.

Noble Hunters

As Leo Tolstoy described in *War and Peace* (1869): 'Fifty-four coursing hounds were taken with six mounted horsemen and keepers of hounds. Apart from the Master and his guests, another eight huntsmen took part, with more than forty hounds. In the end, there were one hundred and thirty hounds and twenty horsemen in the field.' Tsar Peter II kept a pack consisting of 200 coursing hounds and more than 420 Greyhounds. Prince Somzonov of Smolensk had 1,000 hounds at his hunting box, calling himself Russia's Prime Huntsman. Better known was the hunt with the Perchino hounds near Tula on the River Upa, where Archduke Nicolai Nikolsevich established a hunting box in 1887 and hunted two packs of 120 par force hounds, 120 to 150 Borzoi and fifteen English Greyhounds. To ensure sufficient hardiness for winter wolf hunts, both horses and hounds were kept in unheated stables or kennels.

Wolf Coursing

Hunting wolves using Borzoi involved not just conserving their numbers by killing them in areas of over-abundance but actually capturing many for releasing elsewhere. Capturing a wolf that believes it is fighting for its life could not have been easy. At the end of Winifred E. Chadwick's *The Borzoi Handbook* (1952), is a chapter entitled 'The Perchino Hunt' by Dmitri Walzoff, in which he describes wolf capture, using leashes of both Borzois and Greyhounds imported from England. Targeted wolves were pursued, run down, bowled over and quickly secured by several hounds, to enable the mounted hunters to arrive and pinion them with leg-bindings and muzzle-ties. The hounds were chosen from those that seized but did not tear the wolf, allowing a relatively unharmed, and somewhat relieved wolf, to be released at a selected site further away. The English Greyhounds were renowned for going for the throat, achieving a 'wholly detaining grip' that firmly held the quarry yet did not rip the flesh. This is instinctive sighthound behaviour, many losing interest in the 'kill' once the quarry has been seized and held.

Summer Coursing
Usually twenty leashes of Borzois were taken to a hunt, each consisting of two males and a bitch. The hunting season was summer coursing (June to early August) on hare or fox, then summer training for Borzois in August. This consisted of 20km walking or trotting with the hunt horses, followed by advanced training on captive wolves in early September, then the wolf-coursing season from mid-September to the end of October. But the real all-round 'hunting by speed' field dogs from Russia are the mid-Asiatic Tasy or East Russian Coursing Hound and the Taigan or Kirghiz Borzoi. The Circassian Greyhound, also known as the Crimean, Caucasian or Tartary Greyhound, is more Saluki-like, understandably so, as the Circassians, as a people, could be found as far afield as Syria and Iraq. It is of interest that the report on Barzois (sic) in *The Kennel Gazette* of December 1891, for the Birmingham show, stated: 'She [Lebedka] was certainly rather curly in coat on the hindquarters, which according to some Russian authorities … is a defect … who shall decide when Russians disagree? Whether Lebith and Lebedka are different breeds, the former being Siberian and the latter Circassian, is more than I can decide.' Were they actually, by modern kennel club criteria, two different breeds?

Steppe Coursing
The Tasy and the Taigon, both over two feet at the withers, are fast, robust, determined, all-purpose hunting dogs, and, like the similar breeds of Chortaj (pronounced Hortai) and the Steppe Borzoi, remain unrecognized by most international registries. This means that their breeding remains in the hands of the hunters, not the exhibitors. The Tasy hails from the desert plains east of the Caspian Sea, and has a ringed tail and heavy ear feathering, with a likely common origin with the better known Afghan Hound, sometimes called the Tazi in its native country. Used on hare, fox, marmot, hoofed quarry and even wolf, the Tasy is remarkably agile, with a good nose as well as great speed and legendary stamina, often being used with the hawk, providing fur pelts as well as meat. One famous Tasy was valued at forty-seven horses, such was its prowess in the hunt.

High-Altitude Coursing
The Taigon operated further east, in the high Tien Shan region on the border with China. Used, sometimes with falcons, to hunt fox, marmot, badger, hare, wildcat, wolf and hoofed game, these sighthounds could follow scent too but were renowned for their extraordinary stamina at high altitude. They may disappear as more urban living consumes their fanciers but their blood could be so valuable to the inbred pedigree sighthounds of the west. Sadly, breed purity comes ahead of performance in today's canine agenda, despite the health dangers of close inbreeding for over a century.

Unspoiled Hounds
Further south, the time-honoured Cossack tradition of coursing is conducted on the vast steppes from the north Caucasus, west of the Caspian, up through the Volga and Don river estuaries, where abundant game is available, and the Chortaj and the Steppe Borzoi excel. The mounted hunters use a brace of sighthounds and a falcon instead of a gun, a style taken further west by the Tartars. Neither breed has achieved registration and this has permitted the best hunting dogs to be used as breeding material rather than the prettiest poseur in the ring. These hounds are prized for what they can do, once the only test for any sporting dog. The steppe sighthounds are famed for their ability to sprint over huge distances, for their remarkable eyesight and for being able to show great speed at the end of a lung-bursting long chase. Not surprisingly, they possess supremely tough feet.

20th Century Borzois. Arthur Wardle, 1920.

Physical Features

In 2009, Dr Anne Midgarden DVM (USA) presented a paper at an American breed seminar on 'Conformation and Speed in Borzoi'. She concluded that the most important factors were: a short back combined with a long loin, tight, elastic skin and high-set ears, and symmetry at the 'back end' – that is, a proportionally larger croup angle, to a smaller hock angle. Most of the distinguished audience, after discussion, agreed. The essentials in this running dog's anatomy can be summed up as: sound shoulder layback and upper arm angulation; good pasterns with sufficient slope to act as shock-absorbers; strong, hare-shaped feet with robust, well-arched toes; a sound rib-cage, no slab-sidedness and noticeable spring of rib. One expert has stated that the Borzoi's ribs should be like a weather-board, with discernible 'ribbing' along a good length, to allow the best possible lung-room. It is worrying,

Borzoi or Russian Wolfhound. 'Velsk was sired by Korotai'.

Mrs Borman's Borzoi, Champion 'Ramsden Rajah' (1910).

then, to read a 2011 show judge reporting: 'What concerns me most is the number lacking in correct hind angulation, some had little or none and of those who did, many were still not correctly put together – which I am sorry to say appears to be creeping into the breed and accepted as the norm.' A faulty back end in a sighthound is surely a disqualifying fault.

A correspondent in *The Field* magazine in 1887 pointed out that 'the depth of these dogs through the heart is quite extraordinary, giving them, with their enormous strength of loin, a very powerful appearance … he has the long sling trot of his born enemy, the wolf'. In *Hounds and Dogs* (1932), in the Lonsdale Library series, the Duchess of Newcastle recounts her briefing by the Grand Duke Nicholas, whilst in Russia researching the breed and assessing hounds for purchase. In his Perchino kennels he had superlative hounds and to her he stressed: the immense importance of wide powerful hindquarters, deep ribs, good sloping shoulders, a strong, muscular neck and an arched back, with the arch starting gradually from the shoulder blades, not half-way down the spine.

The distinctive topline of this breed is a defining feature. I have seen wheel-back, sway-back, flat-back and camel-back, but it is only correct for the curve to be over the loin and not further forward. Without this vitally important positioning, the sporting hound is compromised. The neck should be the same length as the head and its depth greatest where the neck joins the body. To withstand the stresses of hunting at great pace, immense strength is essential in the lower neck and really strong, not heavy, bone where the neck blends into the shoulders. The back's thoracic vertebrae anchor the ribs, the flexibility coming from further back, with the power seated in a muscular loin. Speed in this breed has to be matched by endurance.

Unique Gene Pool

Many of the working Borzoi and especially the South Russian sighthounds, have never known food manufactured just for dogs, have never experienced veterinary care and have always been bred for hunting performance; their survival indicates their anatomical soundness and physical robustness and they represent a unique gene pool, a source for good both from a sporting and a health point of view. As we increasingly impose our moral vanity on the underdeveloped world and show increasing disrespect to unsophisticated hunters, whether they are seeking fur clothing or food for their table, merely to survive, we need to take stock. These robust, virile hunting dogs possess valuable genes, especially as so many western breeds succumb increasingly to heritable defects. They are prized breeding stock.

To continue to breed from closed gene pools in the pedigree world when top geneticists strongly advise against it is a form of madness. To go on recycling old genes in the hope that magically some rejuvenated produce will ensue is irrational wishful thinking. All over the world the hunters have the best dogs; the South Russian sighthounds in particular are superlative hounds bred for performance by knowledgeable owners. If this new century is going to restore some common sense to dog-breeders then the introduction of blood from high-performance, highly robust, remarkably effective hounds will again be valued. Commendably the KC is promoting a 'fit for function' campaign; these Russian hounds certainly meet that stipulation – that is how they survive!

> If for nothing else, we have at least one thing to be grateful for to Russia – she has given us the Borzoi, one of the most beautiful of the canine race, combining at once strength, symmetry, and grace. The manner in which in recent years the Borzoi has steadily advanced in the public favour, while other foreign breeds, and unfortunately some of our own (e.g. the Mastiff) have gone to the wall, is in itself evidence that this breed, at all events, has come to stay.
>
> W.D. Drury, *British Dogs* (1903)

> Borzois owe their standing in this country to the Duchess of Newcastle, who was stimulated to form a kennel towards the close of the last century, after one had been given to her mother by a Spanish nobleman. In doing so she had the advantage of receiving advice from one of the Russian Grand Dukes, and so well did she follow her mentor and exercise her judgment that the breed was established on proper lines. That they are aristocrats of high degree is apparent from their elegance of form and demeanour. Tall, and covering as much ground as they stand, they show that they are built for speed.
>
> A. Croxton Smith, *British Dogs* (1945)

Afghan Hound: The Himalayan Sighthound

If the Saluki is the canine aristocrat of the desert, then surely the Afghan Hound is the canine aristocrat of the mountains. Those mountains determined the coat of the Afghan Hound, unique amongst sighthounds for that longer, thicker jacket. I have read of this breed being developed in isolation because of the location of its homeland. Th is is contradicted by the perpetual invasions; Afghanistan, like Poland, is one of those 'crossroad' countries, where invaders are either entering from the west or east or coming in from the south and north too. The Arabs brought their Salukis, the Tajiks their Tasys and, no doubt, Alexander the Great some Greek hunting dogs. More primitive dogs resemble each other; when restricted to purebreeding, they unsurprisingly take on the exaggerations that define them. The Afghan Hound has emerged as a very distinctive breed but this has, sadly but inevitably, led to its coat being prized ahead of its sighthound capabilities.

Confusing Nomenclature

In *The Kennel Encyclopaedia*, Volume 2 (1908), edited by J. Sidney Turner, under the section entitled Greyhounds (Eastern), there is extensive coverage of the Afghan Hound but under the title Persian Greyhound, with good illustrations of early import Zardin. The text contains these words:

> From Seistan, in Persia, are obtained very heavily coated hounds, mostly fawn in colour, with black

Afghan Hound of 1900.

faces … Dogs of this type are to be found at Chageh (Biluchistan-Afghan border); at Nasratabad (Persian-Afghan border) – both places wide apart; as well as over a large area on the Eastern Persian borders. The Afghan hound, also known as the Barakzai, Kurram Valley hound, and Kabuli hound, is to be found in more or less numbers all along the borderland and Northern India. It is often kept even further South for hunting purposes, where it eventually loses the greater part of its coat.

Zardin, on whom the fi rst Afghan Hound breed standard was based, came from Chageh in the vast Mekram area of Persia, not from Afghanistan.

Terrain Influence

As with all such breeds, a different type, slightly heavier-boned and more coated, evolved in the mountains, with the plains variety developing as

Zardin, imported from Persia, 1908.

Major Bell-Murray with three of his Afghan Hounds.

Miss Bell-Murray with Pushum (left) – note wide front on Begum.

lighter-framed and less coated. Major and Mrs Amps imported the former, the Ghaznis, Major and Mrs Bell-Murray the latter. Half a century ago, Gulbaz, writing in Kabul, records:

> The greyhound or 'Tazi' as it is called all over Afghanistan … There are three popular breeds of this dog. One is called 'Bakhmull' meaning velvet because it has a long silky coat which covers the whole body including the ears. Another is called 'Luchak' or smooth-coated, and the third one is 'Kalagh' (rhyming with 'blast') which has long silky hairs on its ears and legs, but the rest of the body is smooth-coated.

This Saluki-like Afghan Hound shows that hunters need dogs to suit quarry, climate and country and have little time for the luxury of breed points or cosmetic whim.

Aboriginal Afghan Hound

The Bakhmull variety is favoured in Russia, where it has its own breed club and separate breeding programme. White or ivory-coated, often with a darker fawn saddle, it is around 28in high and weighs 44–75lb. The head is more Saluki-like than classic Afghan Hound. Its fanciers regard it as the original Asian Sighthound, developed in the mountainous areas of mid and central Asia, reaching down to the Punjab of northern India. It has been used on wild ram, goat, big cats, wolves, foxes and hares, hunting in a brace, not in a pack. Not over-coated or exaggerated in any way, it would provide an excellent outcross for the pedigree breed of Afghan Hound, should one be needed.

Afghan Hounds owned by Jat tribesmen in Northern Afghanistan.

Afghan Greyhound, from Tirah – a 1908 depiction.

Barukhzy Hound. Property of Major Mackenzie (1888).

Racing Afghan Hounds

I give our Afghan enthusiasts many plaudits for staging race meetings for their hounds. In a recent report on an Afghan Hound race meeting at Ellesmere Port, these words were used in the introduction: 'Those of you who have never taken your dogs racing – you really do not know what you are missing – find your nearest meeting and go along and see what happens. They – and you! – deserve the fun.' But Afghan Hounds have a special heritage; they had to run fast over some of the rockiest, most uneven, toe-crunching, tendon-testing ground in the world. If they were not successful hunting dogs,

A modern Afghan Hound.

they simply did not last! Sadly, unlike sporting dogs, the best athletes are not preferred in breeding plans here, the needs of the show ring and the desired 'breed-type of the day' receiving a higher priority.

Versatile Hunters

As far as their use in the hunting field goes, Sir Harry Lumsden, when with the British Army in Kandahar at the time of the Indian Mutiny of 1857, was not impressed by the hounds he saw, writing:

> The dogs of Afghanistan used for sporting purposes are three sorts: the greyhound (Afghan Hound), Pomer and Khundi. The first are not formed for speed and would have little chance on a course with a second-rate English dog, but they are said to have some endurance and, when trained, are used to assist charughs (hawks) in catching deer, to mob wild hog, and to course hare, fox, etc.

Later, a Major Mackenzie wrote to advise Drury for his *British Dogs* of 1903, to say that 'The sporting dog of Afghanistan, sometimes called the Cabul Dog, has been named the Barukhzy Hound from being chiefly used by the sporting sirdars of the royal Barukhzy family. It comes from Balkh, the north-eastern province ...', going on to describe how one hound killed a leopard that had seized her pup. This would have been some hound, both in size and determination. Drury provides an illustration of such hounds.

Mackenzie went on to describe the hounds in the hunting field:

> They usually hunt in couples, bitch and dog. The bitch attacks the hinder parts; while the quarry is thus distracted, the dog, which has great power of jaw and neck, seizes and tears the throat. Their scent, speed and endurance are remarkable; they track or run to sight equally well. Their long toes, being carefully protected with tufts of hair, are serviceable on both sand and rock.

He gave their size and weight as 24–30in and 45–70lb. The ones he used were fawn or bluish-mouse, always darker down the spine, with a smooth, velvety coat texture.

Use with Hawks

In Croxton Smith's *Hounds and Dogs* (1932), Mrs Amps also gave an idea of their sporting use:

> The quarry, a small very swift deer called Ahu Dashti, is hunted by Afghan Hound with the aid of hawks ... The young birds and Afghan puppies are kept together, fed on the flesh of deer. When fully grown, the hounds are loosed after a fawn and the hawks flown at it ... The Ahu Dashti or chinkara, as it is known in Indian, is so swift that it is said that, 'The day a chinkara is born, a man may catch it; the second day a swift hound; but the third, no one but Allah.'

She went on to describe hearing of a pack of chinchilla hounds, always grey with black points. She wisely stated that:

A group of Afghan Greyhounds – a 1913 depiction.

Today's Afghan Hound.

Many of our breeders and judges today clamour for size, for bigger hounds at any cost. The Afghan Hound is, or should be, of the greyhound type but sturdy, compact and capable of endurance in order to enable him to hunt all day over the barren, rocky, precipitous mountains of his own land. The struggle for height so often results in coarseness or weediness at the expense of quality. The origin of the Afghan Hound is lost in the mists of antiquity but his Afghan master has kept the breed unaltered for some two thousand years. It seems a pity to alter it now for the English show bench.

There goes a lament echoed in so many sporting breeds of dog.

Show Reports

Mrs Amps would not have liked the show reports on her breed in recent years. One, in 2010, read: 'It has

Stripped down Afghan Hound.

Full-coated Afghan Hound.

been a few years since I judged our breed and I was very shocked and disappointed to see some drastic faults which are coming in. Several were very narrow throughout, bordering on slab-sided and very thin … a lot had soft muscle'. Another 2010 judge reported: 'Quite a few of the entry lacked forechest and depth of chest'. A year earlier, one judge wrote: 'Having started with two male Afghans in the 1960s, each decade I see less of what attracted me to this wonderful hound. The smooth springy gait is being replaced by short jerky movements more befitting Zebedee on Magic Roundabout'. Another wrote: 'I found the front assembly of many hounds was disappointing'. A third one gave the view that: 'We are I think at a crossroads and if we are not careful the qualities we have in our breed could easily be lost'. These comments from experts in the breed are worrying and the faults listed extremely serious in a sporting breed, a sighthound especially.

Worth Saving

It seems perverse for fanciers here to see a distinctive breed from a remote country, to admire its features and characteristics developed by faithful devotees over many centuries, only to disrespect its heritage by breeding hounds quite incapable of carrying out their original function. It was that function that gave us the hound; in the evolution of sporting dogs function always decided form. The challenge now for Afghan Hound breeders is to restore the breed to its classic phenotype and stop breeding for false points like profusion of coat, flashy movement and purely cosmetic appeal. This is a sighthound breed well worth saving and the challenge is on.

> The Afghan is specially designed, with relatively long powerful limbs, deep roomy chest, tucked-up loins permitting a maximum reach of the hind legs when in action, feet peculiarly adapted to suit the rugged terrain, and terribly powerful jaws … and therefore a dog coming from stock which hunted by sight, the Afghan uses his nose quite a lot when in the chase. He is truly a great hunter well able to track a spoor unseen until the time comes for the final sprint when he speeds after his prey with fascinating finality.
>
> Clifford Hubbard, *The Afghan Hound* (1951)

CHAPTER 4

SIGHTHOUND CRITERIA

The Anatomy for Speed

The sighthound silhouette is unmistakeable: long legs, long back, long muzzle – it is hardly surprising they are often all called longdogs! But the seeking of great pace creates the need for those features, with the requirement for endurance only just a secondary requirement. Foxhounds, huskies and wolves, especially, have great endurance but do not rely on sheer speed; the sighthound build and its musculature demonstrate the priority. It is an anatomy for immense pace, sustained pace, but not for mile after mile, as the packhounds, wolf packs and the sled dogs need. Of a Greyhound's live weight, roughly 57 per cent is accounted for by muscle. This compares with around 40 per cent for most mammals. During exercise, a Greyhound can increase its packed (blood) cell volumes by between

The unmistakeable Sighthound phenotype.

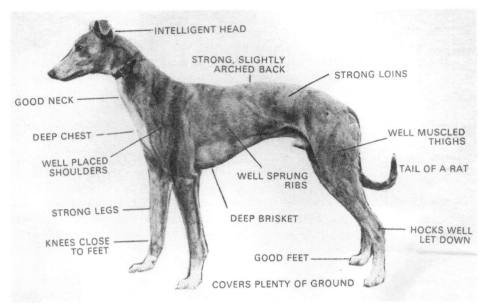

The specialized musculature of the sighthound.

INTELLIGENT HEAD

STRONG, SLIGHTLY ARCHED BACK

STRONG LOINS

GOOD NECK

DEEP CHEST

WELL PLACED SHOULDERS

WELL MUSCLED THIGHS

WELL SPRUNG RIBS

TAIL OF A RAT

STRONG LEGS

DEEP BRISKET

KNEES CLOSE TO FEET

HOCKS WELL LET DOWN

GOOD FEET

COVERS PLENTY OF GROUND

60 and 70 per cent, and increase its heart beat from below 100 to over 300 beats per minute; this allows a much more effective blood flow to its muscles than is the case in most other breeds. The Greyhound's thigh muscles are far better developed than in most other breeds, facilitating pace.

Unique Build

The particular function of each sporting dog not surprisingly led to the development of the physique that allowed the dog to excel in that function. That is why sighthounds have a muscular, light-boned build, the terriers a low-to-ground anatomy and the flock guardians substantial size. Sighthound breeds, wherever they were developed, project the same silhouette, display the same racy phenotype. The Azawakh of Mali, the Harehound of Circassia, the Sloughi of Morocco and the Tasy or Taigon from central Asia would never change hands if they did not look like fast-running dogs. If they

Cretan Hound – ears exaggerated for a purpose. Lavrys.

Circassian Harehound – well clothed.

did not possess this anatomical design they could not function as speedsters. The hounds from the Mediterranean littoral have upstanding 'bat' ears to maximize their already acute hearing; this is an ear shape not favoured further north, partly because of the harm inflicted to such ears by freezing winds and driving rain.

Breed Differences

Whilst the sighthound breeds have a common silhouette, the differences in their hunting styles, hunting country and the local climate have produced small but key differences, such as ear shape, between the various breeds in the group. All need the long loin to provide flexibility in the fast gallop, a deep chest to enable lung power and immense propulsion from the rear. Sighthounds need length in the forearm to facilitate the fast double-suspension gallop. The Ibizan Hound has a different front from most of the sighthounds, designed to allow greater jumping agility. It displays a noticeable 'hover' in its gait. The Whippet has more tuck-up and loin arch than the Mediterranean breeds. The Greyhound, from the side view, shows the anatomy its users have learned provides speed in the gallop. The shoulder blade is not as well laid-back as in, say, the 'endurance' breeds,

like the sled dogs, and the upper arm is more open than in a non-sporting breed, with a proportionately longer forearm. The Greyhound's front pasterns are long and sloping due to the immense 'bend' needed there at great pace. Many Saluki owners prefer the smaller, more energy-efficient type, since the breed is expected to cover substantial distances in the heat at the trot. The ratio of weight to height matters when speed with stamina is sought.

Weight Significance

The weight of successful coursing Greyhounds is worth a glance. The renowned Master McGrath was around 53lb, Bit of Fashion was 54lb, Golden Seal, Staff Officer, Guards Brigade, White Collar and Fitz Fife were each around 65lb but Shortcoming only 49lb. Lobelia won in 1867 weighing just over 44lb. I believe that Coomassie was the smallest Greyhound that ever won the Waterloo Cup, weighing in at just 44lb. (A little bitch called Swift was very successful at Plumpton in the period 1879–1882, weighing a mere 34lb.) Cerito, a white bitch weighing 50lb, won in 1850 and twice subsequently. In 1881, a dog described as 'very smart and clever', Princess Dagmar, won the Waterloo Cup and was considered to be a big bitch at 58lb. The truly great track dog,

Coursing stars: Fullerton and Bit of Fashion, by John Charlton, 1893.

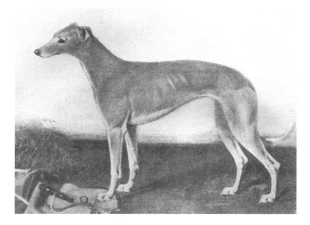

Coomassie. Winner of the Waterloo Cup, 1877–78.

Mick the Miller, was 64lb at peak fitness. Alvaston Lulu Belle weighed only 45lb when she broke the track record for 810yds at Catford. More recently, Cash for Dan weighed 89–90lb when winning the 1969 BBC Television Trophy.

Our show Greyhound has no stipulation regarding weight but its ideal height, for a male dog, is 28–30in. A Deerhound dog of 30in at the withers would weigh around 100lb. Does a Greyhound need to be 30in high and approaching a hundredweight? At the end of the last century, the Waterloo Cup was twice won by dogs weighing over 90lb; this has been put down to the Irish breeding for sheer speed in 'park' coursing (hares released in an enclosed setting). The American KC standard sets the Greyhound's weight at 65–70lb for a dog and 60–65lb for a bitch. I do not believe that the giant lurchers I see at some country shows would make effective hare-hunters, however fast in the short sprint.

Fit for Function

I do see more correctly constructed 'greyhound-lurchers' than I do show Greyhounds. This is a comment rather than a criticism, because I see many more of the former than the latter. It is worrying, however, to see a lack of muscle on show Greyhounds and at times a slab-sidedness that affects type as well as function. Sporting breeds must be judged in any ring on their ability to carry out their specific historic function; if not then there is really little point in breeding them. This ability was summed up by the esteemed 'Stonehenge', when writing on the Greyhound anatomy over a century ago:

> This framework, then, of bones and muscles, when obtained of good form and proportions, is so gained towards our object; but still, without a good brain and nervous system to stimulate it to action, it is utterly useless; and without a good heart and lungs to carry on the circulation during its active employment, it will still fail us in our need.

Running dogs need heart in every sense.

Pace Based on Extension

The sighthound build is a superb combination of bone and muscle, a unique balance between size/weight and strength and quite remarkable coordination between fore and hind limbs. The Greyhound sprints in a series of leaps rather than running in a strict sense. It is what is termed a 'double-flight' runner, where the feet are all off the ground at the same moment. This is unlike a 'single-flight' animal like the horse, which, when racing, nearly always has at least one foot on the ground. The Greyhound's leaping gait is rooted in quite exceptional extension, especially forward with

The importance of front legs at speed.

The Waterloo Cup – the supreme test of anatomy.

the hind legs, but also rearwards with the front legs. Anatomically, the most vital elements in such a dog are the shoulders and their placement, and the pelvic slope, which determines the forward extension of the all-important hindlimbs. That is where the power comes from. It always saddens me to see a sighthound in the show ring displaying upright shoulders and short upper arms, together with a lack of pelvic slope. It is even sadder when such an exhibit is placed by an ignorant judge – having been entered by an ignorant owner! I see these fundamental anatomical faults being condoned at far too many championship dog shows, but why cannot the owner/breeder see such basic flaws?

Forequarter Construction

The racing front involves an extremely long upper arm, often dropping the elbow below the brisket line. I have heard show judges declare this feature to be undesirable, even 'shelly'. But most of the desert Salukis I have seen hunt with great success possessed this feature, as do many quality lurchers. In the Dachshund front, the whole forehand structure is reduced in length of bones; the elbow action arc being actually *above* the brisket line. Many dogs that are loose at elbow are tight at the shoulder joint, the forelegs tending to be thrown out sideways in a circular movement. If the dog is tight at elbow the whole leg inclines outwards, making the dog 'paddle', that is, move the feet in an arc to the side. Loose elbows are often accompanied by other front leg faults: slack pasterns, splayed feet or feet that turn in or out. Dogs with correctly sloping shoulders and compatible upper arms rarely have such a problem. Yet Oliver Coughlan's coursing Greyhound Spring Tide stood with both front feet turned outwards, but was unbeaten as a puppy, going on to win the Waterloo Purse. He never suffered from lameness, often associated with such a foot feature. Pigeon toes generally go with a strong front, able to cope with impact from, say, a rolling tumble or a straightforward collision.

Shoulder Angulation

For over a century, dog writers and show judges have insisted that the correct angulation for the forequarters of the dog, the slope of the shoulder, should be 45 degrees. (This originally referred to a 45-degree angle between the slope of the scapula and the horizontal, *not,* as some state, the angle between the scapula and the upper arm.) This has never been the case in sighthounds and is being vigorously challenged in all sporting breeds, after compelling evidence from cineradiography or moving X-rays. American experts Rachel Page Elliott and Curtis M. Brown have produced convincing evidence to show that the standing dog, in most breeds, displays a 30-degree slope, which in sighthounds can be as much as 10 degrees less. An exaggerated long forward reach is not essential for the sighthound, but immense extension is, both fore and aft. In a letter to *Dog World* in 2009, lurcher expert Jackie Drakeford, quite rightly corrected the words of a contributing vet-author by stating:

> Any working-bred hound or terrier will show how far forward the forelimbs need to be set, and there is never a 'ship's prow' chest in a true working dog … Anyone who has ever seen a running dog tight on the tail of hare, fox, rabbit or deer would know just how well they can twist and turn with those long backs and forelimbs set for forward reach.

Those valuable words sum up so succinctly the importance of the front assembly in all sighthounds. The power will always come from the back, but the manoeuvrability comes from the front.

Quality in the Neck

In his little-known book on the Greyhound of 1937, B.A. McMichan, the official vet to The Greyhound Breeders and Trainers Association in Australia, covered the sighthound's neck quite admirably, writing on this physical feature:

> [It] is peculiarly graceful, and its length, symmetry, and set-on are of vital importance. It must be of sufficient length and flexibility to enable him to strike his hare without losing his stride. A ewe-neck, i.e. one that is concave above and convex beneath instead of the reverse, is a terrible fault, and one seldom met with, for the simple reason that all puppies so afflicted are, as a rule, promptly destroyed. If the tape is run from the point of the nose to that of the shoulder, the junction of the head with the neck, will, in a well-formed dog, be found to be midway. This fact is mentioned by 'Stonehenge' and is well worth

remembering; for when the test fails it will be found that either the head or the neck is too short for well-balanced symmetry. A long, graceful, and well-set neck adds to that vague (but to experts, well understood) term, quality.

There is knowledge, experience and wisdom behind these words.

Handicapping Features

When shoulders are correctly sloped, the topline runs through much more smoothly, giving a far cleaner look. The shortening of the neck from the forward placement of the shoulders does seriously impede a working dog. In retrieving, for example, a sighthound with such a feature has to make so much more effort to pick up game or carry it over an obstacle. Short-necked dogs tire far more quickly than soundly constructed ones. No working dog deserves incompetent breeding bestowing handicapping features on it. When moving, 60 to 70 per cent of a dog's weight is distributed on the front legs; the forequarter construction decides the soundness of the dog's movement. Long-arched necks provide flexibility for the head carriage and usually go along with good shoulder placement, the two combining to give the sighthound a look of quality and style. Long cervical bones, long dorsal bones, good neck length, adequate upper arm length and a gap between the scapulae at the withers are not difficult to detect when viewing and 'going over' an exhibit.

R.H. Smythe, sportsman, vet, writer and exhibitor, once owned a brace of highly successful show Greyhounds, both over 27in in height, which could outrace a hare but never catch one. He also had a coursing Greyhound, 25in high, with two and a half fingers' width between the blade bones, which once picked up fifty-seven rabbits in three hours 'lamping' in similar country. The show Greyhounds were handicapped dogs, in the physical sense.

Keystone 'Bridge'

For me, shoulders and loins are the crucial ingredients for a quality sighthound. The flexibility needed when, say, a Greyhound is racing is quite astounding: the hind feet 'overtake' the fore feet, with the loin and the thigh both curved into just about a semi-circle when the hindlimb is stretched forward to its very limit.

The elasticity which permits this is astonishing, but the soundness of construction and muscularity of the dog allows it. The loins have no support at all from any bones other than the seven lumbar vertebrae and act as the crucial link, the keystone 'bridge', between the front limbs, from the ribs forward, and the rear limbs – the legs, pelvis and tail. For structural strength, a slight arch here is essential, but too great an arch is a weakness. That is why the gift of 'an eye for a dog' puts one judge in a different class from another. A desirable arched loin can be confused with a roach or sway back.

Most Important Single Factor

A dog may get away with a sagging loin in the show ring or even on the flags at a hound show; but it would never do so as a working or sporting dog. It would lack endurance and would suffer in old age. Yet it is, for me, comparatively rare to witness a judge in any ring in any breed test the scope, muscularity and hardness of the loin through a hands-on examination. For such a vital part of the dog's anatomy to go unjudged is a travesty. It does not take much imagination to appreciate the supreme importance of the loins to the speedsters, the sighthound breeds. Some Greyhound experts have argued that the muscular development of the back is probably the most important single factor in the anatomical construction of the Greyhound, ahead of the muscular hindquarters.

Through the centuries, the writers' words have been consistent: Berners – 'Backed lyke a beam'; Markham

Ch Deepridge Mintmaster, generally agreed to have been one of the most perfectly proportioned of Whippets.

Borzoi Ch 'Mythe Maxim' displaying the spinal arch.

– 'A square and flat back, short and strong fillets'; Cox – 'Arched, broad, supple and showing enormous muscular development'; 'Stonehenge' – 'The loins must therefore be broad, strong and deep, and the measure of their strength must be a circular one'. In his informative book on the Greyhound, Edwards Clarke writes: 'The very first test that any trainer makes of the condition of a greyhound is to run his hand over its back and loins … The first impression by touch should be one of supple firmness, of well-developed muscular tissue of a rubber-like consistency.' He sought a little trough or valley along the backbone. He looked for arching of muscle not any arching of the skeleton, a common fault in our show sighthounds, especially in Whippets and Borzois.

Clarke termed the roach or 'camel' back a skeletal malformation, a form of spinal curvature that 'militates against any possibility of smooth-flowing, free-striding movement'. At a championship show a few years ago, I saw a lady exhibitor proudly posing her winning Greyhound for the dog-press photographers despite its very obvious camel back! The somewhat brief breed standard for the Greyhound stresses an arched loin both in the General Appearance and the Body sections; perhaps a few more words on the need for a muscular arch rather than a skeletal arch would be a better guide.

The standard of the Borzoi actually demands a back that is bony, free from any cavity and rising in a curve.

Bull lurcher with strength of loin.

Top quality Whippet: Ch Lily of Laguna.

The Whippet is expected to feature a definite arch over its loin; the Borzoi, however, is supposed to possess the highest point of the curve in its back over the last rib, that is, forward of the loin. Both are sighthounds built for speed. The American standard for the Borzoi calls for a back that is 'rising a little at the loins in a graceful curve'. That is more than a little different from ours and more likely to produce an efficient sighthound. There is a world of difference between a bent skeleton over the last rib and a curve of muscle over the loins, the latter benefiting the dog! The lumbar vertebrae are quite literally the backbones of the loins, *lumbus* being Latin for loin. Any arch should be over the lumbar vertebrae and not further forward.

In an attempt to appreciate the value of the loin to the dog, I think of the dog as a four-wheel drive, rear-engined vehicle with its transmission in the loins. They are an absolutely key feature of the canine anatomy relating to movement. If we prize movement then we must understand the loins. But just try researching the subject, even in weighty books on dogs. It is vitally important for any serious sighthound breeder to learn about loins. Coursing men did, as Frank Townend Barton MRCVS states in *Our Dogs* (1938): 'All coursing men pay particular attention to depth of chest, quality of back and *loins,* and still more to the hindquarters – i.e. the rump, the first and second thighs as well as the hock joints and pasterns. It is almost impossible to be too insistent regarding highly developed muscles and broad loins, where so much action is brought into play when a Greyhound is running and twisting after the hare.'

Bo Bengtson's book on the Whippet (1985) also provides surprisingly rare coverage of this vital part of a dog's anatomy: 'To acquire the perfect silhouette the dog must obviously have sufficient length of loin to avoid the cramped, wheel-back stance which has periodically been quite common. This extra bit of loin is what makes the dog cover a lot of ground and was what Mrs McKay at the Laguna kennels always impressed on me made all the difference between an ordinary whippet and a top-class one.' It is good to see a knowledgeable show ring judge and international Whippet expert appreciating the value and importance of this vital area of the anatomy of the running dog.

Visible Power

One hundred and fifty years ago, in the early days of showing, running dogs were regularly exhibited: the winner of the Waterloo Cup in 1855, Judge, won second prize at the 1862 Islington conformation show. Twenty-five years later, Bit of Fashion, dam of the celebrated Fullerton, was exhibited at Newcastle, winning first prize. I find it hard to believe that a specialist Greyhound judge would not admire the powerful hindlimbs, strong sloping shoulders and rounder rib cage of the sporting type. All Greyhounds were once like this; where is the rationale of being attracted to a breed and then wishing to change its shape? Symmetry, gracefulness and beauty are not the essence of a sporting breed, however pleasing to the eye. Every Greyhound should demonstrate physical power, really look like a superlative canine hurdler – a genuine fast hunting dog.

Physical Flaws

In *The Kennel Gazette* of July 1888, the Greyhound critique made mention of 'a showy black, but flat in ribs' and a bitch of 'beautiful quality and style, but decidedly short of heart room'. Does 'showiness' compensate for flat ribs? Can a sighthound, designed to run very fast, combine beautiful quality with a lack of heart room? Five years later, a critique praised a 'niceish' black bitch with 'rather upright shoulders' (which came second!) and the reserve card winner a 'pretty' dog 'somewhat cow-hocked'. A critique on the breed just a year ago stated that front movement was really bad, with another observing that muscle tone was very hard to find. A recent Crufts critique on the breed commented on the absence of muscle tone and a lack of spring of rib in the entry. This is depressing.

In *The Whippet* (1976), C.H. Douglas-Todd wrote: 'An upright shoulder in a Whippet is like a man with hunched shoulders. Just try hunching your shoulders and then, with your shoulders up round your ears as it were, try to walk forward smartly and see how you feel.' Front movement depends on well-placed shoulders, well-muscled but not 'loaded'. A good judge will always spot the difference, but a knowledgeable exhibitor really ought to know such basic flaws.

Feet for Function

Ever since Dame Berners' much-quoted description of a Grehound (sic) included the words 'Fottyed lyke a catte', the sighthound breeds' foot has tended to be desired as 'compact', as in the Deerhound standard. The cat foot has been blurred with the compact foot. The Irish Wolfhound is expected to have round feet. The Borzoi is required to have hare-like rear feet and oval front feet. The Whippet needs oval feet. The Sloughi is preferred with the hare foot and I think this is right. I always associate the cat foot with endurance and the hare foot with speed. Condition can affect the appearance of the feet, with an unfit, out-of-condition dog looking splay-footed and slack-pasterned. In the dog the toe-pads do most of the footwork.

The main difference between a hare foot and a cat foot is the length of the third digital bone. In both shapes of foot this bone should be parallel to the ground but the second digital bone in the cat foot should lie at 45 degrees. Exercise, too, when carried out entirely on soft ground can cause the dog's foot to look more spread out. Hunting country can also influence foot shape, with the Afghan Hound required to display large, strong, broad forefeet and long hindfeet, to suit the terrain it hunts over.

'No foot, no dog' is as applicable to the sighthound as is 'no foot, no horse' to that family of animals. It is crucially important to appreciate that there is a fundamental difference between the locomotive system of the horse and that of the dog; the horse uses what is called the transverse gallop, the dog uses the rotary gallop. A veteran huntsman once gave me the view that 'horses run with their legs, dogs with their backs.'

Superb Eyesight

Rotary gallop, muscular power, energy storage and soundness of feet apart, the speedsters of the dog world need superlative eyesight. Dogs easily outperform humans in detecting movement, their motion sensitivity allowing them to recognize a moving object from a distance of 900–1,000yd away. Motionless, the same object will only be picked up by the dog's vision at roughly half that distance. Dogs have far superior peripheral vision to us, around 250 degrees, against our 180 degrees maximum. It is no accident that all the cursorial breeds have the same skull outline. Their better depth perception and enhanced forward vision come from longer nasal bones resulting from a longer nasal-growth period that occurs at an earlier age. As biologists Raymond and Lorna Coppinger point out in their perceptive book *Dogs – A Startling New Understanding of Canine Origin, Behavior and Evolution* (2001), when selecting breeding stock for rabbit-catching hounds: 'I would sort through my dogs and pick those that worked best, and breed the best to the best. I might not realize that all I am really doing is selecting for longer nasal bones. The eyes themselves are no better than in any other breed. They are just in a better position to see forward.'

All animals active at night, whether predators or prey, have a 'back-up' visual support system, which gives the retina two opportunities to catch light, greatly enhancing night vision. A highly reflective layer of cells, the tapetum lucidum, underlies the retina and behaves like a mirror. Light is reflected back through the retina, the tapetum offering the photoreceptors a second chance to capture light. This mirror effect, reflecting light back out through the eye, makes predatory animals' eyes shine in the darkness. Photographs of them pick this up.

Dogs' low-light vision is far superior to that of humans but is still not as good as that of the cat family, which detects light levels six times dimmer than our eyes can. Cross your coursing dog with a cheetah and you have the hunter by night as well as the hunter by sight! (In 1937, the founder of the Romford track, Archer Leggett, launched a new attraction: cheetahs racing against Greyhounds. After a cheetah bitch had covered the 355yd course in 15.86 seconds, easily a track record, the experiment was discontinued, allegedly because the cheetahs became bored with inedible prey!)

Breed Standards

It could be argued that the group of dogs above all others that need sound eyes is the sighthound group, if only by name. But if you examine the wording of the various sighthound breed standards over the years, there have long been amendments needed. The Afghan Hound eyes have to be 'nearly triangular', without the shape of triangle being specified; that is not helpful to a tyro breeder. The punctilious could well argue that 'nearly triangular' is a contradiction in terms; a triangle cannot be 'nearly' anything else. Who decides how flat or upright the nearly triangular eye of the Afghan Hound has to be? Of what *value* is such a loose term? The Saluki and the Sloughi have to have 'large' eyes, but how large? The Greyhound and the Borzoi are expected to feature eyes which are 'obliquely set', that is, diverging from a straight line, but by how much? The eyes of the Cirneco dell'Etna have to be relatively small – but relative to what? Imprecise wording in a description intended to be instructive can be dangerous. The Kennel Club, to be fair, is reviewing the wording of all breed standards, with clearer guidance, especially with health issues in mind, but descriptions, however well-meant, can lead to misguided and sometimes ignorant breeders pursuing a flawed word picture of their breed.

The Skull of the Sighthounds

This collection of sighthound head studies show the skull construction and eye placement that allows the best possible vision for the hot-pursuit hunting

Greek Hound – head study.

Cretan Hound. Lavrys.

The Irish Wolfhound.

Greyhound Heads.
C. Graeme, 1892.

Sloughi sapling.

Saluki of 1912.

Deerhound Heads. C. Graeme, 1902.

Ibizan Hounds.

The Afghan Hound.

dog. These long lean but not too narrow heads – often with a prominent occiput, broadest at the ears, tapering to the muzzle, always with a powerful jaw, displaying little stop, with well-set never prominent eyes and always held high, ever ready to scan the middle distance, are a unique feature of the speedsters. In *The Illustrated Natural History* (1928 edition), the Rev. J.G. Wood states: 'The narrow head and sharp nose of the Greyhound, useful as they are for aiding the progress of the animal by removing every impediment to its passage through the atmosphere, yet deprive it of a most valuable faculty, that of chasing by scent.' He overlooked the fact that sighthounds use *air scent* and operate

in country where ground scent is minimal. The hounds from the Mediterranean littoral seek air scent, using the high head posture, and have bat-ears, relying much more on their hearing and being less vulnerable to icy winds; their heads resemble a blunt wedge and they are usually broader-headed than their northern cousins.

The sighthound breeds have more refined skulls than most hunting dogs, facilitating that sighthound aloofness, so much a characteristic of the group. But the whole skull construction is built to permit the best possible *vision,* probably stereoscopic – like ours – from a high head position, rather than to demonstrate canine elegance.

Borzois of 1900. Arthur Wardle.

Dimensions

Measurements of the Coursing Greyhound Master McGrath:

(taken from *The Coursing Calendar,* volume xxi).

Head: From tip of snout to joining on to neck, 9½in; girth of head between ears and eyes, 14in; girth of snout, 7½in; distance between eyes, 2¼in.

Neck: Length from joining on of head to shoulders, 9in; girth round neck, 13¾in.

Back: From neck to base of tail, 21in; length of tail, 17in.

Intermediate points: Length of loin from junction of last rib to hip bone, 8in; length from hip bone to socket of thigh joint, 5in.

Fore leg: From base of two middle nails to fetlock joint, 2in, from fetlock joint to elbow joint, 12¼in; thickness of foreleg below the elbow, 6in.

Hindleg: From hock to stifle joint, 9¾in, from stifle joint to top of hip bone, 12in; girth of ham part of thigh, 14in; thickness of second thigh below stifle, 8¼in.

Body: Girth round depth of chest, 26½in; girth round loins, 17¼in; weight, 54lb.

Master McGrath won thirty-six out of his thirty-seven courses, winning £1,750 in four years (1867–71). His fame was such that he was taken to Windsor Castle and presented to Queen Victoria. He was descended from the Bulldog-blooded King Cob (bred 1839).

Master McGrath, as is well known, was a small dog, weighing generally, when he ran, about 54lbs. He

The legendary coursing Greyhound Master McGrath.

was however, stoutly built, with good neck and shoulders, capital barrel, and rare legs and feet; he had a somewhat plain and short head, and a very short and fine tail. He was an example of what inbreeding will do from good strains, as he combined four strains of King Cob…three on his dam's side and one on his sire's.

Thomas Jones, *The Courser's Guide* (1896)

I think I saw the immortal black run all his courses in public after his initial effort in his native land, and certainly no other greyhound ever made my blood tingle in the same way … During one of his courses, I was out in the running field … McGrath was driving closely … with marvellous movement, the entire length of his back being in visible play, just as though it were a mass of hingework …

'Vindex', writing in the *Irish Field* (1919)

The Ibizan Hound is described as simply 'slightly longer than tall'. The forechest or breastbone is sharply angled and prominent, however the Ibizan's brisket is approximately 2 and a half inches above the elbow and the deepest part of the brisket is rearward of the elbow. The Ibizan's front is entirely different from that of most Sighthounds, however in the field the Ibizan is as fast as the top hounds and without equal in agility, high jumping, and broad jumping ability.

Robert W. Cole, *An Eye for a Dog* (2004)

The Ibizan Hound – different forequarter build.

Generally speaking, the top-class greyhounds are not necessarily perfect specimens, but they are so evenly balanced that no outstanding defect is exhibited in their conformation. With very few exceptions, the top-class greyhound embraces symmetry, elegance, balance, condition, and freedom from all forms of coarseness. We could not believe for a moment that a coarse bushy tail, a rough coat, over- or under-shot jaws, or a coarse thick head could affect the speed of the greyhound, but I am in agreement with the many authorities who are of the opinion that these signs exhibit a lack of quality and are signs of degeneracy.

Anne Rolins, writing in her *All about the Greyhound*, Rigby Publishers, 1949.

All coursing men pay particular attention to depth of chest, quality of back and *loins,* and still more to the hindquarters – i.e. the rump, the first and second thighs as well as the hock joints and pasterns. It is almost impossible to be too insistent regarding highly developed muscles and broad loins, where so much action is brought into play when a Greyhound is running and twisting after the hare.

Frank Townend Barton MRCVS, *Our Dogs* (1938)

Judging the Sighthound

Judging Criteria

Among cattle and sheep-breeders it is generally admitted that certain leading qualities shall be considered all important, such as the propensity to carry flesh of good quality on the parts most valuable to the butcher, early maturity, and, in the sheep, quantity and quality of wool. But in horses and dogs, and more especially in the varieties of the latter, there is not the same unanimity, even in the leading principles; and in matters of detail, as may naturally be supposed, the difference of opinion is very great.

Those words, written by 'Stonehenge' in his *Dogs of the British Islands* (1878), could be rephrased nowadays, when so many dog breeds can be judged on their 'wool' and their 'flesh'. Fortunately the sighthound breeds are spared this false appraisal, overweight exhibits being easily spotted and appropriately devalued, although the 'wool' on the Afghan Hound can be excessive.

Variety classes: a handsome, exotic or unusual breed very often does well in variety classes.

Knowledge of Purpose

To judge a breed by working-type standards involves a deep knowledge of its particular purpose in the canine world, be it to follow a line of scent and tenderly retrieve game, or to point and set the position of game unseen, or to face and set a fox or badger in his den, or to match the speed and nimbleness of a hare until it escapes from sight. Each of these functions requires and calls for special physical and mental faculties with which the appropriate breed is naturally endowed.

Those wise observations by H. Edwards Clarke, in his book *The Greyhound* (1965), should be engraved on the thinking of not just sighthound judges but those who appoint them. Fitness for function may be a new Kennel Club cry, but in the world of the sporting dog it has always been the ultimate judgement.

Breed shows: a scene during the Afghan Hound Association's Show, 1947.

Salukis at Crufts, 1991.

The sighthound breeds at dog shows are not always the best 'showers'; most of them resent such immodest blatant exhibitionism, as they might see it, preferring activity and expecting to be judged on performance not pushiness. Judges who know such breeds usually acknowledge this, although many lurcher judges at country shows lack the experience to see past this group reluctance to perform artificially. Assessing any breed of dog in a ring is always going to be a combination of judgement, ideally objective, knowledge and

technique. Sadly, far too many judges that I see appear to base their decisions on 'gut feeling' or by taking a shine to a particular dog on the day, or concentrating on fad breed points. One sighthound judge at Crufts in 2010 reported: 'When I first judged Salukis in 1966 one could see all the characteristics that govern Salukis. Now it is difficult to find the ruff, the long tails, the bright oval eye, the dignified gentle expression and the unique shaped foot.' Would such details matter to a Bedouin hunter? Only as an afterthought did this judge add: 'Some movement leaves a lot to be desired.' Now that would bother the Bedouin hunter!

Need for Technique

A judge with knowledge is always going to triumph over one just hoping to get his decisions right. A judge with a technique is more likely than any other one to make sound decisions. Fanciers who pay money to enter a ring and travel a long way to get there deserve a competent judge. But time and time again, especially at lurcher and terrier shows, I watch judges at work in the ring who apply a different sequence to each exhibit, only check one aspect of movement and fail even to examine some parts of

Salukis at the Hound Show, Stafford, 1987.

Hands-on judgement of a Whippet. Crufts, 1991.

the dogs' anatomy. Consequently I do not believe that their judgements are soundly based. In any field of human activity knowledge applied through a tried and tested technique will surpass gut instinct every time. Assessing quality by eye alone is far better when the visual image is tested by a hands-on examination. In this regard, I believe that the Kennel Club show ring routine of a systematic, close-up physical check is potentially far more accurate than, say, a hound show judge viewing packhounds at Peterborough,

Hands-on judgement of a Whippet lurcher, 2010.

Honiton or Rydal solely from a few yards away, with no closer 'hands-on' examination.

Need for Ringcraft

Far too many exhibitors at country shows expect the judge to see merit in their entry when they themselves have done little to prepare the exhibit for the ring. Some terriers and many gundogs are natural show-offs, most sighthounds are not. Dogs need to be schooled for the ring – not slavishly prepared, but trained to walk briskly on the lead and stand still during closer scrutiny. A future judge's examination of the bite is made easier by previous rehearsal. Why should your dog unquestioningly allow a complete stranger to look inside its mouth? Jaw construction really does matter and a competent judge will always want to check this important feature of a sporting dog. The judge can better apply his judging technique if the exhibitor's ring technique has been practised and the exhibit rehearsed. This can significantly affect placings. Why exhibit a really good dog but make no attempt to school it in the requirements of the ring? Why not help it win?

Identifying Breeding Material

The most valuable purpose for me in showing dogs in any ring is to identify future breeding material. The most important factor for me is: could this dog carry out its breed function? We all like a handsome dog but handsome, unsound dogs, sadly, do win. I attended the 2003 World Dog Show in Dortmund and spent several days at the show. I have never seen so many unsound dogs under one roof in my entire life, and some of them won prizes! Sportsmen expect their dogs to *function*. This capability is so much more important than beauty or breed type, the latter originating in function, but is so regularly betrayed by human whim. Hounds of all types, sighthounds especially, must never be judged on cosmetic appeal but on their anatomy's ability to carry through their function. Those breeding for flashy markings beware! The best show ring judges make their decisions on soundness and conformation to the breed standard, not showmanship.

Overall Soundness

Fault judging is no help to anyone – breeder, owner, the status of the show, the sport of showing itself.

Overseas faults are often listed according to their seriousness, that is, from disqualifying ones down to merely undesirable ones. No sighthound should ever win in the ring if it features incorrectly sloping shoulders, short upper arms, a weak neck or loins, poor feet, a short body (especially with a long back) or shoulder blades that touch when the dog stoops to put its nose to the ground. There is no such thing as the perfect dog; it is vital to judge the *whole* dog, not descending on the animal, oozing praise just because it is in superlative condition, has powerful hindquarters or a superb head. The sporting dog

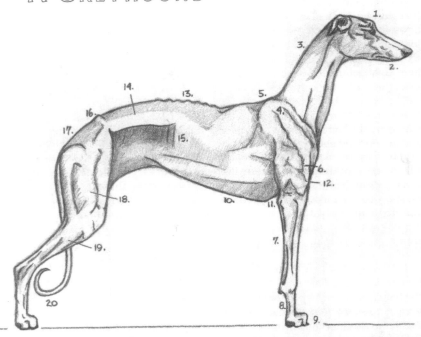

Faults In A Greyhound

Listing of Faults

1. Prominent frontal bones (nasal sinuses)
2. Lacking underjaw
3. Ewe neck
4. Short, upright shoulder
5. Lumpy, short, low withers
6. Short, upright upper arm
7. Bowed foreleg
8. Upright pastern
9. Cat foot
10. Herring gut, poor underline
11. Shallow chest
12. No front fill
13. Arch starts too far forward; rise too extreme; too many visible vertebrae; roached
14. Shallow loin
15. Upright ribs; slab-sided
16. Hipbones set too low
17. Short, steep croup
18. Narrow hindquarters, inadequate muscling
19. Narrow, weak second thigh
20. Ringed tail

From Sue LeMieux's The Book of the Greyhound (TFH, 1999).

Ch. Okeford Queen (1928).

The Champion of Champions St. Ronan's Rhyme.

needs every part of its body to be sound! In KC show rings far too many breeds are judged solely on their heads or their coats or their flashy gait. Far too many judges ignore poor condition in the entry before them. This, when sporting breeds are on parade, is an insult to the heritage of these breeds.

Learning from the Past

It often pays to look at portrayals of the top dogs of the past to establish in your mind's eye what the dog before you in the ring should resemble. In his *Dogs and I* (1928), the show judge and coursing Greyhound expert Harding Cox used an illustration of Champion Okeford Queen to show what he considered 'a perfect specimen of the show Greyhound'. In early Edwardian times, the Deerhound Champion St Ronan's Rhyme, born 1903, bred by the great Deerhound breeder Harry Rawson, was described as 'probably the most perfect dog of any breed living in her time'. Both dogs had wonderful symmetry, a hint of athletic power and no sign of the slightest exaggeration. Neither of these quite outstanding dogs was shown with its hindfeet in the next county! The famous Saluki Champion Sarona Kelb and the two exceptional coursing Greyhounds Master McGrath and Fullerton also showed these qualities. But being able to spot faults is clearly not within every show judge's range of skills – the placings by some being strangely faulty in themselves. In her perceptive book, *The Book of the Greyhound* (1999), Sue LeMieux sets out the 'Faults in a Greyhound' both succinctly and with clarity. It is worth comparing her illustration, with its eighteen key points, with the depictions of the great sighthounds listed above.

Hunting Requirements

Judges must start by accepting the fundamental fact that a hound that hunts using its speed must have the physique to do so. Immense keenness for work will always come first but the build to exploit that mental asset comes close second. A sighthound judge must look for, at the front, a long strong muzzle with powerful jaws and a level bite. How else can the hound catch and retrieve its quarry? The nose should be good-sized with well-opened nostrils, for, despite some old-fashioned theories, sighthounds hunt using scent as well as sight. A long muzzle permits better scenting. For any sighthound to succeed, its eyes should be fairly prominent and be set slightly oblique, to the side of the head. One eye should look away to the right and one to the left so that, like any good rangefinder, both eyes can be used for long distance marking. It is likely, however, that at close range only one eye is used at a time. The neck should be long but symmetrically so, muscular and firm. Length of neck does not improve 'pick-up'; flexibility in the 'swoop' comes from the placement of the shoulder blades. Good judges look out for such points.

Sighthound Anatomy

A sighthound must have powerfully set shoulders; I always apply the 'two fingers' width' test to the

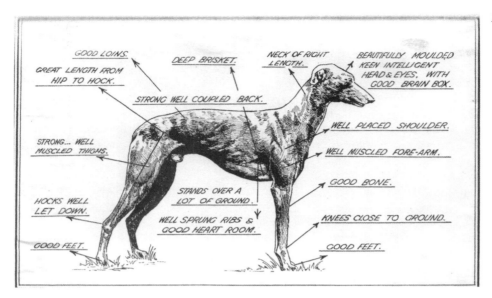

Points of the Greyhound.

space between the shoulder blades of a stooping dog. Many show Great Danes have to spread their feet to drink from a bowl of water on the ground because of excessive narrowness in the set of their shoulder blades. The sighthound's back should hint at suppleness and power, be slightly arched in the lumbar region, yet have a mainly level topline. The chest should be deep from the withers to point of elbow but be fairly flat, with the underpart of the brisket fairly broad across. The ribs should be well separated, with good lung room and space between the last rib and the hindquarters to allow a full stride. At full stretch, the impress of a hare's hindfeet is implanted in front of that of the forefeet; the sighthound should have the same capability. There must also be freedom of suspension in the ribcage or thorax in the way it is 'cradled' by the scapulae – the dog needs to utilize this when hurdling a farm-gate or turning at high speed. What a sighthound is expected to do must constantly be in the judge's mind.

Sound Angulation

Inequality between the length of the rear stride and the length of the front stride is producing ugly unsound movement in an ever-increasing number of breeds as the contemporary fad for hyper-

Ch. Shalfleet Stop That Tiger.

Ch. Shalfleet Sir Lancelot.

angulation in the hindquarters gathers more and more momentum. In far too many sporting breeds the hind feet have difficulty keeping tally with the front ones. This, combined with inflexibility in the spine, produces a failure of synchronization behind. In soundly constructed dogs sufficient angulation in the hindquarters and adequate length in the tibia enables the hock to flex and the hind foot to advance beneath the body enough so that balance is maintained. The side effects of excessive angulation in the hindquarters of a number of pedigree breeds are increasingly manifesting themselves. Why, then, is it becoming almost de rigueur in breeds like the show Greyhound, the Great Dane – a running mastiff – and the show Whippet? Top judges always look for a *balanced hound;* exaggeration in sighthounds hinders great pace and that is never good for the dog.

In every animal walking on four legs the force derived from pressing the hind foot into the ground has to be transmitted to the pelvis at the acetabulum, and onwards to the spine by way of the sacrum. In over-angulated dogs the locomotive power is directed to an inappropriate part of the acetabulum. In addition, in order to retain the required degree of rigidity of the joint between the tibia and the femur, other muscles have to come into use. In the over-angulated hindlimb, the tibia meets the bottom end of the femur at such an angle that *direct* drive cannot ensue. The femur can only transmit the drive to the acetabulum *after* the rectus femoris muscle has contracted, enabling the femur to assume a degree of joint rigidity when connecting with the tibia. This means that the femur rotates anticlockwise whereas nature intended it to move clockwise. The knowledgeable judge will know of this; novice judges need to learn of it.

Excessive angulation in the hindquarters, with an elongated tibia, may give a more pleasing (to some) outline to the exhibit when stacked in the ring, but in the long term it can only lead to anatomical and locomotive disaster. Such angulation destroys the ability of the dog's forelimbs and hindlimbs to cooperate in harmony in propelling the body. Yet I have heard it argued by breed specialists at seminars that it will increase the power of propulsion operating through the hindlimbs and on through the spine. If it did, the racing Greyhound fraternity would have pursued it with great vigour. I have heard a dog show judge praise an over-angulated dog because it 'stood

Ch. Shalfleet Stop the World.

The successful coursing Greyhound bitch Age of Gold by Fabolous Fortune–Mona Milrea.

Lauderdale: a very successful show dog, 1873–1880.

over a lot of ground'. So does a stretch limousine – but it is designed to do so! It is worth comparing top-class show Greyhounds from the Shalfleet kennel, such as Stop That Tiger, Sir Lancelot and Stop The World, with portrayals of great dogs from further back: Tom Sharples's Lauderdale, a very successful show dog in the period 1873–80, and the superb coursing Greyhound bitch Age of Gold from around that time. The proportions in each of these dogs are roughly the same; the balanced anatomy is there. Sighthound judging requires knowledge!

The hindquarters must be powerfully constructed if they are to propel the dog forward in the chase, but symmetry and balance fore and aft are the key to turning ability. Every sighthound depends upfront on good long arms and forearms, and, in the hindlegs wide and muscular thighs and second thighs, length of stifle and *sound* angulation. Many of the early breed standards were based on the knowledge of those better acquainted with horses. The expression 'hocks well let-down' refers to the heel bone itself, that is, the point of hock, and not to the rear pastern as a whole. It means a short heel bone, not the distance between the foot and the heel. The feet should be compact, with well-knuckled toes and short claws, naturally worn from working or sound exercise. Some old-school Greyhound experts used to assess a dog by looking at the tail first, noting any sign of coarseness, desiring the tail of a rat in appearance, long and whip-like with little hair. I suspect that some of them were checking on alien blood rather than signs of excellence.

Immense Flexibility
In his most informative book, *An Eye for a Dog* (2004), conformation expert Robert Cole writes:

> The Greyhound demonstrates in profile the conformation man has selected for speed at the gallop. The shoulder blade is not as well laid-back as endurance trotting breeds and the upper arm is more open … The Greyhound's front pastern is long … At the fast double-suspension gallop this pastern bends 180 degrees to lie flat on the ground, shortening the leg as the shoulder passes over it. After the Sighthound's shoulder passes over the paw, this pastern springs back up contributing an upward thrust. Each of these forequarter styles has been selected by man to perform a specialized function resulting in a certain structure …

The immense flexibility needed in the sighthound physique has to be foremost in every breeder's mind. Robert Cole was the creator of the much-misunderstood expression TRAD – tremendous reach and drive – in judging Salukis. He himself pointed out, however, that 'it must be remembered that long distances on the hunt are covered by the Saluki at the trot, not the gallop, therefore action at the trot should appear seemingly effortless, conserving energy for the final fast gallop'. In designing for great speed, there is still a need for the sighthound to get to the crucial final stage of the hunt; a sighthound on the move is not just a sprinter and its anatomy has to permit the sustained trot as well as the dynamic dash. Judges really do need to have 'the moving dog' in their mind's eye in the ring.

Under-Exercised Exhibits

In his informative *The Practical Guide to Showing Dogs* (1956), Captain Portman-Graham writes:

> The fact that a dog is structurally sound is not in itself sufficient to ensure that it will always win at shows. It is of paramount importance that it must be … at the highest standard of condition … Perhaps one of the biggest advantages which dog showing confers on the dog as an animal is the care which must be bestowed upon it.

If unfit dogs with poor muscular condition can win at dog shows, then the whole argument that such shows improve dogs is totally destroyed. Dogs that are inadequately exercised and merely wheeled out for the next show can be spotted so easily by any competent judge and quickly thrown out of the ring that such an insidious practice, both for dogs and the dog game, can be ended. Sighthounds are first and foremost *hunting dogs*. Unfit, unexercised sighthounds look just that and reveal more about 'the other end of the lead' than most exhibitors realize! Judges must rate condition as much as form.

Portman-Graham went on to write: 'exercise is a vital consideration in maintaining any breed of show dog in bloom, health and vigour … When one watches the beautiful muscles of a racehorse one sees a similarity between a dog's muscles which have been developed correctly and naturally, and ripple in movement'. Yet there is evidence of lack of muscular tone and development in so many sighthound rings, even at many lurcher shows today. One of the saddest sights at a pedigree dog show has to be an unfit, under-muscled, unexercised exhibit from a sighthound breed; these dogs were born to run! What value would such a neglected, undervalued hound have for a hunter? That is the ultimate query for any competent judge; the whole exercise of showing a dog is the pursuit of top-class animals, the identification of future breeding material, and not a parade of possessions.

Value of a Sequence

Movement demonstrates soundness, or reveals flawed physiques; the initial overall appraisal can reveal symmetry and allow assessment of the whole dog. The closer hands-on examination allows the slope of shoulder, the strength of loin, the muscular development, the skeletal frame and the construction of the jaw to be checked. The sequence of the examination is crucial. For me, it is logical to view the whole dog standing and moving *before* a closer look is given. And by moving I mean three-dimensional: going away, going across and then heading directly for me. I am seeking effortless locomotion, a balanced harmonious economical gait and no excessive action, either to the side or off the ground. Does the dog look as though it could go on like this for miles? Would the judge want to take the dog home?

Any closer examination has, for me, to follow a set sequence: head, jaw, eyes and ears, neck and shoulders together, back and loins together, set of tail and pelvic slope together. Then to the lower case: spread and elbows together, front legs *and* feet, thorax and tuck-up, hindlimbs *and* feet, then coat and character. Judging character is not straightforward; I go for the look in the eye, the tail action and the confident body language. We all surely want keen, willing, up-on-their-toes sporting dogs.

Without a set sequence I would be worried that I would miss something. In the end, of course, what the dog can do will always be more important than what it looks like. But sound construction, backed by physical fitness, will always allow a sporting dog to excel, and that is the task of every sighthound judge: to reward soundness and fitness for function, not showiness. Winning show dogs get bred from; but, truly, who is honestly proud of a kennel full of incapable exhibitionists, useless show-offs?

Sighthound Good Fortune

The sighthound breeds, the early show Greyhounds, Deerhounds and Borzois particularly, came to us from the coursing fields of the world and that is their good fortune. Function and performance shaped their form and ensured their perpetuation. Some companion breeds are the result of man's whims and can range from the cuddly baby-substitutes to sheer oddities in appearance. Not every courser was happy when the show ring claimed the sighthound breeds. In *The Greyhound* (1930), James Matheson writes: 'As a sporting dog, the show greyhound has all but ceased to exist. It is not only that his conformation militates against his chances of success in the chase, but his very inclinations to pursue and kill are sadly lacking through disuse.' Some modern welfarists might welcome the latter but no sighthound admirer wants to lose the essential conformation of the coursing dog. In *The Greyhound and Coursing* (1921), Adair Dighton writes:

> Someone, possibly more than one, will criticize this chapter and say, or write, that I have said nothing about shape or make … They run and win in all shapes and of all makes, and so long as a greyhound can gallop and work it does not matter what he looks like. This work is not written for the owners of those apologies, 'The Exhibition Greyhound', but for the coursing man, and he, I know, will under-stand my point.

Dual-Purpose Hounds

Stars of the track and coursing field have also triumphed in the show ring from the very beginnings of the show scene, as I have set out in Chapter 2 and above in this one. In *The Courser's Guide* (1896), Thomas Jones writes:

> Many of the most worthless greyhounds in the cours-ing field take prizes at shows. One or two exceptions to this rule I will, however, mention; the first being Jenny Jones, who was as good-looking a bitch as ever went out of slips … After her running career she was shown a great number of times, and her record in this way, I believe, beats any greyhound who has been on the bench either before or since. The second one is that good-looking bitch, Bit of Fashion, whose per-formances are well known to all coursing men … She

may be set down therefore as not only being a perfect model, but also as possessing all the good qualities of a first-class greyhound in the coursing field.

All true devotees of the sighthound breeds are surely seeking 'a perfect model' – handsome, yes, but essentially a *running* dog.

The subject of judging opens up a wide range of discussion, and there is no gainsaying the fact that there are a great number of inefficient young judges about. One can't get a real knowledge of dogs in a few months, or even in a few years; and although I am always out to give the novice a chance, discrimination should be used. To see some of these 'gentry' at shows makes one positively shiver. Many a time I have seen them 'performing', when giving an exhibition of how a dog should not be judged…

T.W. Hancock Mountjoy, *Points of the Dog* (1927)

Your turn may come to be a judge one day. It is a great responsibility. An unsound criterion of one individual of points necessary to make a dog a winner can influence a breed for the worse for generations, and slowly eliminate it from the scene by the demand made on stamina if the faulty criterion is persisted in. Is it too much to ask that the standards of Show points should be revised, with the well-being of the breed in mind? And may the committee that does this beneficent task have among its members an experienced veterinary surgeon accompanied by a geneticist?

R.C.G. Hancock, BSc, MRCVS, *The Right Way to Keep Dogs* (1956). Half a century later, this is now happening.

It is well to remember that 'perfection of form' does not ensure perfection of movement, nor necessarily any great improvement in stamina. A vast number of greyhounds fulfil all the requirements of the most exacting standard until such time as they are called upon to move.

Anne Rolins, *All About the Greyhound* (1982)

Movement, on some that I know have won well, was all over the place, wide coming and going or two legs coming out of the same hole … Muscle, some carried far too much, a show Whippet should have long, flat

muscle not racing dog bulgy muscle. At the other end of the scale dogs so narrow that you could not get your hand between their forelegs and had the appearance of two shadows glued together.

Critique on a championship Whippet show, 25 September 2011

Now I myself shall tell you by what means you should judge the fast and well-bred ones … First, then, let them stand long from head to stern … Let them have light and well-knit heads … Let the neck be long, rounded and supple … Broad breasts are better than narrow, and let them have shoulder-blades standing apart and not fastened together…loins that are broad, strong not fleshy, but solid with sinew … flanks pliant … Rounded and fine feet are the strongest.

Greek historian Arrian, *Cynegeticus*, second century AD

So handsome are greyhounds, so graceful in outline, that they would be worthy of the chisel of a Phidias. At their best, in the form cultivated for the show ring by breeding for beauty rather than performance, they are particularly pleasing, and a really good one seldom fails to catch the eye of those who judge the variety classes open to all breeds. The points desired in the show dogs are such as should be required in the coursing or racing dogs. The general description prefacing the standard of points drawn up by the Greyhound Club of Great Britain reads: 'In judging greyhounds it is essential that the judge should bear in mind that the beautiful lines of the breed are one of its biggest assets. This breed is essentially built for speed, ability to bend and turn with his game, and possess the build (or formation) which will fit him for his work in the field in combination with the graceful lines of a thoroughbred. It is absolutely essential that he should be well balanced throughout.'

A. Croxton Smith, *Sporting Dogs* (1938)

The more one judges the more one comes to appreciate that truly outstanding dogs are a rarity and that the standard of most of the dogs that one is asked to judge falls somewhere between acceptable and very good. A great dog once gone over is never forgotten and lives on in the memory forever. When judging dogs that are perhaps best described as average, one has to be prepared to compromise. Judges do vary in the extent to which they choose to penalize specific faults and this can easily result in a multiplicity of opinion with regard to the placing of the same exhibits by different judges or indeed by the same judge on a different day.

Critique from the Saluki judge at the Manchester Championship Show, 2011

Breeding Real Sighthounds

Because dogs similar to tesems (i.e. slender, erect-eared, curly-tailed hounds) were known in antiquity to accompany the pastoral peoples of the Eastern and Western Deserts, and erect-eared sighthounds are shown in rock art of the Atlas countries, the range of this dog is thought to have extended across much of ancient North Africa. Whether the original parent stock from which the Old Kingdom form evolved was indigenous to East Africa or was introduced from western Asia is unknown, although the recovery of skeletal remains of a similar sighthound from the Ubaid Period in Mesopotamia tends to favour southwest Asia as the source. During Dynastic time however, there is evidence that tesems were imported into Egypt from the south (modern day Nubia and Somalia).

Douglas Brewer, Terence Clark & Adrian Phillips, writing in their *Dogs in Antiquity, Anubis to Cerberus, The Origins of the Domestic Dog*, Aris & Phillips, 2001.

Revealed in Performance

Early hunters bred dogs for their performance. That is how the sighthounds earned their keep – they were bred to be useful, never to be primarily pretty. Increasingly in the modern world, appearance is all; image matters more than substance and physical looks can outweigh character and performance. This has sadly long been the case in the canine show ring. We all like a handsome dog but a dog that can do nothing else but pose has a limited appeal to sportsmen. The highly successful racing Greyhound Mick the Miller and the impressively effective coursing Greyhound Master McGrath were always described as rather plain and unremarkable – until they started running, that is! Master McGrath was rather thick-set, with a shortish neck and, for some, was too compact. Mick the Miller had no obvious outstanding features but

Wall painting from grave of Rameses VI, 3,000 years ago.

also no significant defects. They have been referred to as the ugly ducklings of the leash and turf but only out of envy. Both had wonderful symmetry of build and superb balance; these are essential attributes in a running dog but are usually only revealed in performance.

Angulation for Exhibition

Neither of these outstanding hounds displayed any sign of physical exaggeration. At Crufts in 2010 one sighthound judge commented: 'I am concerned that over-angulated hindquarters seem to be becoming more prevalent, too long from the point of stifle to the hock. Not only does this spoil the balanced and symmetrical outline but is a serious fault as far as the functional capability of the Whippet is concerned.' This is a point very well made.

In his most informative book, *The Dog – Structure and Movement* (1970), vet and sportsman R.H. Smythe, writes:

Lord Lurgan's Master McGrath, winner of the Waterloo Cup 1868–1869.

In the running dogs such as the Greyhound, the change [to extra angulation], whatever it produced in the matter of appearance, has certainly done nothing to improve performance. The racing Greyhound of today has a straight hindlimb and tibia of moderate length and it executes a large number of short, rapid strides, attaining a very high speed. The exhibition Greyhound with exaggerated angulation, 'standing over a lot of ground', and with a very much longer hind stride, both behind and beneath the body, actually carrying the hind feet past the shoulders in the forward section of the stride, cannot catch the smaller dog with the straighter stifle and hock, simply because the fewer, longer strides cannot compete with the many shorter ones.

In these few words, he makes many points on conformation, but the key point lies in the bare fact that if you wish to perpetuate a real sighthound breed, as the pioneers in that breed strove mightily to do, you have to ignore show ring fads and breed for function. A sounder animal emerges, quite apart from the genuine hound.

Visualization

The design specification, as always with a hunting dog, a sighthound especially, is to find the ideal match between quarry, country and conditions on one hand and speed, determination and hunting instinct on the other. The best judge of a sighthound is a man who has hunted one himself, a man who visualizes the dog before him in the ring in the chase. He has to possess

Lord Lurgan's Master McGrath.

some basic knowledge of the fundaments of hunting dog anatomy or he has no right to be in the ring as a judge. I see judges at shows who never look at the feet, never test the condition of the loin, fail to examine the bite, and reward entrants with slab-sides, an incorrect slope to the shoulders and ribcages that lack lung room. That can only reward bad breeding, leading to a production line of mediocre dogs; winning dogs get bred from! Lurcher shows may be mainly a bit of fun, but KC-approved shows for the sighthound breeds identify future breeding stock.

Abnormal Gaiting

The seeking of unnatural movement in the ring is also a curse. In her book on the Saluki, Ann Chamberlain writes, on 'gaiting': 'The Saluki is a hunting breed, used for thousands of years in every terrain imaginable. To attempt to define the 'show gait' or the 'proportion' of the dog [in the breed standard] after all these years seems not only unnecessary but also superfluous.' I doubt if such a wise opinion will be heeded.

In her book on the Afghan Hound, Margaret Niblock writes:

> The Standard succinctly describes the gait of the Afghan as 'smooth and springy with a style of high order' with a proud head carriage, far-away gaze and raised tail. This cannot be achieved if the animal is restrained by a tight grip on a short lead, or 'strap-hanging' as can be seen in terrier handling. It is miserably uncomfortable for the dog, which, choking and coughing, leans even more heavily against the collar in a frantic effort to put his feet on the ground for balance. The result is an unnatural, stilted, flailing or 'knees up' action in front and unbalanced over-thrusting from the hindlegs, often accompanied by knocking hock joints and leaning away from the handler. This misuse of hind muscles particularly in gangling youngsters, may cause permanent damage and unsoundness.

She was writing this over thirty years ago; if anything, abnormal 'gaiting' and stringing exhibits high up on choke chains is even more prevalent now than then. I have even witnessed it at lurcher shows.

Needless Size

I do not understand the justification for so many sighthounds, including lurchers, being so huge! It is worth remembering that the main reason that show Deerhounds tend to be enormous is not need but origin. Deer hunters found that dogs over 28in at the withers lacked performance and quickly passed them on to the early show breeders. No Waterloo Cup winner has ever been 30in high. I regularly see lurchers at shows which stand 30in and which must weigh 90–100lb. I would have thought that even on Salisbury Plain or around Newmarket, 60–70lb was easily big enough. I have written earlier that the superlative coursing Greyhound Master McGrath, three times winner of the Waterloo Cup, believed by many to have no equal for pace, cleverness and killing power, weighed 52–54lb. Wild Mint weighed 45lb and Coomassie only 42lb; both were superbly effective coursing dogs. They were judged and rated entirely on their performance, the sternest and most valid test of all. Any breed prized and valued purely for its size, from a hopelessly bulky Mastiff to a needlessly giant Great Dane is going to pay a penalty too in bone problems, and not just late in life.

Shaped by Function

Whatever their size it is possible to judge these admirable dogs more effectively. If we are going to assess them, let us do it properly. If we betray all the remarkable work, carried out not just by the pioneers in each pedigree breed but in longdogs the world over, we will gradually lose a precious feature of the timeless man–dog relationship, as well as an ancient hunting feature. A hound that hunts using its speed *must* have the anatomy to do so. Immense keenness for work will always come first but the physique to exploit that mental asset comes close second. Hunting ability rests not just on pace. A sighthound *must* have a long strong muzzle with powerful jaws and a level bite, with strength right to the nose end of the muzzle. How else can it catch and retrieve its quarry? The nose should be good-sized with well-opened nostrils, for, despite some old-fashioned theories, sighthounds hunt using scent as well as sight. Their function shaped their design, a function demanding performance, both from the quarry and the owner.

Protective Coats

Smooth-coated sighthounds are sometimes handicapped by too little coat, lacking protection from wire and chill winds. Whilst not advocating a

Linty-coated lurcher.

Lurcher with weatherproof coat.

change of jacket in any sighthound breed, I can see operational merit in a stiff-haired, wire-haired or linty coat. Ibizan Hounds can carry such a coat, but it is one not favoured in the show ring. The jacket of any sporting dog should shed the wet, not hold the wet. Waterproofing comes from hair density and texture, not profusion of coat; if you look at the originally imported Afghan Hounds and Borzois and then compare their coats to today's specimens, you can see how function has been sacrificed to fashion. Salukis develop a different coat in our climes, but that does not mean a needless handicap in their primary function – as a cursorial hound. We need them to feature what is best for them, here, not for us.

Fitness for Function

The best physique is squandered without keenness in the chase and immense determination; an alert eager expression in the eye indicates this and is essential. Every sighthound judge has to ask himself: will this dog hunt? Can this dog hunt with this anatomy? Better function-judging, based on a more measured assessment, should lead to the production of better dogs. With coursing here confined to the past, we owe a great deal to the rich sporting heritage of our sighthounds and must breed canine sprinters to be just that. Country sportsmen have too much sense to allow the show ring sighthound breeds to degenerate into the pretty-polly state prevalent in far too many pedigree dog breed show rings. Lurcher shows, for example, are more a day out than any identification of future breeding stock: a bit of fun; the only real test

for such a dog is in the chase. But that 'bit of fun' can raise standards too if the judges' critiques are sound. Who wants to win with an unsound, incapable dog?

In her book *Sighthounds Afield* (2004), Denise Como writes:

> Whether lure coursing, oval track racing, sprint or straight racing, open field coursing, hunting, hiking for miles, or any combination of these activities, an unfit hound is going to get injured. These are strenuous sports. An out-of-condition hound is a prime candidate for pulled and torn muscles, ligaments, and tendons, cramping, heat exhaustion, dehydration, and other forms of extreme unpleasantness.

The condition of your sighthound should always be a matter of great personal pride and I am saddened when I hear of a show exhibit in one of these breeds being knowingly under-muscled to obtain a 'sleeker' dog for the ring. To own a sporting breed is a privilege that should never be taken lightly. Every sighthound judge must honour their impressive sporting heritage and reward only those exhibits displaying the physique of a fast-running hound.

Breed Points

Much is made in the show fraternity of breed points, or those physical characteristics that define one breed from another. In all hunting dogs, form is decided by quarry, country and climate. Coursing dogs tended to be stronger-boned than racing ones, with their lighter bones. The Irish Wolfhound and Borzoi needed

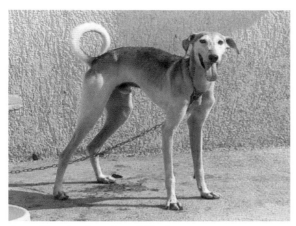

Cretan Hound – almost Basenji-like. Lavrys.

The sharper-muzzled Sloughi.

greater size to engage the wolf. The smaller Cretan Hound, specializing more on hare, can be almost Basenji-like. The Afghan Hound needed bigger feet and a more protective jacket. The Whippet has a relatively deeper chest than other sighthounds. The Mediterranean breeds display less chest depth than most other sighthound breeds.

Owners too exercised a preference in deciding that the Pharaoh Hound was to feature one coat colour, the Whippet any colour, but with some colours associated rightly or wrongly with performance. The Deerhound and the Wolfhound breeds had fewer colours in the gene pool. Syrian Saluki breeders preferred the crop-eared dog. The Borzoi shows a distinct rise over the loin. The Sloughi can be sharper-muzzled. Where such features support field performance then justification is there. Colour preferences usually represent human choice. What is regrettable is for breeders to sacrifice field performance for show gain. Handsomeness purely for its own sake in such loyal, long-serving and ever-willing breeds is a commentary on the owners and breeders concerned. It insults the memory of all those eminent pioneer breeders who strove to bequeath to us outstanding hounds.

Real Sighthounds

In his book on the Greyhound, published half a century ago, the great sighthound expert H. Edwards Clarke wrote:

> It soon became apparent to the early breeders of the Greyhound that their fastest dogs, generally speaking,

were cast in a certain common mould. In the fullness of time they came to associate such physical features as tall straight forelegs, strong loins, powerful quarters, with the fullest endowment of speed and stamina. In their minds' eyes they created a picture of the ideal Greyhound, of the conformation that in their experience had proved to be the most reliable and consistent vehicle of the breed's great intrinsic qualities. This commonly accepted standard of physical perfection was drawn up long before dog shows had ever been thought of.

All sighthounds function as such from the design of their anatomy; if we seek to change that design to suit a contemporary whim, we threaten their claim to be *real* sighthounds.

> A number of people take up the breeding of animals thinking that it is only necessary to purchase a few show specimens in order to turn out innumerable winners. No doubt they very soon find out their mistake … Dog-breeding seems an easy enough matter to those persons who have been accustomed to breeding mongrels or hardy animals of pure breeds. It is not until the novice takes up the breeding of the highly-bred, inbred show dogs that he learns to his surprise how many unsuspected difficulties may arise, and what complications may ensue.
>
> C.J. Davies, *The Kennel Handbook* (1905)

Saluki – power with grace.

The early owners of racing dogs raced them and the fastest dogs were those of a definite type. The fastest were the sires and dams most sought as progenitors. There is an association of bodily features which is conducive of great speed, so the type of dog which we know as the greyhound began to become a breed. And finally by the recognition of the fact that there is a definite association of physical characteristics, leaders found that they could also improve greyhounds by inculcating beauty into the breed without sacrificing speed. Then they began to compare them in groups to see which most nearly approximated what they thought was the composite of beauty and usefulness. In this way cliques were built up around all breeds which were interested not in the usefulness of the breeds but in the appearance. They gradually made their idea of beauty the goal and forgot usefulness. In fact they did the most absurd things and are still doing them ...

Leon F. Whitney, *How to Breed Dogs* (1947) – American veterinarian and the most highly experienced dog breeder of his day

At the beginning of 1945, I was permitted to refer to dogs in a broadcast talk for the first time since I began working for the BBC ... One of my points was that the breeding of dogs was far too haphazard an affair and not sufficiently based on available knowledge. In addition, I pointed out some of the reprehensible things that were going on and cited the crossing of the Borzoi into our Collie in order to secure a long narrow head in place of one of the broadest and brainiest of doggy skulls, with disastrous results on the temperament and intelligence. I gave other instances equally foolish, but the aim of what I said was a plea that all this hit and miss experimental breeding could be put on a much surer and scientific basis if representatives of my profession, geneticists, and the Kennel Club, could meet and discuss the problem ... but the doggy world and its all-powerful ruling body passed me by. I was even the subject of attack in the dog papers ...

R.C.G. Hancock BSc, MRCVS, *The Right Way to Keep Dogs* (1956)

Bend racing, with Greyhounds.

CONSERVING THE SIGHTHOUND

We have every reason to be proud of our sighthound breeds. They are a distinctive and unique part of the canine world, developed by man in the most testing terrain, the most demanding climates in the world and often against the most elusive quarry. Those hunting with dogs have great respect for their quarry, whether it is the humble hare or the grander gazelle, and this has been so throughout man's long hunting history. Hunting with sighthounds was never about the size of the bag but about the quality of the pursuit, with the athleticism of the hounds admired no more than the agile elusiveness of their prey. Urban-dwelling, town-thinking lobbyists, sadly so often with no knowledge of country people, and pursuing a single agenda – the abolition of hunting with dogs, whatever the penalties to wildlife – have, like so many do-gooders, been blind to the custody of our countryside by generations of rural hound-owning sportsmen who had greater regard for conservation than they have ever been credited with.

Humane System

The widely held view that hare-coursing had the sole purpose of *killing* hares, rather than comparing the running and turning skills of a pursuing brace of sighthounds, soon became accepted wisdom. Pro-coursing lobbyists just could not swim against the tide and the 'antis' exploited this quite shamelessly. The most humane system for the control of foxes should not be debased by an irrational dislike of men on horses in pink coats. If it is agreed that fox-control is essential, especially in hill areas, why not employ the soundest method of doing so? Nature is viewed by so many town-dwellers as a place where a collection of lovable animals live in harmony, whereas nature in reality is astonishingly cruel. Human ignorance about

animal welfare is not bliss and no basis for activist energy. Are wild animals ever likely to benefit from innocent ignorance or from conspiring humans with a political agenda?

Maiming Foxes

Have foxes and hares benefited from such conspiracies? Or does the antipathy to hunting have little to do with animal welfare if the truth be known? Sadly, maimed foxes can survive a fox-shoot. Not many hares escape a hare-shoot. A study in the May 2005 issue of *Animal Welfare,* the journal of UFAW (Universities Federation for Animal Welfare), showed that up to 50 per cent of foxes shot with shotguns were wounded not killed. I understand that in no coursing season in the last two decades of the twentieth century were more than 300 hares, of the 2,000 coursed, killed. Just under 400,000 hares were shot annually on non-coursing estates for control purposes during that time. And the hare was welcome on coursing estates. Sport is about seeking a contest, not extermination; the coursing community respected hares. It is the hunter's natural instinct to preserve what he hunts. The Veterinary Association for Wildlife Management has stated that hunting is the natural and most humane method of controlling populations of all four quarry species and is a key element in the management of British wildlife in general. That is how our sporting dogs were fashioned.

Punishing Wildlife

The management of British wildlife in general has been in the hands of countrymen throughout our history, but now the town-dwellers are the masters, whatever the effect on our precious wildlife. Coursing is over 2,000 years old; suddenly, modern man, whilst rapidly destroying the planet, knows best. The biggest single component attending the Waterloo Cup comprised working-class men from the north of England, Liverpool especially. Their elected representatives have achieved what no Danish king or Norman knight could do: deny the humble countryman his right to catch his own supper. The ban on hunting with dogs has been called an act of class war, but the class worst hit has been the working man, not the wealthy man. It takes near genius to draft one Act that punishes both wildlife and the ordinary far-from-wealthy countryman to a greater degree than hitherto obtained in history. But by far the greatest punishment has been handed out to sporting dogs, sighthounds more than most. They have lost their reason to be, their historic role, their spiritual release, their usefulness.

Importance of Regulation

A highly regulated country sport with very strict rules, like coursing, brings with it respect for the quarry and the country being used. As Professor Roger Scruton, writing in the winter 2009 issue of the magazine *Hunting* put it:

> The opponents of hunting see it as a kind of primitive battle, in which the quarry is overcome by unfair military tactics and a cruel war of attrition. For the hunt followers, however, the hunt is an equal contest, governed by rules of engagement which respect the hunted animal while giving the greatest possible scope to the hounds that are pursuing it. True, the quarry is singled out for a life and death struggle which it did nothing to provoke. But this 'singling out' exalts the fox or stag in the eyes of its pursuers and imposes on them the ethic of fair play.

This 'ethic of fair play' used to be the leitmotiv of country sports and a way of bringing young adults into maturity with respect for nature and the countryside around them. The young tyro hunter off with his lurcher for a day's sport once demonstrated the timeless trinity of man, dog and the land.

Doing Good or Not

In his masterly *Rural Rites, Hunting and the Politics of Prejudice* (2006), Charlie Pye-Smith writes:

> Anyone who wishes to ridicule the Act, and test it to the limits, will have no trouble doing so. Take, for example, the hunting of hares. It is illegal under the

Act to hunt hares with dogs. However, you can hunt hares with as many hounds as you like providing you are pursuing hares which have been shot.

If any perverse sadist elected to maim hares with a high-powered air rifle, he could then legally course them. Is this truly how animal welfare should be enacted? Do-gooders so often end up being evil-doers. The rules of coursing did more for animal welfare than any legal action arising from the words

The Whippet was born to run.

Whippet leaving the traps.

of this vengeful Act could. Many of those opposing field sports have the strange concept of nature being left alone and being better for it. Not in twenty-first-century over-populated Britain! Without man's intervention, most wild creatures would starve or die of disease. They rely on human control for their needs to be met, and in enlightened, not prejudiced ways.

Need for a Rethink

The Hunting Act (2004) became so closely associated with the prohibiting of fox-hunting that the ancient sport of coursing became relegated; not many sportsmen spoke up for this well-regulated sport. In Victorian times Delabere Blaine was writing in his immense tome *Rural Sports*: 'Coursing, like other field sportings, has its advocates and its enemies; it also presents its bright and cloudy sides. It is not, indeed, fit that we should all be enamoured of the same pursuit; but it is proper that we should not underrate the amusements followed by others.' Those who respect and practise our ancient country sports failed to close ranks when this badly drafted bill was being framed; there should have been a realization that 'once the pistol was loaded, it could point in any direction'.

The war poet Charles Causley once wrote a heart-rending poem about a recruiting sergeant, to the effect that 'he's already taken our Tommy and Kate – and he's coming back for more'. The law concerning hunting with dogs is in a real mess; this is neither good for animal welfare nor for country sports. Before the highly vocal opponents of country sports 'come back for more', we, as a nation, need to put this house in order, for the sake of our wildlife just as much as for our ancient country sports. Once hunting in its widest sense is outlawed, sporting dogs become victims. There are no native sighthound breeds in mainland western Europe because coursing with dogs is banned in those countries. Yet breeds designed to conduct coursing are very popular there. Humans want the companionship of such splendid animals but not their spiritual happiness.

Veterinary View

The fact that the Veterinary Association for Wildlife Management has stated that hunting is the natural and most humane method of controlling populations of all four quarry species (deer, fox, hare and mink)

Farndon Fancy, Fairy Footsteps and Fabulous Fortune, 1902.

and is a key element in the management of British wildlife in general, is surely a lead for us all. The ban has affected more working-class hunters than any number of men mounted and in pink coats. Look again at those depictions of the Waterloo Cup, whether on canvas or in old black and white photographs; the vast majority of the spectators wore cloth caps not top hats. They have been badly let down by those feigning to protect their interests.

Harry Wright with his four famous charges: Wellaway, Champion Times, Full Pete and Cotton King.

Four Famous Waterloo Cup winners: Fabulous Fortune, 1896; Fearless Footstep, 1900, 1901; Farndon Ferry, 1902; and Father Flint, 1903.

Fighting Force, Waterloo Cup winner, 1920. A.G. Haigh, 1922.

So has our wildlife, if the vets are to be believed. In four successive years in the 1980s, the winners of the blue riband event of coursing, the Waterloo Cup, each won without killing a single hare between them. The coursing community had great respect for the hare, safeguarding their interests through tight regulation and being more conscious of their ultimate conservation than any urban-dwelling activist.

Lost Expertise

In many sporting dog circles, remarkable families crop up. In the coursing world, from the 1880s to the 1900s, the Wright family stands out. Edwards Clarke, the great Greyhound expert, admitted he learned most from them. Joe Wright trained the Waterloo Cup winner of 1888, Burnaby, and the 1895 winner, Thoughtless Beauty. This latter final saw Joe Wright the trainer of the winner, a younger brother Tom the trainer of the runner-up, and another brother, Robert, acting as slipper for the contest. Tom trained five winners of this famous cup, for the Fawcetts and their famous 'F&F' kennel: Fabulous Fortune (1896), Fearless Footsteps (1900 and 1901), Farndon Ferry (1902) and Father Flint (1903), a quite stunning record for any sporting family. Farndon Ferry and another dog from the same kennel, Fiery Furnace, were considered by Edwards Clarke 'to be the tap-roots of all Greyhounds that have either coursed or raced in the twentieth century'. Harold Wright trained Dee Rock, the Waterloo Cup winner of 1935. The Wrights, between them, possessed enormous knowledge of Greyhound training, conditioning and welfare, and especially, their health care. Will we ever see their like again? The loss of such immense

The author meeting racing Greyhounds, before their road walk, at Maurice Walsh's Bampton kennels.

Italian Greyhounds lure-racing. Dogs in Canada *magazine.*

A lurcher – not an Ibizan Hound.

A lurcher – not from Egypt!

expertise from the sporting dog scene, without new blood coming through, is hugely worrying.

Preserving Sighthound Skills

We are now faced with an unprecedented challenge to our sighthounds, with the law of the land against the function for which they were bred and used for over several thousand years. When a highly regulated

Lurcher owned by Mrs Frater of Keigthley, Yorkshire – so like the Podengo type.

field sport becomes proscribed, unregulated illegal hunting, with no respect for the quarry, replaces it. This will be a disaster for our wildlife and a major setback not just for sighthounds but for the quarry species too. But in the time it takes to realize legislative folly and then restore sanity to the scene, what can we do to preserve the sighthound skills? Track racing, lure-chasing and hound matches need to be supported; these superlative hounds need to be tested, if only to identify the best breeding stock. (Despite being classified as a Toy breed, even the Italian Greyhound needs to sprint!) We need the same dedication that developed their amazing talents now to be devoted to their preservation, and not just for their sakes, but that of their quarry too.

Sporting Salvation

As with a number of scenthound breeds, the future of the sighthound breeds is worryingly uncertain. Greyhounds have their racing side, Whippets have their admirable working Whippet club, lurchers have both a national body and a racing organization, Afghan Hounds have their racing set-up, with other breeds encouraged to go along too – but the loss of the coursing clubs leaves a big hole. No one body is caring for the sporting future of the sighthound. The kennel clubs of the world are not established to do this and could end up being the 'Avon Ladies' of the dog world, concerned only with cosmetic appeal, more focused on presentation than performance.

Their inability to understand the origins of the sighthound breeds illustrates their lack of real appreciation. In just one national kennel club's official publication, the Ibizan Hound's history is 'traceable back to approximately 3400BC, with the glory that was ancient Egypt the most fitting setting for this regal hound, which was owned and hunted by the Pharaohs'; the Pharaoh Hound is 'considered one of the oldest domesticated dogs in recorded history, tracing his lineage to roughly 3000BC. Fortunately, the history of Egyptian civilization was well documented and preserved through paintings and hieroglyphics and from these we learn that this unique dog ...' and the Saluki is described as 'The Royal Dog of Egypt ... a distinct breed and type as long ago as 329BC when Alexander the Great invaded India.'

What do they think went before? How can they ignore the Sumerians and not mention the Hyksos?

A lurcher – not a Pharaoh Hound.

Prick-eared Whippet lurcher.

The ancient Egyptians may have had the artefacts but the steppe nomads had the dogs! I shudder to think how they would have covered, say, a discovery of carvings at Stonehenge of dogs like the bat-eared, purely British-blooded lurchers illustrated here! Sporting dogs, sighthounds especially, whatever their provenance, are easily lost to us once their founding function is removed; the survival of pedigree *breeds* by itself is only half the answer.

Breed Care

I believe that it is entirely fair to state that most breed clubs exist to serve the exhibition side of the breed's affairs. To care comprehensively for a breed, especially a sporting one and a sighthound one in particular, there is, however, a distinct need for each breed club to have an archivist – who really must know the difference between a Tesem and a Tasy; a health watch scheme – which at long last the Kennel Club is urging; a proactive rescue system; a consultant morphologist – who really knows what the breed should look like and is guided by the KC's commendable 'fit-for-function' campaign; and last but far from least, a sporting wing, running lure-racing, speed-racing – rather as the admirable Afghan people do – and any other physical activity for these remarkable hounds. From such a structure would come a renewed appreciation of what these dogs are for, where they came from, what they should look like and how to promote their well-being. These breeds must be conserved as *hunting dogs*.

Unwise Policy

In his book *Medieval Hunting* (2003), Richard Almond writes:

> Man needs to hunt to release the pressures of being human, to appreciate the countryside, the seasons, to be aware of the beauty and brevity of life, and the inevitability and sadness of death … We are the inheritors of hunter-gatherers from not so long ago and the streams of consciousness of our ancient ancestors still run deep and powerful.

When the next sizeable meteorite hits Mother Earth, as it surely will, who will be more likely to survive, the simple hunter with his efficient hunting dogs or a city-dwelling merchant banker? When a distinguished diplomat and Saluki breeder is prevented from importing desert Salukis from the sheikhs by our Kennel Club because their purebreeding is in question we have clearly lost our way. When Bloodhound fanciers object to hounds from the packs being registered as Bloodhounds with the KC because their purebreeding is disputed, we have, in the modern idiom, lost the plot.

Community Event

It is so often overlooked by scholars that hunting in medieval times was very much a community event; the tenantry and those living in the countryside all took part in the chase. The poet Wordsworth picked this up in his words:

> Up, Timothy, up with your staff and away!
> Not a soul in the village this morning will stay;
> The hare has just started from Hamilton's grounds,
> And Skiddaw is glad with the cry of the hounds.

There has long been a democratic basis to the hunting field that overcomes the different levels of class and social position, valuing instead capability and prowess. Hunting in the Middle Ages was much more inclusive, embracing every stratum of society and filling a larger social need than some historians will admit. As Henry Savage pointed out in his contribution to *Speculum,* the journal of the Medieval Academy of America, in 1933:

> The hound of the middle ages was for use. It would have been strange for the medieval 'venator' to have thought of wolf-hounds without thinking of wolves, of deerhounds without thinking of deer. Our fathers protected the game to hunt it; we do not protect it, and are reduced to the necessity of pursuing anise-seed bags! If we are coming to a realization of the importance of conservation, we are only finding out what our fathers knew.

Moral vanity and the dislike of the chase by academics often ignores not just social history but what courses through our primeval veins.

Greyhounds, 'Raymond Ways' and 'Alamein Express' by Stuart Tresilian 1950.

Loss of Working Anatomy

The handlers of sighthounds at Crufts are unlikely to know of the medieval fewterers who held the sighthounds in the chase or the criteria they worked to. The hound judges at Crufts in 2008 made these comments on the hounds before them: Afghan Hounds: 'the breed has been getting further away from its origins and although there are many glamorous coated hounds there are fewer and fewer that display the true essence of the breed …' and 'he is a hunting hound not a dressed up puppet'; Borzoi: 'The Borzoi has to be able to chase and hold down a large formidable animal, could yours?'; Pharaoh Hounds: 'This is a running hound and I was disappointed to find only a handful of dogs who were well muscled and fit …' What were those like that did not qualify for Crufts! It is foolish to leave a sighthound breed entirely in the hands of its show ring fraternity. Most of the latter would welcome the involvement of and advice from those who *use* their hounds. The future of these outstanding hounds is threatened as never

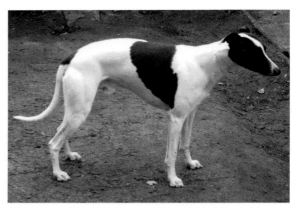

No poseur – Jeff Hutching's top-quality working Whippet Stars Strike Heart and Soul of Pennymeadow.

before; it will take both vision and dedication to retain them as true sporting hounds still able to carry out their historic role. I trust this book will contribute to securing their *sporting* future.

> In the world of dogs the sighthounds certainly constitute the most striking illustration of the adage 'Beauty is born of the adaptation to function'. Today most are no longer utilized hunting by sight, a type of hunt forbidden almost everywhere or supplanted by the gun.
>
> *Chiens de France* (No. 9, 1994)

> There is little doubt but that the greyhound gallops purely for galloping's sake, and when he is fit and well it takes little to induce him to do so. Even when not sent to exercise with another, a single greyhound in a field will go for all he is worth, simply out of sheer ecstasy of spirit and the joy of bringing into play the whole of his active organisation.
>
> *The Greyhound - Breeding, Coursing, Racing, Etc.,* by James Matheson, Hurst & Blackett, Ltd.,1930.

The Span of the Sighthound. Dogs in Canada *magazine.*

POINTS OF A GOOD SIGHTHOUND

The points of a good greyhound: (from Clarke's The Greyhound (1965) by kind permission of Popular Dogs).

1. Long, lean, intelligent head
2. Full, bright-spirited eye
3. Strong, well-coupled back
4. Oblique shoulders
5. Loins powerful, slightly arched
6. Flanks well cut up
7. Great strength from hip to hock
8. Thighs – second thighs wide and muscular
9. Stifles well bent
10. Hocks well let down
11. Covering a lot of ground
12. Well-sprung ribs
13. Deep brisket
14. Good tight feet
15. Knees close to ground
16. Good timber
17. Long, straight, well-muscled forearm
18. Long, strong, flexible neck.

GLOSSARY OF TERMS

Action Movement; the way a dog moves.

Angulation The degree of slope or angle of the shoulder blade in the forequarters and in the sharp angles of the interrelated bones in the hindquarters – thigh, hock and metatarsus.

Back Area of the dog between the withers and the root of tail.

Balanced Symmetrically proportioned.

Barrel-hocks Hocks turned outwards, resulting in feet with inward-pointing toes (similar to bandy-legs).

Barrel-ribbed Well-rounded ribcage.

Blanket The coat colour on the back from the withers to the rump.

Blaze A white patch of hair in the centre of the face, usually between the eyes.

Bloom The sheen of a coat in prime condition.

Bodied up Well developed in maturity.

Brace A pair, a couple.

Breed points Characteristic physical features of a breed, often exaggerated by breed fanciers.

Brisket The part of the body in front of the chest.

Button ear The ear flap folding forward, usually towards the eye.

Cat-foot Rounded, shorter-toed, compact type of foot.

Champion A dog achieving this level of merit under KC-approved judges.

Chest The area from the brisket up to the belly, underneath the dog.

Chiselled Clean-cut, especially in the head.

Chopping Exaggerated forward movement through abbreviated reach.

Close-coupled Comparatively short from the last rib to the leading edge of the thigh.

Coarse Lacking refinement.

Cobby Short-bodied, compact in torso.

Conformation The relationship between the physical appearance of a dog and the imagined perfect mould for that breed or type.

Couples Connection of hindquarters to torso.

Coursing The practice of racing (usually two) sighthounds in pursuit of a hare.

Cow-hocks Hocks turned towards each other (similar to knock-knees).

Crossbred Having parents from two different breeds.

Croup (rump) Region of the pelvic girdle formed by the sacrum and the surrounding tissue.

Dewlaps Loose, pendulous skin under the throat.

Down at pastern Weak or faulty metacarpus set at an angle to the vertical.

Drive A solid thrust from the hindquarters, denoting strength of locomotion.

Drop ears The ends of the ears folded or falling forward.

Elbows out Elbows positioned away from the body.

Even bite Meeting of both sets of front teeth at edges with no overlap.

Feathering Distinctly longer hair on rear line of legs, back of ears and along underside of tail.

Flank The side of the body between the last rib and the hip.

Flat-sided A noticeable lack of roundness in the ribcage.

Flying trot (suspended trot) Fast gait in which all four feet may be off the ground briefly during each stride.

Forearm Part of foreleg extending from elbow to pastern.

Forequarters Front part of dog, excluding head and neck.

Front Forepart of body viewed from the head-on position.

Furnishings Long hair on ears, trailing edge of legs and under part of tail.

Gait Pattern or rhythm of footsteps.

Gallop The fastest gait, with a four-beat rhythm, propelling the dog at great speed, with all four feet off the ground in the pursuit of sheer pace.

Gazehound Par force hound accompanied by mounted hunters; *not* synonymous with Greyhound or sighthound.

Grizzle Bluish-grey or steel-grey in coat colour.

Hackney action High-stepping action in the front legs (named after the carriage horse).

Hare-foot Longer, narrower foot, usually with an elongated third digit.

Haunch Rump or buttock; bones of that area.

Height Distance or measurement from the withers to ground contact in the standing dog.

Hock Joint on the hindleg between the knee and the fetlock; the heel in humans.

Hound-marked Coat colouring involving a mixture of classic Foxhound coat colours – white, black and tan – in varying proportions, usually mainly white, especially underneath.

Hound-tail Tail carried on high, up above the rump.

Irish spotting White markings on solid coat, usually on the blaze, throat and toes.

Knee Joint attaching forepastern and forearm.

Layback The angle of the shoulder compared to the vertical.

Lay of shoulder Angled position of the shoulder.

Leash Three or more hounds.

Leather The flap of the ear, smaller in sighthound breeds, but larger and much more erect in the Mediterranean breeds.

Level back When the line of the back is horizontal to the ground.

Level bite (pincer bite) The front teeth of both jaws meeting exactly.

Loaded shoulders When the shoulder blades are pushed outwards by over-muscled development (often confused in the show ring with well-muscled shoulders on a supremely fit dog).

Lumber Superfluous flesh and/or cumbersome movement arising from lack of condition or faulty construction.

Mask Dark shading on the foreface, most usually on a tan or red-tan dog.

Moving close When the hindlimbs move too near each other.

Occiput The peak of the skull.

Out at elbow *See* elbows out.

Overreaching Faulty gait in which the hindfeet pass the forefeet on the outside due to hyper-angulation in the hindquarters.

Overshot jaw The front upper set of teeth overlapping the lower set.

Oversprung ribs Exaggerated curvature of ribcage.

Pace Rate of movement, usually speed.

Padding Hackney action due to lack of angulation in forequarters.

Paddling Heavy, clumsy threshing action in the forelegs with the feet too wide of the body on the move.

Pastern Lowest section of the leg, below the knee or hock.

Pedigree The dog's record of past breeding; sometimes used as shorthand for purebreeding.

Pile Dense undercoat of softer hair.

Pincer bite *See* level bite.

Plaiting (or weaving or crossing) The movement of one front leg across the path of the other front leg on the move.

Prick ear Ear carriage in which the ear is erect and usually pointed at tip.

Racy Lightly built and leggier than normal in the breed.

Ribbed-up Long last rib.

Roach- or carp-backed Back arched convexly along the spine, especially in the hindmost section.

Root of the tail Where the tail joins the dog's back.

Rose ear A small drop ear with the leather folding over and back, often showing the inner ear.

Saddle A solid area of colour extending over the shoulders and back.

Saddle-backed A sagging back, caused by extreme length or weak musculature.

Scissors bite When the outer side of the lower incisors touches the inner side of the upper incisors.

Second thigh The (calf) muscle between the stifle and the hock in the hindquarters.

Self-coloured A solid or single-coloured coat.

Set on Where the root of the tail is positioned in the hindquarters.

Shelly Weedy and narrow-boned, lacking substance.

Short-coupled *See* close-coupled.

Shoulder layback *See* layback.

Sickle-hocked Lack of extension in the hock on the rear drive.

Slab-sided Flat ribs, with too little spring from the spinal column.

Snipiness Condition in which the muzzle is too pointed, weak and lacking strength right to the nose-end.

Soundness Correct physical conformation and movement.

Splay feet Flat, open-toed, widely spread feet.

Spring of rib The extent to which the ribs are well rounded.

Stance Standing position, usually when formally presented.

Standard The written word picture of a breed.

Stifle The joint in the hindleg between the upper and lower thigh, equating to the knee in humans, sadly weak in some breeds.

Stop The depression at the junction of the nasal bone and the skull between the eyes.

Straight-hocked Lacking in angulation of the hock joint.

Straight-shouldered Straight up and down shoulder blades, lacking angulation or layback.

Strain A family of related dogs throwing offspring of a set type.

Symmetry Balance and correct proportions of anatomy.

Throaty/throatiness An excess of loose skin at the front of the neck.

Tied at the elbows When the elbows are set too close under the body, thereby restricting freedom of movement.

Topline The dog's outline from just behind the withers to the rump.

Trot A rhythmical two-beat gait, with hind- and forequarters working in unison.

Tuck-up Concave underline of torso, between last rib and hindquarters; lack of discernible belly.

Type Characteristic attributes distinguishing a breed or strain of a breed.

Undershot Malformation of the jaw projecting the lower jaw and incisors beyond the upper (puppies with this condition appear to be grinning).

Upper arm The foreleg bone between the shoulder blade and the elbow.

Variety Subdivision of a breed.

Well-angulated Well-defined angle in the thigh-hock-metatarsus area.

Well-coupled Well made in the area from the withers to the hip bones.

Well-knit Neat and compactly constructed and connected.

Well-laid Soundly placed and correctly angled.

Well laid-back shoulders Oblique shoulders ideally slanting at 45 degrees to the ground.

Well let-down Close to the ground, having low hocks.

Well ribbed-up Ribs neither too long nor too wide apart; compact.

Well-sprung With noticeably rounded ribs.

Well tucked-up Absence of visible abdomen, as in most sighthound breeds, but especially so in Whippets and Greyhounds.

Wheel back Excessive roaching; marked arching over the loins.

Wire-haired A coat of bristly crispness to the touch, hard in texture.

Withers The highest point on the body of a standing dog, immediately behind the neck, above the shoulders.

Yawing (crabbing) Body moving at an angle to the legs' line of movement.

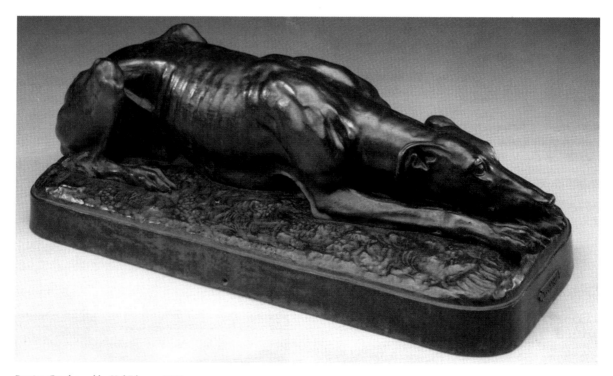

Resting Greyhound by Val D'osne, 1875.

BIBLIOGRAPHY

Allen, D. and K., *The Complete Saluki* (Ringpress, 1999)

Almirall, L.V., *Canines and Coyotes* (1941)

Almond, R., *Medieval Hunting* (Sutton, 2003)

Apsley, Lady V., *Bridleways through History* (Hutchinson, 1936)

Ash, E., *Dogs: Their History and Development* (1927)

Bengtson, B., *The Whippet* (David & Charles, 1985)

Berners, Dame J., *The Boke of St Albans* (1486)

Bingham Hull, D., *Hounds and Hunting in Ancient Greece* (University of Chicago Press, 1964)

Blaine, D., *An Encyclopaedia of Rural Sports* (1870)

Borzoi International Magazine (1990)

Borzoi International Magazine (1993)

Brander, M., *The Hunting Instinct* (Oliver & Boyd, 1964)

Brewer, D, Clark, T. and Phillips, A., *Dogs in Antiquity, Anubis to Cerberus* (Aris & Phillips Ltd, 2001)

van Bylandt, H., *Dogs of all Nations* (1904)

Caius, Dr, *Of English Dogs* (1576)

The Sportsman's Cabinet or a correct delineation of the Canine Race (1803)

Chadwick, W.E., *The Borzoi Handbook* (Nicholson & Watson, 1952)

Chamberlain, A., *Saluki* (Interpret Publishing, 2001)

Chiens de France (1984)

Chiens de France (No. 9, 1994)

Clark, D. and Stainer, J., *Medical & Genetic Aspects of Purebred Dogs* (Forum, USA, 1994)

Clark, Sir T., Derhalli, M., *On Hunting (Al-Mansur's Book)* (Aris & Phillips Ltd, 2001)

Cole, R.W., *An Eye for a Dog* (Dogwise Publishing, USA, 2004)

Como, D., *Sighthounds Afield* (Authorhouse, USA, 2004)

Compton, H., *The Twentieth Century Dog* (Grant Richards, 1904)

Compton Reeves, A., *Pleasures and Pastimes in Medieval England* (Sutton Publishing, 1997)

Coppinger, R. and L., *Dogs – A Startling New Understanding of Canine Origin, Behavior and Evolution* (Scribner, 2001)

Coren, S., *The Intelligence of Dogs* (Headline, 1994)

The Countryman's Weekly (7 September 2011)

The Coursing Calendar (Vol. xxi)

Cox, H., *Dogs and I* (Hutchinson, 1928)

Cox, H., Lascelles, G., Duke of Beaufort (ed.), *Coursing and Falconry* (The Badminton Library, Longmans, Green, & Co., 1892)

Cox, N., *The Gentleman's Recreation* (1674)

Croxton Smith, A. (ed.), *Hounds & Dogs,* Lonsdale Library Vol. 13 (Seeley, Service, 1932)

Croxton Smith, A., *Sporting Dogs* (Country Life, 1938)

Croxton Smith, A., *British Dogs* (Collins, 1945)

Croxton Smith, A., *Dogs since 1900* (Dakers, 1950)

Cummins, J., *The Hawk and the Hound: The Art of Medieval Hunting* (Weidenfeld & Nicolson, 1988)

Cunliffe, J., *Sighthounds – Their History, Management and Care* (Swan Hill Press, 2006)

Cupples, G., *Scotch Deerhounds and their Masters* (Blackwood & Sons, 1894)

Dalby, D., *Lexicon of the Medieval German Hunt* (De Gruyter & Co., Berlin, 1965)

Dalziel, H., *The Greyhound* (Upcott Gill, 1887)

Daniel, Rev. W.B. *Rural Sports* (1802)

Davies, C.J., *The Kennel Handbook* (The Bodley Head, 1905)

Dighton, A., *The Greyhound and Coursing* (Grant Richards, 1921)

Doherty, B., *Working Deerhounds, Lurchers and Longdogs* (Goldfinch Publications, 2006)

Douglas-Todd, C.H., *The Whippet* (Popular Dogs, 1976)

Drury, W.D., *British Dogs* (Upcott Gill, 1903)

Edwards Clark, H., *The Greyhound* (Popular Dogs, 1965)

The Field (7 February 1891)

Gardner, P., *The Irish Wolfhound* (Murphy, 1928)

Genders, R., *The Greyhound and Greyhound Racing* (Sporting Handbooks Ltd, 1975)

Gilbert, J.M., *Hunting and Hunting Reserves in Medieval Scotland* (John Donald, 1979)

Gilbey, W., *Hounds in the Old Days* (1913)

Goldsmith, O., *Animated Nature* (1770)

Griffin, E., *Blood Sport: Hunting in Britain since 1066* (Yale, 2007)

Hall, L., *Fifty-Six Waterloo Cups – Greyhounds and Coursers* (1922)

Hamilton Smith, C., *The Naturalists' Library,* Vol. 19 (1840)

Hancock, R.C.G., *The Right Way to Keep Dogs* (Elliot Books, 1956)

Hancock Mountjoy, T.W., *Points of the Dog* (Eveleigh Nash & Grayson, 1927)

Harding, A.R., *Wolfe and Coyote Trapping* (A.R. Harding Publishing Co., Ohio, 1909)

Hartley, A.N., *The Deerhound* (Peterborough, 1972)

Hartley, O., *Hunting Dogs* (A.R. Harding Publishing Co., Ohio, 1909)

Hogan, E., *History of the Irish Wolfdog* (Gill & Son, 1897)

Hubbard, C., *The Afghan Hound* (Nicholson & Watson, 1951)

Hunting magazine (Winter 2009)

Hutchinson, W. (ed.), *Hutchinson's Dog Encyclopaedia* (1934)

'Idstone', *The Dog* (1880)

Jesse, E., *Anecdotes of Dogs* (Henry Bohn, 1858)

Jesse, G., *Researches into the History of the British Dog* (Robert Hardwicke, 1866)

Jones, T., *The Courser's Guide* (Cawney House Bank, Dudley, Worcs.,1896)

The Kennel Gazette (July 1888)

The Kennel Gazette (December 1889)

The Kennel Gazette (August 1890)

The Kennel Gazette (April 1891)

The Kennel Gazette (December 1891)

Lee, R., *Modern Dogs* (series; 1890s–1900s)

Leighton, R., *The New Book of the Dog* (Cassell, 1912)

LeMieux, S., *The Book of the Greyhound* (TFH Publications Inc., 1999)

Lewis Renwick, W., *The Whippet Handbook* (Nicholson & Watson, 1957)

McBryde, M., *The Magnificent Irish Wolfhound* (Ringpress, 1998)

McMichan, B.A., *The Greyhound – Training, Management, Diseases* (Angus & Robertson Ltd., Sydney, 1937)

Martin, W.C.L., *The History of the Dog* (Charles Knight, 1845)

Matheson, J., *The Greyhound – Breeding, Coursing, Racing, Etc.* (Hurst & Blackett Ltd, 1930)

Niblock, M., *The Afghan Hound: A Definitive Study* (K&R Classics, 1980)

Phillips, A.A. and Willcock, M.M. (eds.), *On Hunting with Hounds, Xenophon & Arrian* (Aris & Phillips Ltd, 1999)

Pitscottie, R.L., of, *The History and Chronicles of Scotland* (1749)

Plummer, B., *Hunters All* (Huddlesford, 1986)

Plummer, B., *The Complete Book of Sight Hounds, Long Dogs and Lurchers* (Robinson, 1991)

Plummer. B., *Secrets of Dog Training* (Robinson, 1992)

Portman-Graham, R., *The Practical Guide to Showing Dogs* (1956)

Pye-Smith, C., *Rural Rites, Hunting and the Politics of Prejudice* (2006)

Raymond-Mallock, L., *Toy Dogs* (Dogdom Publishing Co., USA, 1907)

Revista del Perro

Rice, M., *Swifter than the Arrow: the Golden Hunting Hounds of Ancient Egypt* (Tauris, 2006)

Ritchie, C.I.A., *The British Dog: Its History from Earliest Times* (Robert Hale, 1981)

Rolins, A., *All About the Greyhound* (Rigby Publishers, 1982)

Sabaneev, L., *Hunting Dogs: Borzoi and Hounds* (1899)

Salmon, M.H. Dutch, *Gazehounds & Coursing: The History,* *Art and Sport of Hunting with Sighthounds* (High-Lonesome Books, 1977)

Science magazine (2004)

Scrope, W., *Days of Deerstalking* (1838)

Shaw, M., *The Modern Lurcher* (Boydell, 1984)

Shaw, V., *The Illustrated Book of the Dog* (1879)

Sheardown, F., *The Working Longdog* (Swan Hill, 1999)

Sidney Turner, J. (ed.), *The Kennel Encyclopaedia* (1908)

Smythe, R.H., *The Mind of the Dog* (Country Life, 1958)

Smythe, R.H., *The Dog – Structure and Movement* (Foulsham & Co., 1970)

Soman, W.V., *The Indian Dog* (Popular Prakashan, 1963)

Speculum, Journal of the Medieval Academy of America (1933)

The Sportsman's Cabinet (1803)

Stables, D., *Our Friend the Dog* (Dean & Son, 1907)

'Stonehenge', *The Dog in Health and Disease* (1867)

'Stonehenge', *Dogs of the British Islands* (1878)

Thacker, T., *The Courser's Companion* (1834)

Thomas, J.B., *Observations on Borzoi* (Houghton Mifflin, 1912)

The Times (21 June 1927)

Thomson Gray, D.J., *Dogs of Scotland* (James P. Mathew, 1891)

Townend Barton, F., *Hounds* (1913)

Townend Barton, F., *Our Dogs* (Jarrolds, 1938)

Vesey-Fitzgerald, B., *The Book of the Dog* (Nicholson & Watson, 1948)

Walsh, E.G., *Lurchers and Longdogs* (Standfast, 1977)

Walsh, E.G. and Lowe, M., *The English Whippet* (Boydell, 1984)

Walsh, J.H., *Manual of British Rural Sports – the Pursuit of Wild Animals for Sport* (1856)

Waters, H. and D., *The Saluki in History, Art and Sport* (David & Charles, 1969)

Watson, J., *The Dog Book* (Heinemann, 1906)

Wentworth Day, J. *The Dog in Sport* (Harrap, 1938)

Weston Bell, E., *The Scottish Deerhound* (David Douglas, 1892)

The Whippet Club's Jubilee Show catalogue (1950)

Whitney, L.F., *How to Breed Dogs* (Orange Judd, 1937)

Wood, J.G., *The Illustrated Natural History* (1928)

The Working Whippet Yearbook (2007)

York, Duke of, *The Master of Game* (1406)

Youatt, W., *The Dog* (1854)

Zeuner, F., *A History of Domesticated Animals* (Hutchinson, 1963)

INDEX

Related Titles From Crowood

Hunt, Point Retrieve Dogs for Work and Showing

N.C. Dear

ISBN 978 1 84797 082 4
160pp, 70 illustrations

The Lurcher

Jon Hutcheon

ISBN 978 1 86126 976 8
112pp, 100 illustrations

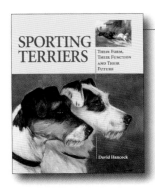

Sporting Terriers

David Hancock

ISBN 978 1 84797 303 0
176pp, 270 illustrations

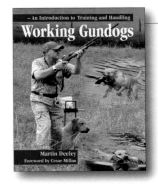

Working Gundogs

Martin Deeley

ISBN 978 1 84797 099 2
192pp, 150 illustrations

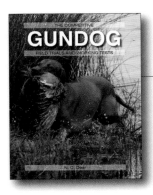

The Competitive Gundog Field Trials and Working Tests

N.C. Dear

ISBN 978 1 84797 282 8
192pp, 115 illustrations

Rabbiting with Ferret, Dog, Hawk and Gun

Seán Frain

ISBN 978 1 86126 802 0
144pp, 110 illustrations

In case of difficulty in ordering, contact the Sales Office:

The Crowood Press Ltd
Ramsbury
Wiltshire
SN8 2HR
UK

Tel: 44 (0) 1672 520320
enquiries@crowood.com
www.crowood.com